RACE WALK LIKE A CHAMPION

Technique, Training, & History

Written by Jeff Salvage

Edited By Bernadette R. McNulty

D1605133

ISBN: 0-9655328-3-6
Copyright 2004
Walking Promotions
79 North Lakeside Drive
Medford, NJ 08055

Printed in the USA
First Edition

Dedication
This book is dedicated to all those who most influenced my race walking career: John Toy, Ken Hendler, Gary Westerfield, Troy Engle, Jake Jacobson and Jeff Popyack (the college professor who let me miss an exam to race. Having blown my knee out in that race, I deem Popyack to be more responsible for my entry into coaching than anyone else.)

Acknowledgements
One cannot limit the time and effort put into writing a book to the period between penning the first idea and rolling the final product off the presses. When I started race walking 20 years ago, my sole hope was to walk an 8:00 mile. I never dreamed that creating race walking books, videos, and DVDs was in my future. To give credit where credit is due, I must go back through the years to all of the people who influenced and imparted knowledge to me.

Race Walking Knowledge
John Toy, my high school teammate, taught me the basics of technique. Ken Hendler, my high school coach, instilled a training ethic and motivation that carried me through my race walking career. Gary Westerfield not only coached me through most of my competitive career, but also became a mentor and primary sounding board for many of my race walking projects. Troy Engle coached me for only a short time, but taught me to relax and enjoy it. Finally, Coach Jake Jacobson has been a true friend and advisor on race walking and life.

My Athletes
Coaching is the single best way to perfect your knowledge of race walking. Over the years, many athletes have trained under my guidance. Ed Gawinski has the honor/burden of walking with me longer than anyone else. Jack Starr, my idol: I only hope I can walk like him when I am 75. Karen Charles, my athlete, co-coach, and friend. Josh Ginsburg taught me how to be patient with young athletes. Lisa Kutzing, Marie Woodland, Keri Cohn, and Al Cataldo, who still walk with me, keep me on my toes—literally and figuratively. Finally, John Nunn, my star pupil, has been like a son to me.

Writing Influence
Gathering enough knowledge to write a book does not ensure a quality text. An instructive book requires a unique combination of writing, imaging, layout, and editing. Although they had no direct involvement in this text, I thank Susan Hartman-Sullivan, Michael Hirsch, and Patti Mahtani from Addison-Wesley. Their guidance and nurturing of my three previous textbooks greatly expanded my writing skills and knowledge of effective page layout.

Photographs
I must thank my photography mentor Stephanie Kirk who is an incredible influence in my photographic journey. While I photographed most of the quality images used to convey the enclosed text, these images are all influenced by the lessons and encouragement provided by Stephanie. Images containing myself were taken by either Stephanie Kirk or Nelson Brown. Thanks go to my models: Lindsay Bellias, Judy Meyers, and Jack Starr.

The collection of historical photographs came from a wide array of contributors: Eli Attar, Nancy Benjamin, Sue Broddock, Lynn Campilli, Ron Daniel, Tom Dooley, Victoria Herazo, Ray Kuhles, Hilda Laskau, Jake Jacobson, Allen James, Herm Nelson, Dave Romansky, Maryanne Torrellas, Gary Westerfield, and Larry Young.

Medical Advice
As a coach and writer, I am always careful about giving medical advice. Nadya Dimitrov, DPM, Dr. Kim Nagle, and Susan Holowchak, C.M.T. and Exercise Physiologist, all assisted with medical-related material in this text.

Assistance with Research
Many thanks to those who assisted me in my research: Bob Bowman, Sal Corrallo, Tom Dooley, Tom Eastler, Josh Ginsburg, Ray Kuhles, Bruce MacDonald, Rich Torrellas, Gary Westerfield, and Steve Vaitones.

On Location at
Special thanks to The Body Shop for the use of their facilities.

The All Important Editor
Finally, the single person who had the biggest influence on the text of this book, Bernadette McNulty. The countless hours editing and struggling with word choice cannot be summarized in a few short sentences. An editor can make or break a book; I am fortunate enough to have the best.

Additional Review and Editing Help
Another set of eyes always helps. Thanks go to Michael Roth, Gary Westerfield, Dave McGovern, Elaine Ward, and Sandee Griffith.

Chapter 1: Introduction

What Is Race Walking?
You're a what? That's the typical response I get when I tell people I am a race walker.

If they have heard of my beloved sport, they don't know much about it. While race walking has been in the Olympic Games since 1904, the first evidence of a walking competition can be traced back to an Egyptian hieroglyphic record from 2,500 B.C. But the public image of race walking faces many challenges; chief among them are its lack of good PR and its unorthodox gait. Although many walkers believe their sport is on the rise, in the U.S. it seems to have a relatively small loyal following that maintains its base without much growth.

The small friendly community of race walking suits me just fine. As an injured runner in high school, I looked for an outlet for my competitive energies. The race walking community welcomed me with open arms. My first race walking experiences were all competitively minded. After a successful competitive race walking career in college, I joined the real world and focused on my non-athletic career. However, race walking remained a major part of my life. The many health benefits of race walking keep me walking, and in shape, lo these many years.

Whether you're competitive-minded or interested in improving your health, race walking offers abundant opportunities for fun, fitness, and personal challenges.

Benefits for the Competitor
For those who are competitive-minded, race walking provides opportunities at all ability levels. For the novice, many running races offer walking divisions, or you can try race walking against some of the slower runners in a local 5K or 10K race. More advanced race walkers typically gravitate to the many regional championships, national championships, and age group competitions organized by USATF (United States Track and Field). At the top of the competitive pyramid, elite race walkers strive to compete in international competitions such as the Olympics, World Cup, Pan Am Games, and the World Championships.

The elite of our sport race walk at incredible speeds. The world record for the mile is well under 6 minutes, while the longest Olympic distance of 50K (31 miles) is covered in less than 3 hours and 40 minutes. If you want to walk this fast then read on.

Benefits for the Health Conscious
Race walking offers greater health benefits than most people realize. Forget fad diets; race walking helps you lose weight and keep it off. Race walking burns more calories per hour than pedestrian walking and more calories per mile than running at the same pace. It improves cardiovascular conditioning and muscle tone while increasing range of motion. All that, without the excessive jarring and stress caused by running.

Race walking involves major body movements, I working your arms, legs, buttocks, and hips. More dynamic than pedestrian walking or running, which use roughly 70% of the body's muscles, race walking uses a whopping 95% of your muscles. Talk a little while you walk and you might get those last few muscles working too.

About the Book
Race Walk Like a Champion is the culmination of 20 years of race walking, as well as the combined experience bestowed on me by my coaches and mentors. It picks up where *Walk Like an Athlete*, co-authored in 1996, leaves off. *Walk Like an Athlete* was aimed at the recreational race walker. *Race Walk Like a Champion* is focused on instructing the competitive race walker. However, whether you are a novice race walker or an elite competitor, *Race Walk Like a Champion* will provide all the information you need.

While race walking has not changed much since my first race walking book, the technology utilized to explain race walking has changed dramatically. Eight years ago, black and white computer graphics provided effective illustrations for *Walk Like an Athlete*. Today, however, the advent of digital photography–rivaling film-quality photos–and improved color-printing production facilities make possible professional, full-color photographic explanations of race walking technique and training. In addition, my own knowledge of expository writing has grown considerably. Since the publication of *Walk Like an Athlete,* I have written three computer science textbooks, while continuing my teaching career at Drexel University. Thus I have learned much about the art of precisely explaining seemingly complex concepts.

Race Walk Like a Champion is more than just a book. It's a complete package when you add the two accompanying DVDs. The DVDs take the printed pages of this text, expands them with over 100 training schedules, from 5K to 50K, and brings them to life in a complete audio/video presentation.

Pedagogy
Photographs

The single most important element of this text is the use of full-color, high-resolution photographs and illustrations to demonstrate proper race walking technique. *Race Walk Like a Champion* contains nearly 400 photographs and illustrations to detail every aspect of proper technique as well as demonstrate common mistakes. The following is just a sample of the images used to clarify the meaning of the definition of race walking:

Is this visible to the human eye?

Zoomed in view

Tips

Throughout the chapter, coaching tips highlight key issues:

 COACH'S TIP

While racing, opening energy bar or gel shot wrappings is difficult. Make sure you pre-open your carbo-source to save time and frustration.

Warnings

Common mistakes are highlighted in a warning box:

 COACH'S WARNING

Never try something for the first time right before or during a race. Experiment with nutritional supplements, different foods, or electrolyte drinks during your training. What works for another athlete may not work for you.

The Red X

To insure you do not accidentally mimic the technique demonstrated in an image showing incorrect form, all incorrect figures will have a small red x in the upper corner.

Spotlights

Throughout the text, key contributors, publications and resources are highlighted via my spotlight breakout boxes:

 SPOTLIGHT ON

Team in Training (TNT) is the world's largest endurance-sports training program in the world. I have had the pleasure of coaching and helping the program since 1994. Words can not express the sense of joy and accomplishment TNT brings to its participants.

TNT trains novices as well as seasoned athletes to participate in ...

Chapter 2 - Proper Race Walking Shoes

Offering advice on selecting proper shoes for race walking presents a daunting task. By the time this book hits the printed page, any shoe mentioned could already be discontinued. Add to this problem the variations in individual needs and body types, and the task becomes even harder. So, instead of making recommendations about specific models, below I present general guidelines to use for selecting the best shoes.

Don't Be a Slave to Fashion

Buy shoes for quality only. Do not pick shoes because they look cool or coordinate well with an outfit or uniform. If you look at the NB 110s below, you might wonder whether New Balance made the shoes ugly on purpose, so only serious athletes would wear them.

Don't Wear Race Walking Shoes to the Mall

Anyone belonging to a race walking newsgroup knows that at least twice a month, the topic of finding the perfect walking shoe surfaces. Like the Holy Grail, perfect shoes are hard to find. Once located, wear them only when working out. Try to remember, shoes wear out very quickly, even without added use. Ideally, walkers training consistently should alternate between two pairs of the same or different model walking shoes; this protects the feet and helps to prevent blisters, as each shoe wears differently. Also, with two pairs, you can usually avoid training in wet shoes.

How Much To Spend on Walking Shoes

Of course, sporting shoe manufacturers proliferate by convincing people to buy the latest celebrity-endorsed shoes, often at prices of one hundred dollars or more. But does paying more really guarantee a higher-quality shoe? Probably not. Budgets usually determine the price we are willing to pay for any item. If your budget allows, buy a pair between sixty and eighty dollars. Shoes with higher prices exist only because companies know that some consumers will buy them. Often, expensive shoes perform marginally better; however, quality does not necessarily increase proportionally with price. While obeying a budget usually proves prudent, pursuing a "great deal" may not. Very inexpensive shoes typically wear out quickly and provide little support, stability, or comfort.

Anyone wishing to conserve money can purchase discontinued shoes without compromising quality. Few technological advances occur from one shoe generation to the next, with fashion the leading reason shoe models get discontinued. However, these shoes remain fully functional at any price and usually cost at least 30 percent less.

How To Pick a Shoe

Want to know a little secret? There are no perfect race-walking shoes. Usually, you can find a nearly perfect shoe, and that will suffice. Below are four almost perfect shoes. The New Balance 110 is actually a race walking shoe. The New balance 713 is a runner's training shoe, while the Asics Tiger Paw is a well-established runner's racing shoe. The fourth shoe, made to order by Bart Hersey, represents a significant financial investment for the average race walker. However, many elite athletes prefer the superb fit, durability, and individualized design of this shoe.

NB 110's

Asics Tiger Paws

NB 713's

Hersey Racing Shoes

Pick your shoe by the following characteristics, tailoring requirements to meet specific needs.

Low Heel

All four of these shoes are built with a relatively low heel: a key for fast, efficient race walking technique. Running shoes generally possess higher, more shock-absorbing heels because of the excessive stress caused by running mechanics. While the NB 110s, Asics Tiger Paws, and Hersey's all have an effectively low heel, the NB 713s are comparatively higher. Still, the NB 713s have the lowest heels I have recently seen on training shoes designed for running, and should be seriously considered by race walkers looking for stability, cushioning and longer life. In contrast, the heels of the NB 823 (the more typical running shoe) are roughly twice as high as the NB 110s.

NB110's low heel as compared with the NB823's

Stable Heel Counter

Most quality shoes provide some form of stabilizing heel counter. With a stable heel, the shoe prevents excessive motion when the heel strikes the ground. Race walkers need more motion control than runners; therefore, we must be careful if selecting a running shoe. To test for heel stability, squeeze both sides of the shoe's heel together; the heel should not collapse.

Sturdy Sole

A sturdy sole is essential to injury-free walking. Amazingly, few shoes offer one. See if your shoe passes this simple test. Use one hand at each end of the shoe to flex it up from the toe. A stable shoe will bend where the ball of the foot rests in the shoe, just like the NB 713s. In fact, the NB 713s add a plastic support to this area for added stability. In contrast, the unstable NB 110s bend under the arch, collapsing under the middle of the weight-bearing foot and causing the hamstring muscle to elongate. This repeated action can lead to senseless injuries.

NB 713 shows a sturdy sole

NB 110 shows a sole without stability

Although rare, some shoes are too stiff. Without ample flexibility in the toe box, it is difficult to get a good push off with your rear foot.

Ample Toe-Box

Self-explanatory. Your foot needs plenty of space to spread out, so make sure you have enough room in the toe-box. Remember, all feet swell during the day and certainly during a long race. Shoes that fit precisely early in the morning cause trouble as your feet swell. After a few miles into a race or training walk, you may realize your shoes are not large enough.

Shoe Last

When a walker's foot strikes the ground, it lands on the outer corner of the heel. As the stride progresses, the foot rolls towards the big toe. The degree that the foot rolls inward indicates the degree of pronation in a walker's stride. Walkers with an overly inward pronation require a straight-lasted shoe, while walkers without enough inward pronation (supinating or underpronating) require a curve-lasted shoe. If you are fortunate enough to pronate normally, then select a semi-curved last.

The difference between a curve lasted and straight lasted shoe, taken to the extreme, is obvious. The figures to the right clearly show how the different lasts live up to their name. However, real shoe lasts are more intricate, often neither easily classified as straight or curved. It is best to ask the advice of a qualified salesperson to determine the last of your shoe.

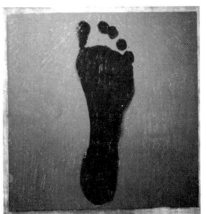

Straight Lasted Shoe   *Curve Lasted Shoe*

So, do you excessively pronate or supinate? Here's a simple test. Soak your foot in water and make a footprint on a clean flat surface. While you might not match your footprint exactly to one of the three patterns shown below, use the pattern that matches most closely to determine your level of pronation.

Normal Foot   *High Arched – Supinator*   *Flat Footed - Over Pronator*

Room for Your Achilles

You can easily inflame your Achilles tendon if the back of your shoe is not cut out in the manner shown (see figure at right). Although most shoes provide this cut out, always check to make sure yours do.

Other Issues

Use of Orthotics

Foot orthotics are shoe inserts designed to help control irregular foot motion. When used for race walking, they add stability to lighter, overly flexible shoes. Orthotics fall into three broad categories: rigid, primarily for changing foot function; soft, serving chiefly for protection; and semi-rigid, combining functional control and protection. They also vary in length. More flexible orthotics offer greater comfort but deteriorate quicker. More rigid orthotics often last many years, but beware: they can cause blisters.

On the following page is one of my own orthotics: rigid and very durable. I cannot race walk without them. Having bad knees since high school, I comfortably walk many miles in less supportive shoes by using orthotics. But if I try to walk even a few miles without them, my knees tighten up almost immediately. Lately I train in Asics Tiger Paws that would fail the *sole flexibility test* out of the box. With orthotics, however, they have arch support and bend near the toe box.

11

Plan ahead if you want orthotics. They tend to take over a month to order and a reasonable amount of time to break in. Typically made by a podiatrist, they can cost several hundred dollars and often are not covered by medical insurance. Though expensive, orthotics can be a very worthwhile investment.

Where Should I Buy My Walking Shoes?

Your search for walking shoes begins at a sports shoe specialty store. Avoid chain stores where inexperienced salespeople offer questionable advice on your single most important piece of race walking equipment. Until you find a suitable pair of shoes, get the best advice available. Once you select a satisfactory shoe, stick with the same model and buy additional pairs as needed. If you wait too long, the pair you like will become discontinued, so shop early. For those who are computer savvy, the Internet is a great equalizer once you know what model is best; virtual shopping saves time and often money.

A Note on Worn Out Walking Shoes

Like all shoes, walking shoes wear differently for each walker. Once a week, inspect your shoes for excessive wear, paying particular attention to the bottom of the shoe near the heel, and the front where you roll off the toes. Also check the shoes from behind. If the midsole of the shoe is compressed or leaning too much to one side, trash them. As a general rule of thumb, replace all walking shoes after about four hundred miles of use.

Not as popular as in the past, home-repairing shoes should not be considered an option. Shoe-Goo and other sole rebuilding products patch just the visibly worn section of a shoe, leaving invisible damage inside to aggravate tired muscles or injuries. Once you feel the need to repair your shoes' problems, don't. Replace them instead.

Everyone's shoe life varies. A person's individual walking style and body weight are just two factors that contribute to the variation in shoe life. Obviously the makeup of the shoe plays a huge factor as well. Most walkers like to train in racing shoes. However, the average life span of a racing shoe is under 100 miles. Therefore, wear them for training and you will be replacing them more than once a month. In contrast, training shoes last about 400 miles. Wearing either type longer than their life span increases the likelihood of injury dramatically.

The Need to *Break In* New Shoes

Most people need to *break in* a pair of shoes to help prevent blisters and other foot ailments. Do so before your old shoes wear out. First, wear the new pair around the house. Progress to a few short workouts, then move on to longer distances. Never wear new shoes to race!

COACH'S WARNING

Beware: racing shoes tend to have a very short lifespan. As little as one hundred miles may be all the use a pair of racing shoes will take—so if you train in them, they will last only a few short weeks.

The Need to *Break In* New Shoes

Most people need to *break in* a pair of shoes to help prevent blisters and other foot ailments. Do so before your old shoes wear out. First, wear the new pair around the house. Progress to a few short workouts, then move on to longer distances. Never wear new shoes to race!

The Hersey Difference

Currently many top race walkers wear shoes custom made by Bart Hersey. Michelle Rohl, Curt Clausen, Al Heppner, and Amber Antonia all use free shoes supplied by Hersey Custom Shoes. The two models available are an interesting alternative to products from the mass-produced brands. The first model, a racing shoe, was worn by Rohl and Clausen in the 2000 Olympics. Unbelievably lightweight at 6 ounces, this shoe is a little too flexible. Keep in mind, this racer is intended to provide just minimal protection for serious competitors who would just as soon race barefoot.

A better alternative is the Hersey training shoe. Also extremely lightweight—9 ounces—it features a minimum heel lift and a super flexible forefoot: the standard training shoe matching most of the criteria I laid out for a good race walking shoe.

Importantly, Hersey varies mid-sole materials and all aspects of shoe construction according to each walker's body weight and customer preference. When placing an order, you specify exactly how you want the shoe constructed. For example, Curt Clausen has had knee problems in the past because of over pronation. Therefore, he requests very straight-lasted shoes. Although the pros do not, request an arch that does not collapse. Protect those hamstrings: order yours with support. Also, consider a denser section under the toe to assist with good push-off.

As you would expect, Hersey's shoes are not cheap, at least initially. He currently charges a one-time fee of $150 to mold the last and pattern. A training shoe costs $155, while racing shoes go for $140. This might seem too expensive, and for some it is; however, Hersey charges only $30 to resole the shoe the first time, and $50 to resole it after that. (He attributes the added cost of subsequent rebuilds to the difficulty in rebuilding older shoes.) The good news is a properly maintained shoe can be rebuilt four to five times. So don't leave them in a car in Southern California when the temperature soars to 100 degrees.

When we look at the math, the price of Hersey's shoes compares well in the long run. When resoling a shoe five times, we pay a total cost of $530, so the amortized cost is $90 per pair. Not a bad bargain, but it gets better. Factor in that, according to elite walkers, resoled Hersey shoes tend to last longer than typical mass-produced shoes. Amber Antonia says that her Hersey shoes lasted three times longer than her previous race walking shoes. After they wore down, she just sent them in and got back a pair that felt like new. She says her feet used to hurt a lot, but not now that she wears a pair of Bart's shoes.

If you decide to try a Hersey, plan ahead. You face a 12-week backlog for initial orders. Resoling, however, takes only one week. You probably need more than one pair of shoes; however, as Hersey says, "If you pay $300 to have a pair of shoes made and you don't want a second pair, we have done something wrong."

For more information check out *www.herseycustomshoe.com* or call Bart at (207) 778-3103.

 SPOTLIGHT ON

USA Track and Field (USATF) is the national governing body of race walking as well as long distance running and track and field. Previously called The Athletics Congress (TAC), it was founded in 1979 to replace the Amateur Athletic Association (AAU) when the Amateur Sports Act prevented the AAU from continuing to govern track and field. In 1992, TAC changed its name to USATF in an effort to better promote those it represents.

USATF comprises 56 local associations that govern the sport on a local level and hold regional championship races. On a national level, USATF sets forth the rules that we must adhere to when competing domestically, produces many publications documenting the rules and promoting the sport, and organizes national championship races.

More information about USATF can be found on their website www.usatf.org.

Dave's World Class Race Walking is where you go if you want to attend a race walking clinic. Holding about 20 weekend clinics a year and one weeklong training camp, Dave McGovern is a traveling clinician.

Books, videos, and DVDs are a great way to learn about the sport, but there is no substitute for in-person hands-on assistance from a coach. McGovern's clinics provide the intense reinforcement of race walking concepts that dramatically impacts a person's race walking style and training philosophy.

> *"I learned more in two days at Dave's Dallas clinic than I did in nineteen years of race walking!"*
> –Fan Benno-Carris, Age 85, World Masters Race Walk Champion

Dave's World Class clinics provide an action-filled weekend. After a brief introduction to the elements of fast, efficient race walking technique, McGovern starts you off with a videotaping session that is next used as a tool to demonstrate areas needing improvement. After he tweaks your form, McGovern tapes you again so that you can see improvements for yourself.

After a brief break for lunch, you head back to the track, where McGovern teaches you dynamic drills, similar to the ones explained in Chapter 3, to improve your walking-specific range of motion.

The end of the first day wraps up with a mock race to see how your technique holds up under semi-competitive conditions.

The second full day of the clinic starts with a lecture on training physiology, followed by a workout designed to approximate your lactate threshold. By approaching this threshold as well as your maximum heart rate, you can develop a solid training program.

The weekend ends with a lecture on how to put it all together. You leave with improved technique, a better understanding of race walking, and a new enthusiasm for our sport.

To obtain the latest clinic schedule from McGovern's web site, visit *www.racewalking.org*.

Dave McGovern practices what he preaches. He walks fast—really fast. A member of the U.S. National Race Walking Team, he has won 13 U.S. National Championships and holds a 20K PR of 1:24:29, one of the all-time fastest 20Ks walked by an American.

Scenes from Dave's World Class Race Walking Clinics

Chapter 3 - Warming Up

Introduction

One of the greatest myths of exercise is that stretching is required beforehand. Never stretch a cold muscle. Cold muscles are tight and easy to strain. Do not interpret this to mean never stretch. Instead, learn to stretch at the proper time.

All workouts start by warming up. Stretching does not warm you up. While you could walk slowly to get the blood pumping, instead perform many of the dynamic drills presented in this chapter. These drills get the blood flowing, warm up the muscles, and increase your range of motion. Repeated practice of these drills prevents injuries and improves your race walking technique.

While practicing all of the drills every day is ideal, it's not likely that your schedule permits that much time to warm up. Each drill specifies a purpose, importance, and intensity. The purpose of the drill assists you in selecting the proper drill for the area of the body in which you wish to increase the range of motion or warm up. The importance indicates, in my humble opinion, the relative merit in performing the drill. The intensity indicates the force that the drill requires.

Some drills are safe for all walkers to perform. Others may not be ideally suited for all walkers. These will be indicated with a *coach's warning*, indicating that walkers with particular physiological problems may choose to skip this drill.

After properly warming up using these drills, stretch any problem areas. Warmed up and stretched, you are ready to race walk. Once you finish race walking, then you must stretch and stretch well. Stretching is detailed in Chapter 7.

 # SPOTLIGHT ON

Since 1986, the North American Racewalking Foundation (NARF) has been promoting race walking in many ways. The Foundation first acted as a referral service for people seeking contacts to learn race walking or to connect with other race walkers. Many magazines and newspapers used the Foundation as an information source and by 1990, NARF was receiving an average of 4,000 calls, emails, letters or faxes a year. The Foundation offers video and telephone coaching, judging information and supplies, as well as information on how to establish clubs, put on races and conduct workouts for different levels of walkers.

Recognizing a need for instructional materials, the Foundation produced numerous videos and books and they are available for sale from the Foundation along with titles from other publishers. Producing a number of newsletters over the years, the Foundation now publishes a Quarterly Bulletin for members and donors supporting the Olympic developmental activities of its nonprofit Institute.

In a two year partnership with the USATF National Race Walk Committee, NARF started a regional/national ranking ladder including Canada in 1993. The ranking was done by five-year age groups with specific time qualification standards as well as judging and certification standards. The ranking ladder was discontinued in 2002.

The Foundation's web site, *http://members.aol.com/RWNARF*, features calculators for calculating times at different distances at different ages. It also provides an age-grading calculator for those using age grading to assess how they are doing in relationship to the best in their age group, as well as how their times hold up over the years. Icabod's Racewalk 101 is equally popular.

If you want to contact NARF, you can write or call them at:

North American Racewalking Foundation
1203 S. Orange Grove Blvd.
Pasadena, CA 91105-3345
Phone: 626-441-5459
narwf@sbcglobal.net

BENT ARM SWING DRILL
Purpose: To loosen the upper-body muscle groups and the hamstrings.

Importance: Medium   **Intensity:** Medium

When the body is cold, this is a great way to get blood pumping to all extremities quickly.

Steps

1. Standing with your feet shoulder's width apart, bend forward slightly, positioning your buttocks just slightly behind your feet. Extend your arms as far as possible to each side, like an airplane (Figure 3-1a).

2. Synchronously swing arms across the front of your body, while bending further down from the waist (Figure 3-1b).

Figure 3-1a

Figure 3-1b

3. Allow your hands to criss-cross one another (Figure 3-1c).

4. Begin to move towards an upright position, to roughly the same height as where you began the exercise (Figure 3-1d).

5. Reverse steps 1 through 4 so you are return to the starting position.

6. Repeat steps 1 through 5 for 20 to 30 seconds.

Figure 3-1c

Figure 3-1d

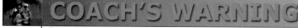

COACH'S WARNING

Do not try this drill if you have any back problems.

SWING ARMS DRILL

Purpose: To loosen the upper-body muscle groups and the hips.

Importance: Medium   **Intensity:** Easy

Another great drill for when the body is cold.

Steps

1. Stand with your feet about shoulder's width apart.

2. Hold both arms straight out in front of your body (Figure 3-2a).

3. Swing your arms from one side of the body to the other (Figure 3-2b to 3-2d). Swing through a full range of motion, so that at the end of the swing you see what is behind your body (Figure 3-2e).

4. Reverse direction and swing all the way to the other side.

5. Repeat this exercise for 20 to 30 seconds.

Figure 3-2a

Figure 3-2b

Figure 3-2c

Figure 3-2d

Figure 3-2e

There are a great many benefits to this drill. Aside from the merits listed above, it also makes a great final warm-up.

Steps:

1. Race walk with normal technique, except place the hands behind the back and walk with very short strides (12 inches or less).

Figure 3-4a

Figure 3-4b

Figure 3-4c

Figure 3-4d

Figure 3-4e

Figure 3-4f

 COACH'S TIP

This drill is completely safe; However, it is most effective when performed after your other drills.

BEND DOWN HAMSTRING DRILL

Purpose: To loosen your hamstring muscles.

Importance: High   **Intensity:** Medium

Hamstring muscles are tough to stretch. This exercise is a great way to warm them before a training walk.

Steps:

1. Standing straight up, place one extended leg six inches in front of your body with toes pointed up.

2. Bend over slowly and, without bending the knee of your extended leg, reach to touch your toes (Figure 3-5a).

3. If you are flexible, try reaching beyond your toes (Figure 3-5b). To relieve the stress on your back, make sure your buttocks are behind your rear foot when touching your toes (Figure 3-5c).

Figure 3-5a   Figure 3-5b   Figure 3-5c

4. Walk forward, alternating legs (Figure 3-5d and 3-5e).

5. Perform this exercise for 30 yards.

Figure 3-5d   Figure 3-5e

Steps:

1. Use a pole or tree for balance.
2. Extend your opposite arm and leg as shown in Figure 3-6a.
3. Swing leg under the body, while bringing the opposite arm back towards the body (Figure 3-6b).
4. Drive the knee up as high as you can, while bringing your opposite arm back behind your body. (Figure 3-6c).
5. Reverse your arm and leg swing, extending back to your original position (Figure 3-6a).
6. Repeat this exercise 10 times for each leg.

Figure 3-6a

Figure 3-6b

Figure 3-6c

 SPOTLIGHT ON

Team in Training (TNT) is the world's largest endurance-sports training program in the world. I have had the pleasure of coaching and helping the program since 1994. Words can not express the sense of joy and accomplishment TNT brings to its participants.

TNT trains novice as well as seasoned athletes to participate in endurance-sports events while they raise funds to help find cures for leukemia, lymphoma, and myeloma. Some of the benefits the Leukemia and Lymphoma Society provides to participants are:

- A comprehensive training plan, regular coaching and training sessions.
- Travel to the race locations.
- A connection with an honored patient so they know just who and what they're doing it all for.

More information can be found at their web site, *www.teamintraining.org*.

HIP ROCK DRILL

Purpose: **To improve hip flexibility.**

Importance: Low   Intensity: Easy

Steps:

1. Place one hand chest level against a wall or on a pole for balance.

2. Place the other hand on your hip.

3. Keep the front foot on the ground, beginning with toes up and rolling to flat down as you progress to step 4.

4. Rock back and forth, extending your hip, rolling up onto your back toe while raising the heel.

5. Perform this exercise 10 times with each leg.

Figure 3-7a

Figure 3-7b

Figure 3-7c

SPOTLIGHT ON

Elliot Denman may have been one of the few Boy Scouts in NYC who actually enjoyed 14-mile hikes. So, when in 1953 his big brother Marty introduced him to track and field, walking races became a natural attraction. Mentored by Henry Laskau and Bruce MacDonald, he was on his way. By September 1956 he was walking the Olympic Trial 50K. Wonder of wonders, the 50K novice placed fourth and made the team when third-placer Jim Hewson opted for the 20K. So young Elliott went to Melbourne placing 11th.

In 1959, Elliott won both the 3K and 50K Nationals, as a proud member of the magnificent NY Pioneer Club team, but his focus would soon shift. He directed his first race, the National 10K in 1960, and in 1962 went to work as a newspaperman. Journalism and pedestrianism proved an ideal combination. While covering the wide, wide world of sports for the Asbury Park Press, including 10 Olympic Games and each edition of the World Championships, he found time to re-establish the Shore AC track team, organize countless events of all lengths and descriptions - including every 40K National but one since 1964 - and serve the sport of track and field in an array of capacities.

He joined the ranks of the IAAF judges in 1980 and has since carried his paddle to events assuring that the rules of the game were enforced with justice and fairness to all. He's walked the NYC Marathon 25 straight times and plans to do it forever. Sure he's slowing up, but he still gets there.

HURDLER'S DRILL

Purpose: To improve hip flexibility.

Importance: Medium   Intensity: Medium

Steps:

1. Lean against a wall or tree.

2. While facing forwards, swing your leg forward and up, then back and around, as if it was clearing a hurdle placed at your side.

3. Use a prop such as someone's arm to act as the hurdle if possible.

4. Range of motion is important to performing this drill correctly. Be sure to extend your leg in as large a circle as possible.

5. Perform this exercise 10 times for each leg.

Figure 3-8a

Figure 3-8b

Figure 3-8c

Figure 3-8d

Figure 3-8e

Steps:

1. Lean against a pole or tree.

2. Swing leg up and away from the body, kicking the leg as high as you can (Figure 3-9a).

3. Swing the leg down and in front of the body. Lift the heel of your supporting leg off the ground so that you have extra height for clearing your foot as it swings (Figure 3-9b).

4. As the leg swings upwards, in front of your body, extend it as far as your range of motion allows (Figure 3-9c).

5. Reverse your position back to the position in Figure 3-9a.

6. Perform this exercise 10 times for each leg.

Figure 3-9a   Figure 3-9b   Figure 3-9c

 SPOTLIGHT ON

Frank Alongi may be the one contributor listed in this book who never race walked competitively. An Olympic 5K runner, his interest in our sport evolved because his brother Casimiro was a race walker.

For years Alongi opened his house to young upstart race walkers for week-long training camps. He and his wife offered limitless generosity. I should know, I was one of their guests.

For 19 years Alongi organized the Casimiro Alongi Classic. Bringing international athletes to America, often at his own expense, the Alongi Classic showed America what a quality race walk competition was all about. While the Casimiro Alongi Classic is no longer held, the Alongi In Marin Classic 5K celebrates its 11th anniversary this year.

Alongi is a teacher as much as a coach. Writing papers on the biomechanics of race walking and instructing nearly every race walking judge in Michigan, Alongi remains active today, providing race walking seminars at the event that bears his name.

SNAKE DRILL

Purpose: To improve hip flexibility.

Importance: Low   **Intensity:** Easy

Steps:

1. Perform this drill by race walking using correct technique, but with slightly shorter strides than usual.

2. Race walk in an imaginary snake or S shaped line.

3. Walk as quickly as possible.

4. Perform this exercise for 30 yards.

Figure 3-10a

Figure 3-10b

Figure 3-10c

Figure 3-10d

Figure 3-10e

Figure 3-10f

LONG ARMS DRILL

Purpose: Improve hip flexibility; Learn correct forward and back hip motion.

Importance: Low   **Intensity:** Easy

Steps:

1. Hold your arms at your side, one in front and one behind the body.

2. Keep both arms straight and your hands flat with palms back.

3. Race walk with a normal stride; however, keep your arms straight. Focus on driving your hips forward.

4. Perform this exercise for 30 yards. You should feel a connection between your arms and hips.

Figure 3-11a

Figure 3-11b

Figure 3-11c

Figure 3-11d

When the body is cold, this is a great way to get blood pumping to all extremities quickly. In addition, it helps to relax and stretch the upper body, leading to a more fluid arm motion.

Steps:

1. Start with one arm at your side and the other pointed straight up to the sky (Figure 3-12a).

2. Swing the arm at your side up and forward at the same time as swinging the pointed arm back and down (Figure 3-12b).

3. Allow both arms to make circles, keeping your arm close to the side of your head as you swing it back (Figure 3-12c).

4. Walk with the proper lower leg motion of race walking.

5. Perform this exercise for 30 yards.

Figure 3-12a

Figure 3-12b

Figure 3-12c

 ## SPOTLIGHT ON

Chapter 4 - Race Walking Technique

When people approach me to teach them to race walk, they usually fit within one of four broad categories: injured runners looking for an alternative to the wear and tear of running, experienced runners looking for a new sport that provides greater competitive opportunities, fitness walkers looking to get fitter and faster, or non-athletes eager to immediately get off the couch and start a fitness program.

Of the four groups, the last actually has the mental advantage. People in the first three groups often approach race walking technique with predetermined ideas of how fast they should be walking. Ask any runner who has tried race walking and not continued with it, and he or she will tell you: race walking is difficult! While difficult is a very vague term, it reflects the fact that the sport takes a much greater degree of sustained focus and concentration on technical details than running. Nevertheless, once basic technique is mastered, race walking is actually an easier sport to progress within because competitors avoid the injuries that continually plague runners.

Do As I Say

Do not mimic the technique of other people who race walk. Instead, follow the detailed instructions described here and on my DVD. All too often I hear that a race walker tried one thing or another because he or she observed someone else do it. Avoid this temptation. Novice walkers cannot know whether a particular race walker's individual method of locomotion is efficient, admirable, or simply an oddity due to something in the walker's unique body structure.

For example, look at the photo of Kevin Eastler (right). While Kevin exhibits completely legal technique and is capable of walking at incredible speeds, he has a wicked bow in his leg that causes his foot to duck out as he carries his leg under and through. Because Kevin is the 2003 U.S. 20K Champion, you might be tempted to mimic his technique. Don't do it! You will most likely get injured very quickly!

Even if an elite race walker's body is ideally proportioned and he seemingly walks with textbook technique, his technique might not work for you. Are your body proportions the same? Are you strong enough to move your muscle groups in the same manner? Are you correctly interpreting what you see?

 COACH'S TIP

For all of these reasons, please: Do as I say, not as you see.

Patience is a Virtue That Comes to Those Who Wait

In the early days of learning race walking technique, the key is not focusing on your pace. Your slower pace builds solid skills, enabling you to walk faster later. The better your race walking technique, the more you use your body's untapped resources, increase your pace, and improve the safety of your workout.

Remember, like any complex skill, the sport of race walking takes time to master, and not everyone progresses to efficient, legal technique at the same rate. Some aspiring race walkers master the technique in as little as two months or as long as two years. Rushing the learning process causes illegal technique and other inefficient habits. Acquired early in your walking career, such habits quickly become ingrained and difficult to unlearn. So start slow. Master all of the techniques explained in this chapter before attempting any of the training schedules explained in Chapter 6 or on the DVD.

The Rules of Race Walking

In national competition, USATF established an official definition of race walking to formally differentiate it from running. This definition evolved across several decades as officials attempted to better define the sport. Although many rules regulate competitive walking, only this definition (in two parts) serves to characterize legal race walking.

USATF Definition

Race walking is a progression of steps so taken that the walker makes contact with the ground so that no visible (to the human eye) loss of contact occurs.

The advancing leg must be straightened (i.e., not bent at the knee) from the moment of first contact with the ground until in the vertical upright position.

One would think by now this definition would be concrete, but in practice, it is fairly subjective.

Loss of Contact

Let's start by examining the first half of the definition, for a moment excluding the words "to the human eye." A race walker must strike the ground with the leading foot before the rear foot breaks contact with the ground. For a brief moment—the double support phase—both feet remain in contact with the ground.

The photographs below demonstrate race walkers achieving the double support phase at national championship races: proof that walking fast while maintaining constant contact with the ground is possible.

Once referred to as textbook form, today such technique is nearly impossible to find among elite race walkers. Indeed, I sifted through thousands of elite walkers' photos to find just a few with double contact—and found these only because my collection includes shots from longer races of two hours or more. At longer distances, race walkers naturally use a slower pace, increasing the likelihood of the double support phase.

Adding a Flight Phase

Adding the words "to the human eye" back into the definition makes judging more subjective. A race walker may lose contact with the ground as long as this lifting is not visible to the human eye. The problem occurs in defining what is meant by visible to the human eye. Observe the following walker:

Is this visible to the human eye?

Zoomed in view

Zoomed in and frozen in time, it's possible to see that the walker above has briefly broken contact with the ground; but can the human eye catch that in real time? Not likely. Therefore, she is not violating the definition and is legal.

I have argued elsewhere that if a videotaped walker is off the ground for one frame or less, the human eye cannot perceive the lift. My peers, however, may contend that less—or more—time is required to distinguish loss of contact. Thus is the case with all subjective rules. You might therefore reasonably conclude that the rule intends for flagrant lifters to be disqualified. Unfortunately, the definition of race walking is not that simple. For example, observe the photo to the right. Would you disqualify this walker? The question remains unanswerable based on a single photo. Always remember, the definition says *to the human eye*. There is no instant replay in race walking.

Is this legal?

If you are a beginning race walker, odds are you will not lift. Frankly, you are not walking fast enough. To be certain, videotape a workout from a side angle. Make certain the camera is a complete track-width away from you, and walk at race pace.

Study the tape one frame at a time. If you see a double support phase, you have nothing to worry about. In contrast, if you lift for two or more frames, a disqualification awaits in your future. The gray area is if you appear off the ground for only one frame. You probably will receive cautions, but hopefully not the three proposals for disqualification that lead to a removal from the race.

Can You Be Too Legal?

After spending so much time learning to walk legally, you might begin to wonder: is there harm walking too legally? Observe the photographs below.

Both walkers are completely legal. Actually, they are overly legal. By leaving the rear foot on the ground too long, they become inefficient.

Straighten the Leg

The second rule of race walking is the one that gives fledgling race walkers difficulty.

The following six figures show the progression of a legal race walker from just before her rear foot leaves the ground (Figure 4-1a) until just after the same foot strikes the ground in front of the body. When her rear foot leaves the ground, it swings forward with the leg flexed at the knee (Figure 4-1b). She begins straightening her leg as it moves forward, using her quadriceps to extend it (Figures 4-1b to 4-1d). Once her foot makes contact with the ground, the leg must be straightened and no longer flexed at the knee (Figure 4-1f).

| Figure 4-1a | Figure 4-1b | Figure 4-1c |

| *Figure 4-1d* | *Figure 4-1e* | *Figure 4-1f* |

If a walker's leg is still flexed at the knee when the leading foot makes contact with the ground, the quadriceps muscles contract eccentrically over the length of the whole muscle to prevent further flexion of the knee. This is commonly referred to as *creeping*. This can be seen in the lead walker in the figure to the lower left. Compare this to the straightened leg of the walker in the rear of the same figure. When the forward leg of the walker to the rear of the figure makes contact with the ground, it is straightened, with the walker's quadriceps visibly relaxed. For a closer view, look at the figure to the lower right. This walker's obviously relaxed quadriceps muscles and a properly straightened leg clearly demonstrates legal technique. No violations here!

Once the leg has straightened, it must stay straightened until the leg passes the vertical position. Actually, keeping the leg straightened beyond the vertical position is fine and even desirable. Observe the leg position in the image on the right: the walker not only follows the definition, she also keeps her leg straightened after passing the vertical position. This leads to increased forward drive and removes any doubt from the judge that your leg is straightened long enough.

While violations involving loss of contact tend to occur more often at short races, bent-knee calls frequent competition at longer distances. The longer a race lasts, the less lifting occurs; conversely, creeping tends to increase. Inexperienced race walkers typically struggle more with straightening the knee, whereas elite walkers face greater problems with lifting. While strong competitors try to avoid either violation, they usually walk as close to the periphery of the definition of race walking as possible.

Legal at Any Age

We are never too old to maintain legal technique. All too often I hear walkers use their age as an excuse for illegal technique. More likely, violations result from lack of flexibility, strength, or ability to walk within their individual technique limitations—that is, trying to walk at a faster speed than their technique allows.

Check out master's race walking extraordinaires Janet Higbie and Jack Starr at the 2003 50K Nationals (right). Jack sometimes receives bent knee cautions and proposals for disqualification, but his knee is actually knobby, not bent. A careful judge or bystander can distinguish between an oddly shaped knee and one that is bent. (Hint: Notice Jack's relaxed quadriceps muscles.)

Learning to Walk

Obey the Definition First

Becoming a legal race walker requires walking without violating either part of the USATF definition. Most likely, when you start to race walk, the previously underutilized muscles required to execute the technique are not strong enough to propel you properly at fast speeds. Most beginning walkers' initial paces are in the range of 10:00 mins/mile to 15:00 mins/mile; thus initially you are not likely to break the first part of the definition requiring constant (to the human eye) contact with the ground.

The second part of the definition of race walking is the one that gives most novice walkers problems. Therefore, we begin the walking technique lesson here. Once you master the technique required for the second part, then focus on all the other techniques explained here to help you walk faster.

Observe Figures 4-2a to 4-2f. They illustrate the correct positioning of my leg the instant my left leg strikes the ground, as my body passes directly over the leg and beyond, and just as my left foot leaves the ground behind my body.

Figure 4-2a   Figure 4-2b   Figure 4-2c

Figure 4-2d   Figure 4-2e   Figure 4-2f

But what looks simple on the page in front of you can actually be a little tricky to master, as least at first.

Look at Figure 4-2a, where my heel has just made contact with the ground. A few things happened simultaneously. Just before contact, as my leg was swinging forward, it straightened, with toes pointed up (about 45 degrees from the ground), while my heel struck the ground. Achieving this smooth synchronized action is the key to success.

Between Figure 4-2a and Figure 4-2c, the body moves forward, over the left leg. This is the second point at which walkers tend to violate the rules of race walking. The leg must remain straightened until it is in the vertical position. In Figure 4-2c, my leg is almost in the vertical position, while it remains straightened.

Once the leg is beyond the vertical position, as in Figure 4-2d, you may bend it. However, when it comes time to lift your foot off the ground, if your leg is still straightened, you get an extra thrust forward by pushing off your rear foot (Figure 4-2c). Through proper flexibility and strength your leg stays straightened longer and you obtain this advantageous thrust. Ideally, the leg remains straightened until the heel of your rear foot lifts off the ground.

Figure 4-2f shows my stance, just after rear-foot push off, with an obvious bend in my leg. It is impossible to race walk with any efficiency and keep the leg straight as it swings forward. Notice that as my rear (left) leg leaves the ground, my front (left) leg is already in position. Also, note that the legs do not create a symmetrical

33

triangle. More of my stride is behind my body than in front. This is achieved through proper hip action, which will be explained shortly.

Race walk with the techniques explained thus far and you can tell people you are a legal race walker, albeit not a very fast one yet. YET! Keep reading and you'll get faster.

Improving the Lower Body

Foot Placement

Imagine there is a thin, straight line extending in front of you and down the path you walk. (If you go to a track, use one of the lane lines.) When walking at a pedestrian pace, without using any race walking techniques, each foot will land on a different side of the line.

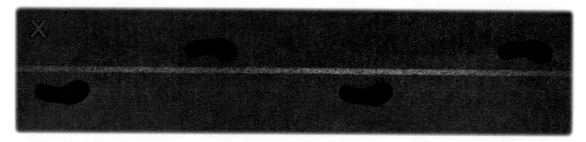

Then, as you increase your pace a little, your feet land just on the edge of the line.

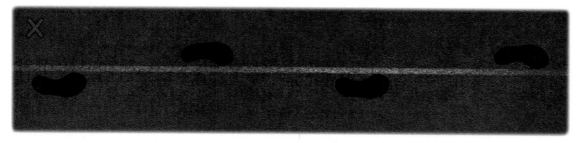

In contrast, when you race walk, your feet land in an almost exact straight line. After you learn to use your hips efficiently, your foot placement changes slightly to imitate this near straight-line placement. But please beware: when you try to mimic this action without using your hips, you place an unneeded stress across your knee.

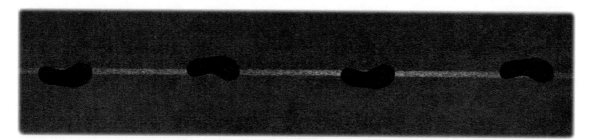

Never allow your feet to cross over the line as depicted below.

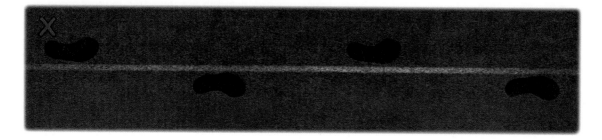

34

Foot Strike

When your foot strikes the ground, land on the back of your heel and point your toes as high as possible. Once your foot makes contact, roll it forward, keeping your toes pointed up and off the ground until the entire leg supports your body's weight.

Figure 4-3a   *Figure 4-3b*   *Figure 4-3c*

The goal when your heel strikes the ground is to position the foot close to a 45-degree angle with the ground. After heel strike, smoothen your stride by rolling onto the midsection of your foot and through to your big toe. Avoid slapping your foot against the ground. If you feel or hear a slap, stop, stretch your shin, and start again.

Figure 4-4a   *Figure 4-4b*   *Figure 4-4c*

When you walk with your toes pointed, you use your shin muscles more. How long you keep your toes off the ground is directly related to the strength of your shin. However, be aware that holding your toe up upon heel strike may cause a burning sensation in your shins. When you feel this soreness, stop and stretch the shins out using the *Seated Shin Stretch* or the *Standing Shin Stretch* in Chapter 7. Slow down a little, walking with pedestrian technique; then, after a few minutes, try the new technique again. The shin pain should go away as you become better conditioned, if it does not seek assistance from a medical professional.

Proper planting of the foot with a smooth roll through also helps avoid premature knee bending. Prove it to yourself. Try to land flat footed with your leg straight. It's not very easy, especially if you race walk with any speed.

Because of body build, some walkers naturally place their feet with toes pointing out or in. Observe U.S. National Team member Sean Albert in the figure to the right. Albert's foot points outward, nearly at a 45-degree angle. It should be pointing straight ahead. Unfortunately, this foot position occurs because of body structure; it may be a contributor to the many injuries that have plagued Albert over the years.

If you face similar problems, do not try to change your foot placement as you learn to race walk. Instead, focus on using your hips properly so that your footfalls occur in a straight line, even if the feet are not parallel. While improper foot positions are less efficient, the alternative—forcing yourself to correct foot placement unnaturally—may cause extra stress on legs, feet, and knees, leading to strain and injury.

Carry That Knee Low

To remain efficient, race walkers must pay careful attention to how their legs swing forward after push off. Drive your leg forward with the knee as low to the ground as possible. While some upwards motion is necessary to break contact with the ground, it should be minimized. Therefore, when the rear foot lifts up, it rises only an inch or two off the ground. This is seen throughout Figures 4-5a to 4-5c. By the time your foot swings under your body, it is almost parallel with the ground (Figure 4-5b).

Figure 4-5a

Figure 4-5b

Figure 4-5c

Driving your knee high as your leg swings forward not only wastes energy, but also gives you the appearance of walking illegally. Appearances are a bigger issue than judges care to admit. Observe the following figures showing a high knee drive. A walker with this style gives the appearance of excessive loss of contact with the ground, even if there is a double support phase.

Figure 4-6a

Figure 4-6b

Figure 4-6c

The Rear Foot

Many race walkers do not hold their rear foot on the ground long enough. The longer you leave your rear foot on the ground, the more efficient your stride, for many reasons:

Your hips are able to pivot, thus lengthening the stride and allowing time for your leg to swing forward and your heel to strike the ground.

The motion stretches your hip muscles as they swing the leg forward, and the resulting reflex pulls the leg forward faster. As the faster-moving swing leg propels your body forward with greater force, you gain even more speed.

Your body exerts a force against the ground due to gravity. When you stand still, this force is completely vertical. By keeping the foot on the ground longer, the ground reactive force of the body's weight becomes more horizontal than vertical when you lift your heel and move to toe off. This force helps maintain contact with the ground while contributing to forward body propulsion.

Figure 4-7a

Figure 4-7b

Toe Off and a Final Push

Efficient race walkers do not let their feet lift passively off the ground; instead, just before the rear foot breaks contact with the ground, they actively push the big toe against the ground. If you add this simple flick, you feel a slight float to your stride. Done properly, overall race walking technique becomes less mechanical and movements feel as if they are flowing together in a forward motion. Done improperly, an overly hard push off causes over-striding and flagrant loss of contact with the ground.

Figure 4-8a

Figure 4-8b

Figure 4-8c

COACH'S WARNING

Be sure not to push off too early. An early push off propels your body upwards instead of forward.

Care must be taken to carry your foot forward in a relatively straight line after you push off. When your foot leaves the ground and is swinging forward, try not to twist the foot to the side as your leg progresses. Observe the following figures that demonstrate proper and improper foot carriage.

Figure 4-9a

Figure 4-9b

Figure 4-9c

Often this improper foot carriage is caused by weakness or tightness of any of a number of muscle groups.

Figure 4-10a

Figure 4-10b

Figure 4-10c

Transitioning From One Leg to the Other

The least-trained eye can readily tell from a distance which race walkers have mastered proper technique and which continue to struggle. Great race walkers look smooth and graceful.

One telltale indication of proper technique is how fluidly an athlete transitions from one leg to the other. A bicycle rider spins a bike crank around and around. If I asked you where the beginning and ending of the cyclist's stride was, what would you answer? Hopefully, you wouldn't come up with one. Identifying a beginning or ending adds an artificial stop to a smooth motion. The same holds true for race walking.

Sometimes a walker feels similar to a car with square tires. When a walker's shins are weak, he or she may land with a pointed toe, only to have the foot flatten quickly. If this happens to you, make sure you do the shin building exercises and stretches explained in Chapter 9 on a regular basis. Strong flexible shins ensure better transitions. When you walk efficiently, the transition flows from one leg to another without any jerky movements. Remember, the goal is to help the body go forward, so any excess motion must go.

Overstriding

Many walkers overstride in front of the body. Overstriders typically reach far in front of their bodies, straightening legs before impact. A straightened leg with nowhere to go hangs briefly, neither pulling nor pushing the body forward. Then gravity pulls it down, sending the foot crashing to the ground. Aside from adding unneeded stress to the body, this crash also gives the appearance of lifting.

COACH'S WARNING

Old school race walkers talk about pulling their bodies forward through the heel. This not only adds stress, it's inefficient.

Overstriding

39

Hips

Gaining Power and Stride Length

Using your legs properly gets you moving, but to go really fast you must learn to use your hips correctly. The hips are the body's primary source of forward locomotion. When we rotate the hips forward, the swinging leg is pulled off the ground. As we repeatedly pivot the hips forward, they act as the body's motor, propelling it forward one step at a time.

Actively swinging the hip forward lengthens the stride from the top of the legs while increasing stride length behind the body. Observe the following two figures. The figure at left demonstrates stride without hip drive, while the figure at right shows the additional length obtained as the left hip extends forward. In a flexible race walker, the gain can be as much as six inches per stride.

Lack of proper hip motion

Proper hip motion

The difference is even more visible from an overhead examination. In each figure below, the front foot is just ahead of the body. But notice the difference created by using the hips. With proper use of your hips, 30% of your stride is in front of your body, while 70% is behind it. This is how I achieved the longer stride behind my body alluded to during the explanation of leg motion.

Lack of proper hip motion

Proper hip motion

Improving technique takes more than just knowing what to do. Walkers must develop and maintain flexibility to gain the full benefit of hip motion. To achieve elasticity and increased range of motion, be sure to practice the drills in Chapter 3, particularly those that indicate high importance for the hips.

When I first learned to race walk, many of these drills were not commonplace. I actually didn't start using them regularly until after I co-authored *Walk Like An Athlete* (1996). After two months of practicing the drills religiously, a race walking judge came up to me after a race and asked what had changed in my technique. She thought I looked great. I hadn't consciously changed anything; it was my added flexibility that made the difference.

Let's Revisit Overstriding

Coaches all agree: overstriding slows you down! On page 39 you saw that overstriding caused the foot to momentarily suspend in the air after the leg straightened; the extra length in stride was inefficient. But isn't lengthening your stride good?

The answer is relatively simple, and highlights the difference between lengthening and overstriding. Yes, a longer stride is good, but only when it's achieved by using the hips. Let's start with a working definition of overstriding.

Overstriding is when a walker takes too long a stride, either in front of or behind the body, such that the extra length actually slows the forward progress.

Proper positioned heel strike

Heel strike of an overstrider

Let's look a little closer at what happens when you use your hips properly. Observe the angle the front leg makes with the ground. The greater the angle, the more the ground pushes you back when you strike it. This phenomenon is known as braking force and will impede your progress. When you reduce the angle the foot makes with the ground, you reduce the braking force. Conversely, the longer stride caused by extending the hips allows your foot to strike the ground with a minimum of braking force. So use those hips!

Common Technique Problems With the Hips

When using your hips, be careful not to swing them out to the side. Some lateral motion is necessary, because the human body does not move in straight lines. However, limit the lateral motion as much as possible.

Correct Hip Motion - Hip swings mostly forward

Incorrect Hip Motion - Hip swings too far out

Proper arm swing must also take into account the way the arm crosses in front of the body. The arm swings forward as if shaking someone's hand.

Get the Feel Using Hip Drills

If you are still having trouble understanding what proper hip action should feel like, try this simple exercise:

1. Find a fairly long and steep hill. Start at the bottom and walk as quickly as you can, folding your arms across your chest like a vampire in a B horror movie. This prevents your arms from counter balancing the forces in your hips.

2. For about 15 yards, maintain this fast pace. Feel the tugging sensation in your hips. Continue walking, but for the next 15 yards, try to exaggerate the sensation you feel in your hips. Allow your muscles to work with your hips, following the motion of the tugs. Be sure the movement is forward and back, not side to side.

3. Finally, bring your arms down into normal walking position. Allow them to swing while continuing to exaggerate your hips. Your hip and swing leg should feel as if they are being whipped forward in conjunction with your arm swinging back.

If you use your hips correctly on the hill, you will feel a dramatic effect. Your stride will be more powerful and longer in the rear.

Arms

Proper use of the arms is key to mastering the hip motion just described. Synchronizing arm and hip motion maximizes efficiency and speed.

Each arm should travel from a couple of inches behind the hip to just above the chest line. You generate the primary power for arm movement by driving the shoulder on the backwards swing of your arm. Do not try to generate power by wildly pumping your arm backward or thrusting it forward. Just use the shoulder as a fulcrum and let the arms swing like a pendulum.

Adjust the angle between your upper and lower arm using your elbow. With the proper angle, when you drive back, your arm swings to proper position a few inches behind your hip. With a relaxed shoulder, your arm recoils forward to the proper position. The cycle repeats with another drive of the arm backwards. Keep in mind that with a relaxed shoulder and proper angle, the effort required to move your arm backwards is not much. Your arms move only as fast as your hips and legs; it's all about synchronicity.

COACH'S TIP

The ratio of upper and lower arm length varies from walker to walker. If you feel you are swinging your arms too far in front of your body, reduce the angle between your upper and lower arms. Similarly, if you have too short an arm swing, increase the angle.

Arms Just Right

Arms Too Short

Arms Too Long

Observe the pictures above. The length of the arm swing is directly related to the angle between my upper and lower arm. As the angle increases, so does the length of arm swing. When my arm swing is too long, I overstride, causing too much of my stride to be in front of my body. In contrast, with my arms too short, the stride is not long enough behind my body. With the proper arm swing, I exhibit the optimal 30% in front, 70% behind ratio.

Proper arm swing must also take into account the way the arm crosses in front of the body. The arm swings forward as if shaking someone's hand.

Correct arm swing

Arms too straight and too long

Arm crossing over body

Crossing directly across the body or too straight inhibits forward hip rotation.

Hand Position

Relax your hands, but do not allow them to dangle or flop with your arm swing. Keep a straight wrist with the hand in a loose fist. As your hands pass by your hips, the fingertips face the hips. If you have trouble relaxing your hands, make a loose fist, then place your thumb between your index finger and your middle finger.

Hands Just Right

Hooked Hand

Hands Out Straight

Relaxed Shoulders

Relaxing the shoulders can be difficult. Many people believe their shoulders are relaxed, but they are not. When we walk, our shoulders often tighten and rise above the desired position. This is like adding friction to the axle of a car.

Observe the height of your shoulders and check whether they are relaxed. Since you won't be carrying a ruler, simply place one hand on your shoulder and lower it as far down as it can go. When your shoulder is all the way down, it is relaxed.

 COACH'S TIP

As a last check, while race walking, try lowering your elbows as if trying to drag them along the ground. Did your shoulders lower in the process? If so, use this visualization to help you relax your shoulders.

Arm Fatigue

When out for a long walk, you may experience your arms or shoulders getting fatigued. When this happens, relax your arms, lowering them to your side and shaking them for two or three seconds. Once you get your blood flowing and feel loosened up, continue race walking regularly. This improves circulation, stretches out the muscles and helps you continue walking comfortably.

It's easy to underestimate how much effort it takes to hold your arm in one position for a couple of hours. When I walk long distances and am not in particularly great shape, my biceps get sore. If your arms constantly feel fatigued, try cross training with some low-weight, high-repetition exercises, as shown in Chapter 9.

Posture

Good posture is very important, and many race walking instructors begin lessons with this topic. However, I usually complete my lessons with posture. I believe people fall into one of two categories. Either they follow common sense and have reasonably correct posture, or they have walked their whole lives with incorrect posture that requires a long time to correct. To maximize efficiency and reduce potential injuries, concentrate on perfecting posture.

Use Common Sense

The principle of good race walking posture is fairly simple. Your body is straight up and down throughout the entire stride. Years ago, walkers believed proper posture meant leaning from their ankles; however, to do so, they often bent from the waist instead. Such bending causes the hips to move backwards, thus reducing the ability to extend the hip and accelerate the stride.

I actually learned to race walk leaning forward from the ankles. The lean forward placed excessive stress on my lower back, and when I walked long distances, the strained muscles constantly felt sore.

Correct Posture	Bent Forward	Sway Back
Figure 4-11a	Figure 4-11b	Figure 4-11c

Many promoters of the forward lean cite traditional sprinters' leaning forms as examples of why race walkers should have the same posture. Conversely, the case of Michael Johnson who set a world record for the 200-meter sprint at the 1996 Olympics might support my argument that an upright posture is best. (Johnson broke the traditional mold of sprinters by maintaining a straight, up-and-down posture, similar to the posture of race walking.) However, race walking and sprinting are two totally different biomechanical activities and should not be compared in this manner.

Sway Back

You still may hear a knowledgeable coach tell a race walker to lean forward. Often this is to correct bad posture such as leaning back, or *sway back*. Aside from adding stress to the back, leaning back causes more of a race walker's mass to be centered behind the hips. The race walker in effect is carrying a weight behind him or her, thus inhibiting forward progress.

Head Position

Many novice walkers, instead of looking ahead, look at the ground five feet in front of them. This causes the neck to bend and stresses the neck and shoulders. Eventually this stress leads to cramping of the neck or shoulders.

Look ahead, not at the ground. Often race walkers claim they look down to make sure they don't trip. By looking ahead, you see enough to prevent tripping. Another common excuse is watching one's own form. While it may be necessary to look at your feet some of the time, this practice should be minimized.

Walking the Varied Road

The techniques presented in this chapter begin with a big assumption: that you are walking on level terrain. While race walking competitions are rarely held on courses with a significant hill, training walks surely lead you to encounter a hill at one time or another.

Hills

How many times have you race walked on a hill that never seemed to end? This phenomenon is especially true if you walk on the same hill more than once in a workout or race. One of the reasons walkers have trouble with hills is that they face a much more difficult challenge in trying to maintain proper form uphill than do runners or health walkers. While most walkers view a hill as similar to another word that varies from hill by only one vowel, learning to walk properly on a steep grade minimizes the pain associated with it.

Pacing yourself as you "climb" involves strategy. Most people attack up a hill—trying to maintain speed—then relax on the downhill. But if you maintain effort instead of pace, you reach the top of the hill more refreshed. As an added benefit, by not relaxing on the downhill, you walk away from the hill with more speed. I like to think of walking on a hill as analogous to an old car's cruise control. Unlike today's modern cars that maintain an exact speed, older cars maintained a constant gas level. Therefore, as you traveled up the hill, you slowed down, and as you traveled down the hill, you accelerated. Like an old car's cruise control, a race walker gains efficiency by maintaining constant effort.

Uphill

Race walking uphill requires slightly different technique than walking on a level surface or downhill. Imagine yourself as a bicycle rider in lowest gear. Bike riders spin their wheels in small gears without great resistance. To get the same effect, shorten your stride. A shorter stride reduces the effort required per step, which helps to counteract the extra effort needed to climb the hill. Also, don't worry about pushing off with your toes as you would on flat ground. The effort would just be sent in the vertical direction. Instead, try to increase the cadence of your legs to compensate for the shorter stride. The faster tempo will assist with maintaining a speed closer to your norm.

Downhill

Once you hit the crest of the hill and head down, you need to shift gears. Elongate your stride, emphasize the hips, and decrease turnover rate. Exploiting hip flexibility, let gravity be your friend and pull you down the hill. For an added surge of speed, allow your swinging leg to attack the ground in front of you. While the braking action mentioned previously slows you down when you overstride, the angle caused by walking downhill counterbalances most of this action.

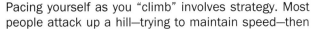
COACH'S WARNING

A final note of caution: if a hill is too steep for you to maintain proper technique comfortably, either jog or health walk down the hill. Remember, race walk competitions do not include sharp hills.

The Crown

While most walkers easily identify a hill along their path, they may be unaware of a less obvious form of uneven surface that causes race walking problems: crowns. A crown is the crest on a road that causes it to be uneven all the way across. Many roads are crowned to prevent puddles forming. While this helps cars, it severely hinders a race walker.

On a crowned road, your foot continually has an unstable landing and must compensate for the improper footing. Over time, this leads to injuries. Choose your roads carefully. Try to walk where there is a sidewalk or no crown in the road. If you have to walk on crowned roads, try to pick those with the least sharp crests in the area of the road you are walking on.

When walking on a crown, walk half the workout with the crown on one side of your body and then turn around onto the same side of the road for the second half of the workout. This balances the stress of the crown on both sides of your body. Be careful, it requires traveling both against and with traffic.

Walking Without a Road

Many people gravitate to a treadmill when the roads or weather outside is inhospitable. In theory there is not much of a difference between walking on a treadmill or road; however, be aware that many treadmills are not long enough to allow a race walker to adequately walk with proper style. When fatigued, treadmills pose another threat. They can force you to extend your range of motion beyond your body's natural range. Obviously, this can lead to additional injuries. If possible, limit treadmill use in your training.

No Weights While Walking

Often the first question asked by beginning race walkers is, "Can I use hand and ankle weights when I race walk?" The perceived benefit of additional weights is that they provide a better or harder workout.

Do not race walk with weights on your ankles, legs, wrists, or hands: the reality is, carrying weights is not beneficial to race walkers. Weights add stress to the body in a way that we are not designed to handle, thus increasing the risk of injuries to an unacceptable level. They also disturb natural cadence, making proper technique difficult if not impossible. Your walking pace will slow with no net benefit. If you want to tone your muscles, add an easy strength training routine. If you want to walk faster, learn the proper technique and then follow the training schedules provided on my DVD.

SPOTLIGHT ON

The North American Racewalking Institute (NARI) is the non profit companion to the North American Racewalking Foundation. NARI has been a major contributor to the race walking program at the ARCO Olympic Training Center in Chula Vista, California, since its inception in 1997. A state-of-the art training facility, the OTC provides a unique resource for both resident and visiting athletes preparing for international competition. Over the years, NARI has also  given financial assistance to high school and collegiate race walking programs, put on training and awareness camps, and sponsored several national championships.

Recently, NARI initiated the Al Heppner Scholarship Fund in honor of this talented and loved athlete. Curt Clausen, Vince Peters, Jeff Salvage, Diane Graham-Henry and Elaine Ward form the Scholarship Committee. The purpose of the Fund is to aid aspiring Olympians.

NARI's activities are made possible by the tax deductible donations of individuals, businesses and charitable foundations. The officers and Board of Directors are volunteers so that all donations go directly to Olympic development programs. Race walking has a true friend in Elaine Ward, the Institute's founder and President. We look forward to enjoying her accomplishments for many more years.

Chapter 5 - Judging

A great many rules govern the judging of race walk events. In fact, USATF devotes an entire book to the topic, The *Race Walk Officiating Handbook*. You can obtain a free version online at *http://www.usatf.org/officials/* (although it may not be the most up to date). If you want a hard copy, order the latest edition from: USATF Order Department, One RCA Dome, Suite 140, Indianapolis, IN 46225.

As a race walker, you need not concern yourself with the minutia of rules governing our sport. Concern yourself instead with those rules most relevant, like how you are notified if a judge records a violation against you.

Notification of Calls

When a judge believes a competitor is violating the definition of race walking, that judge submits a proposal for disqualification (also known as a red card). Prior to 2003, proposal was termed *warning*; the change was meant to increase clarity. If three separate judges issue such proposals, the walker is disqualified. The chief official—and only the chief official—notifies the walker of the disqualification. Disqualifications occur during a race, if time permits; otherwise immediately afterwards. Each judge may issue only one proposal for disqualification per race walker and if practical should inform the walker of the submission.

A judge also has the option of issuing a caution to someone in danger of breaking a rule. A caution means the walker is close to breaking a rule; it does not necessarily result in a proposal for disqualification. A caution can be viewed as coaching advice, although race walkers should not assume they will always receive a caution prior to receiving a proposal for disqualification. Cautions are given at the judge's courtesy.

To inform a walker when issuing either a caution or proposal for disqualification, a judge uses one of the paddles depicted below. The first symbol specifies a loss of contact violation (lifting), while the second paddle indicates a bent leg (creeping). The woeful third paddle is used by the chief official to indicate disqualification from a race[1]. The number of judges per race varies. A race on the track has five judges, while a road race may have between six and nine.

| *Loss of Contact* | *Bent Leg* | *Disqualification* |

When faced with all the mental, emotional, and physical challenges of race walking, some competitors feel overwhelmed by the prospects of keeping track of calls during a race. Fortunately, officials at larger races typically utilize a disqualification board. (This is actually required at championship races.) When a call is entered against a competitor, that walker's race number appears on the board with an X to indicate each proposal for disqualification. Cautions are not recorded on the board. Realize, however, that the DQ board may not be accurate. Racers should not step off the course if they see three Xs next to their name, as the chief official holds the sole responsibility to remove a competitor from a race. Importantly, the DQ board tends to lag behind real time, so a lack of three Xs on the board does not guarantee safety from disqualification.

Factors That Affect Officiating

Ideally, judges should determine legality by studying only a walker's legs and feet. However, draw attention to yourself and they may scrutinize your every motion. Your goal, therefore, should be smooth technique. Do not engage in conversation with the officials: just pretend they don't exist. In fact, you want them to not notice you at all, so avoid clothes that draw attention. Bright or unusual attire not only draws attention to your fashion sense, but also serves as an invite for officials to observe you more attentively.

---

[1] If you wish to order paddles like these, visit *www.walk-usa.com*. They are sold at a nominal cost.

The amount of excessive motion in your stride is unfortunately harder to control than what you wear. If your head bops up and down, arms swing side to side, or hips sway out, you are likely to attract the watchful eye of an official. Trained officials ignore these oddities when determining legality; however, unorthodox motion in your gait may attract unwelcome scrutiny from the judges.

While judges should not determine legality on a comparative basis, all too often such disqualifications occur. Imagine two walkers racing side by side: a common sight at a large race. One walks with good, efficient style and no excessive motion; the flanking walker is equally legal but has an awkward, inefficient style, putting him at greater risk of receiving a call. The lesson is, those who worry about borderline legality should consider walking a safe distance from those with textbook form.

The rules governing acceptable clothing are subjective. If a judge deems a competitor's clothing an obstruction to determining the legality of technique, he or she may issue a proposal for disqualification. For example, tights shown to the left would be acceptable cold-weather attire, while sweats shown to the right would not. As you might guess, baggy sweats prevent a judge from fully observing a straightened leg.

| *Usually Acceptable* | *Highly Subjective* | *Unacceptable* |

The IAAF Difference

International competitions use slightly different wording in their English race walking definition. The IAAF (International Amateur Athletic Federation) definition states:

> The advancing leg shall be straightened (i.e. not bent at the knee) from the moment of first contact with the ground until in the vertical upright position.

This varies by only one word from the USATF definition that states the leg *must* be straightened. The second difference is that a proposal for disqualification is now called a warning; USATF found that people confused the terms caution and warning and thus changed the terminology. In both cases the wording change is semantical; the definitions are essentially the same.

One final IAAF difference is quite a change from our domestic rules. In IAAF races, there is a Chief Judge who may disqualify a walker without other judge's proposals during the last 100m of a race. The Chief Judge does not judge the rest of the race, but supervises the race and the other judges.

Disqualification Controversies?

All this discussion of rules may lead you to believe, as some critics of race walking do, that the sport is inherently flawed with controversial disqualifications. Ignorant TV correspondents utilize slow-motion or freeze-frame images of race walkers to "prove" they are "running." I argue that race walkers violate the rules of their sport no more frequently than basketball and football players. My evidence? Imagine placing a camera on the offensive and defensive lines in football and officiating through the electronic lens. Nearly every play would invoke a penalty. And if cameras tracked basketball players on each possession, the game would face constant interruptions for penalties. (Oh wait, it does. See my point?) Race walking has no flaws that a little education on rules can't fix.

Chapter 6 - TRAINING

Both novice and experienced race walkers face a confusing task when trying to determine a training strategy. Ask one hundred coaches for a training schedule and you get one hundred different training schedules. A race walker's best bet is to select a training schedule that is scientifically based and well thought out. A competitor requires a good idea of what lies ahead in the months leading up to a race. Programs thrown together without forethought usually lead to uncertainty and disappointment.

I believe all training schedules need to be written with one goal in mind: a race to serve as a target for training. You may choose to participate in other races along the way, but the focus of your training must be the target goal. Focusing on too many goals leads to certain doom or at least mediocre performances. No disrespect to some old-school race walkers who promote racing every week, but doing so leads to sub-optimal performance at a given distance.

COACH'S WARNING

Before you undertake a training regimen, be sure you have mastered the basic race walking techniques and form. Focusing on racing before you achieve a solid technical foundation leads to shoddy, inefficient technique that slows you down, and worse: it may get you disqualified from a race.

As a coach I am constantly asked to produce individualized race walking training schedules. Developing such programs requires me to consider a great many factors while leaving room for flexibility as each athlete progresses through his or her schedule. So, how can I sit down and write up one training program appropriate for every race walker reading this book? The answer is, I can't. Instead, I need to write hundreds of pages of training schedules, all based on the same theories and mathematical extrapolations that factor into a program after someone describes his or her goals and current fitness level.

Since including hundreds of pages of training schedules in one book is cost-prohibitive, here we take a different path. This chapter explains the methodology underlying the varied workouts that make up a schedule; it also guides you through a sample schedule for a walker who wishes to race a 10K in 50 minutes.

Once you understand the information presented here, either write your own schedule or use one of the approximately 100 schedules available on the *Race Walk Like a Champion* DVD. The DVD allows you to select your targeted race distance and desired finishing time. It then presents a series of training schedules, similar in form to the sample below, guiding you day by day through your training cycle. If you meet the prerequisites for the program and use some common sense in picking your goals, you should be able to follow the program with a reasonable amount of effort. Trust that following your schedule will lead you to achieve your goals.

If you find as you progress through the schedule that you cannot recover quickly enough from workout to workout, you are probably attempting a training program for which you are not adequately prepared. Shift to a slower schedule at the same race distance, but try not to do the opposite if you find the schedule too easy. If you try to shift to a harder program mid-schedule, you will be unprepared for the increased intensity and duration and thus increase your risk of injury. The exception to this rule is if you attend a clinic or get individualized expert advice. In those cases, improving your technique and increasing your efficiency might enable you to shift to a more aggressive training program.

COACH'S WARNING

Use common sense when following the training programs presented below. Factors such as heat and cold affect how fast or far you can walk. If the temperature is 100 degrees, slow your pace and reduce the mileage. Likewise, on sub-zero days, you cannot expect your body to blast out a speed workout.

Go Out and Walk

The most universally accepted training philosophy for successful race walking is, if you want to be a successful race walker, you need to go out and race walk. Getting up every morning and crunching one hundred sit-ups or pumping out fifty push-ups will not dramatically improve your walking time. Specificity of exercise is the key to improvement. While other exercises help your race walking, nothing helps as much as race walking itself. Think of adding additional exercises as a catalyst for improving an existing race walking program, not as a program in and of itself.

Adapting to Stress

To improve our body's ability to handle stress, we need to improve a number of factors. All of my schedules are based on the concept of periodization. One cannot train the same way every day, week, or even month and expect to get great results. Training requires variation in type, duration, and number of workouts, following a pattern called a phase. Each phase in the training plan works toward a different goal. My plans utilize three phases, with each emphasizing different types of workouts.

My training schedules are color coded, helping you recognize the various workout types. Observe the legend to the right. It indicates the colors for each type of workout in the schedule.

Training Schedule Legend	
Workout	Color
Easy	
Easy Distance	
Tempo	
Interval	
Rhythm	
VO$_2$ Max	
Race	

I break training phases up further, into mini-cycles. A mini-cycle is an interval of time during which you build training intensity and then recover. Most mini-cycles involve adding increasingly more stress to the body for three weeks, with a one-week recovery following. These mini-cycles repeat a few times in each phase. In most cases, each new mini-cycle is designed to stress the body more than the previous mini-cycle.

To understand a training plan, it helps to understand a bit of exercise physiology—don't worry, just a bit. First, let's clear up a common misconception. Many people believe that as we train, we increase our maximum heart rate. This is rarely the case. Instead, we improve the volume of blood the heart pumps over a given time. With more blood pumping, we become capable of exercising harder. The volume of blood pumped over a time period equals the number of beats of the heart during that period multiplied by the amount of blood pumped with each stoke. As we cannot increase our maximum heart rate, we need to increase the *amount* and *volume* of blood pumped. We accomplish this by making the heart stronger.

Training at an easy race walking pace benefits your conditioning in several ways, some of which require a physiology degree to completely understand. Coach Jake Jacobson used to say, do the long stuff because it builds the capillaries. He was right: easy walking promotes increased capillary development, thus enhancing the body's ability to distribute blood, and therefore oxygen, to the muscles. The more oxygen distributed evenly throughout the muscles, the more efficient exercise becomes. In addition, cellular adaptation in the muscles increases the quantity and size of energy-producing mitochondria. Mitochondria are like little energy factories. The more factories in the right locations, the better!

I hope by now you understand the physiological effects of easy walks well enough to acknowledge that they need to be a part of our training regimen.

Easy-paced race walks come in two varieties in my training programs. Some easy workouts are Recovery Days. Their function is to allow the body time to recuperate and rebuild from the stress already placed on it. When the body gets stressed, it breaks down. Given sufficient time to rest, it then rebuilds to a stronger level than before.

Other slower-paced workouts are Easy Distance Days. They serve to add stress gradually, over longer distances, thus improving the body's endurance. The pace for easy recovery days and easy distance days remains relatively similar.

A training program cannot progress along a linear course. Novices often think they will improve the same each week and march lock-step to their goal.

Initially, improvement occurs as a race walker first learns the proper skills required to race walk. Once the skills are mastered, considerable improvement is achieved through increases in training. However, eventually you can no longer add workload or skills and the progression roughly mimics the shape of the curve on the previous page.

The Base Building Phase

Easy workouts of the shorter and longer variety comprise the first phase of training, *base building*. During the base building phase, your goal involves safely increasing mileage to a level your body can handle, and training it to withstand the more-intense workouts that follow. As a rule of thumb, weekly mileage increases by no more than 10% from week to week, with no corresponding increase in intensity. Too much stress too soon causes injuries, leading you to lose more training time than if you progress slowly from the start.

My training programs do not follow a linear progression. In general, you train three weeks, steadily increasing either intensity or distance, with distance as the focus in the base building phase. After three weeks of building endurance, your body needs a rest, so a one-week break that backs off in mileage and intensity follows each three-week mini-cycle.

Distance Workouts for Base Building

During the base building phase for 5K to 20K race goals, you must train your body to walk farther than your selected race distance. By dedicating a long training day each week to adapting your body to long walks, you gain physical, mental, and emotional benefits. The longer distances teach your body to burn fat as a source of energy, increase your capillaries' capacity, and promote those other physiological benefits to which I alluded previously. Walking farther than your targeted race distance allows you to feel comfortable focusing on race pace instead of race length.

With all of this said, the base building phase is the easiest to understand. The hardest part involves determining at what pace to train. Easy miles must be walked at an easy pace. Make sure you can talk comfortably and maintain good race walking technique at this pace for many miles. Do not start out fast and then slow down. If anything, do just the opposite. Start slow, and if you feel good, pick it up a little later. However, do not sprint the end of the workout.

If you maintain a fairly steady pace, the distance makes the workout harder. In the base building phase, the workout really starts only after you walk half the day's distance. Time on your feet, not pace, determines the effort of the workout. Therefore, the first few miles should always seem exceptionally easy.

Observe the following base building schedule for a race walker whose goal is to complete a 10K race in 50 minutes:

Sample Base Building Schedule

Purpose:
 Build a foundation for more intense workouts. Perfect race walking technique.

Starting Weekly Mileage:	Maximum Weekly Mileage:	Easy Pace:
25 miles/week	45 miles/week	10:00/mile

Week	Sunday	Monday	Tuesday	Thursday	Friday	Saturday
1	6 easy miles	3 easy miles	4 easy miles	4 easy miles	3 easy miles	5 easy miles
2	7 easy miles	3 easy miles	5 easy miles	5 easy miles	3 easy miles	5 easy miles
3	8 easy miles	3 easy miles	6 easy miles	6 easy miles	3 easy miles	5 easy miles
4	5 easy miles	3 easy miles	3 easy miles	3 easy miles	3 easy miles	3 easy miles

Week	Sunday	Monday	Tuesday	Thursday	Friday	Saturday
5	8 easy miles	4 easy miles	5 easy miles	5 easy miles	4 easy miles	6 easy miles
6	9 easy miles	4 easy miles	6 easy miles	6 easy miles	4 easy miles	6 easy miles
7	10 easy miles	4 easy miles	7 easy miles	7 easy miles	4 easy miles	6 easy miles
8	5 easy miles	3 easy miles	3 easy miles	3 easy miles	3 easy miles	5 easy miles
9	10 easy miles	5 easy miles	7 easy miles	7 easy miles	5 easy miles	7 easy miles
10	11 easy miles	5 easy miles	7 easy miles	7 easy miles	5 easy miles	7 easy miles
11	12 easy miles	5 easy miles	8 easy miles	8 easy miles	5 easy miles	7 easy miles
12	5 easy miles	3 easy miles	3 easy miles	3 easy miles	3 easy miles	5 easy miles

COACH'S WARNING

Do not increase mileage too rapidly. Focus on technique; you need to master it before you progress to faster workouts.

For a 10K, your base building phase lasts a minimum of three months. During this time you walk six days a week. If you train hard, you must rest hard. Therefore, all of my schedules include at least one day off each week. If your schedule permits walking only five days a week, then skip one of the easiest days in the schedule. Also note, which days of the week you select to serve as workouts or rest days matters little, as long as you do not perform all of the hard workouts consecutively.

Notice the weekly mileage starts at 25 miles. If you have not recently walked 25 miles in one week, then slowly build up to this distance before starting the program. Do not count the time spent increasing mileage to 25 miles per week as part of the actual schedule. The schedule begins *after* you can comfortably walk this distance at the Easy Mileage Pace, the pace at which you walk most miles during this phase of training. If the pace feels too easy or too hard, consider selecting a different training program.

When you look across the schedule, you find that Sunday is the easy distance day. Your mileage on Sundays starts at six miles and builds up to twelve miles, taking a few steps back along the way. Don't rush to get to twelve miles; you will get there fast enough. Walking a slow progression of increasing mileage reduces your chance of injury. While your walks on Tuesday, Thursday, and Saturday are not quite as long, we still regard them as easy distance training. Walk just a few easy miles on Monday and Friday; these represent your recovery days each week.

Do not be compulsive about walking nonstop during base building workouts. On a long walk, you may need to stop for one reason or another, such as alleviating a burning shin muscle. Rather than pushing through discomfort, you improve more in the long run if you stop to prevent injury with a little stretching, or avoid dehydration by sipping some water from a fountain.

Additional Options

If you have additional time in your training schedule—in this scenario, more than three months until your target race—and you wish to add another mini-cycle to the base building phase, feel free to do so. I recommend repeating the last four-week mini-cycle. Race walk all of the same workouts, but increase your pace by 10 seconds a mile. For example, in this schedule, walk at 9:50 per mile during the added weeks, as follows:

Week	Sunday	Monday	Tuesday	Thursday	Friday	Saturday
13	10 easy miles	5 easy miles	7 easy miles	7 easy miles	5 easy miles	7 easy miles
14	11 easy miles	5 easy miles	7 easy miles	7 easy miles	5 easy miles	7 easy miles
15	12 easy miles	5 easy miles	8 easy miles	8 easy miles	5 easy miles	7 easy miles
16	5 easy miles	3 easy miles	3 easy miles	3 easy miles	3 easy miles	5 easy miles

Alternatively, try increasing your weekly mileage to 50 miles without increasing intensity. Consider this option:

Week	Sunday	Monday	Tuesday	Thursday	Friday	Saturday
13	10 easy miles	6 easy miles	7 easy miles	7 easy miles	6 easy miles	7 easy miles
14	11 easy miles	6 easy miles	8 easy miles	8 easy miles	6 easy miles	8 easy miles
15	12 easy miles	6 easy miles	9 easy miles	9 easy miles	6 easy miles	8 easy miles
16	5 easy miles	3 easy miles	3 easy miles	3 easy miles	3 easy miles	5 easy miles

COACH'S WARNING

Do not simultaneously increase intensity and mileage! It causes injuries.

Why Train Faster?

If you want to race at the same pace as your easy distance race walks, then training at your easy distance pace most of the time is fine. However, most people want to race as fast as possible, so their training needs to incorporate faster walks. Race walking faster produces waste products that the body may or may not be able to handle. When your race walking pace remains at or below a certain level—*the lactate threshold*—then your body can process one waste product, lactate, at the same rate it produces this waste. When you race walk faster than your lactate threshold pace, more and more lactic acid builds, eventually slowing your pace. Therefore, to improve performance, you need to train to increase your lactic acid threshold.

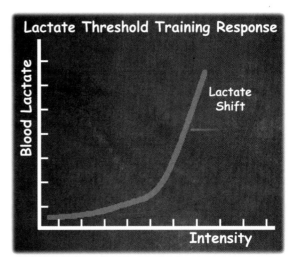

The Interval Training Phase includes workouts that train your body to improve its lactate threshold. Pushing the threshold higher enables you to race faster without overloading on lactate.

Interval Training Phase

Race walking at varied intensity levels trains the many energy systems used by the body during a race. The second phase of training, the *interval training phase*, trains the body to race walk progressively closer to your selected racing pace. A few months into a training program, your body is unprepared to race at your targeted pace. Therefore, you must begin with slower walks and work up to race pace. Completing a full interval training phase and then a *peaking phase* develops your ability to sustain your targeted race pace for your entire race distance.

During this phase, your weekly training consists of three hard workouts and three easy workouts. Notice the significant decrease in weekly mileage when you start this phase. This compensates for the added stress your body takes on when increasing workout intensity.

Distance Workouts for Interval Training

Distance workouts for interval training resemble distance workouts for base building. The distance day cycles from a moderate distance and builds to a longer distance, with the longest walk no farther than the greatest distance walked during the base building phase. The cycle repeats with each cycle increasing your workload for a few weeks, backing off, and then increasing it again. Importantly, your distance days need to be at an easy pace, so do not increase the pace of the distance workout from week to week. Instead, increase your pace at the start of each mini-cycle and maintain it throughout that cycle. As the length of your easy distance walk increases, your weekly workload elevates slightly. While accelerating the pace of your distance workout at the beginning of each mini-cycle adds to your workload, mileage reduction associated with the beginning of each mini-cycle tempers this acceleration. The true increase in workload comes from the other workouts added to your training regimen.

Tempo Workouts

The *tempo workout* is the first workout for which you race walk at a significantly fast pace. Each week of the mini-cycle contains one tempo day. From week to week within the mini-cycle, the tempo workouts get slightly longer, while your race walking pace remains about the same. The added mileage results in the increased workload. Then, after each mini-cycle, the race walking pace increases and your mileage reduces back to the original distance specified at the cycle's start. This helps your body adapt to the new pace as you increase distance. By reverting back to the shorter distance, your body is able to handle the new intensity.

Tempo walks are a great way to raise your lactate threshold, but they are very difficult workouts and must be done properly to reap full benefit. Failure to walk at the proper pace leads to training the wrong energy systems, thus throwing off the training program's balance.

While you should always warm up before working out, when you race walk a tempo workout you really must make sure you warm up properly. To save space, the training schedule omits specific warm-up drills, but you should perform at least the drills with high importance as described in Chapter 3. If time permits, perform the additional ones. After you complete these exercises, race walk one mile at your easy distance pace, using good technique. After the mile, stretch any tight spots or chronically sore areas, as explained in Chapter 7.

Properly warmed up, try to complete the tempo walk at a relatively constant pace, without stopping. Variance in your pace is acceptable if you start slower and finish a little faster than the recommended pace. When race walking a tempo workout, make sure you still can utter a few words, but have difficulty holding a conversation. Once finished, you must take the time to warm down. Walk another mile at easy distance pace and then stretch thoroughly, again using Chapter 7 for guidance.

If you have a watch that stores splits, record them at regular intervals, such as each lap on a track. If you walk on a measured road course, record your time at the locations most convenient to consistently grabbing splits. Splits are important, because walking at a consistent pace or one that slowly speeds up provides more benefits than starting quickly and slowing down. Starting too quickly leads you to use the wrong energy systems, thus eliminating the workout's full benefit. To simulate your target racecourse experience, measure out a 2K or 2.5K loop when you train on the road. The best way to measure a loop is with a wheel, a car odometer is not accurate enough.

Long Interval Workouts

The third hard workout also raises your lactate threshold. It involves simulating a race by walking a number of shorter-than-race-distance intervals, with a rest in between each one. Many people think they need to walk these intervals at race pace; however, as mentioned, during the Interval Phase the body is unprepared to walk at the goal race pace for the entire race distance. Therefore, we walk our first mini-cycle at slower-than-race pace, and each progressive mini-cycle at an increased pace. This schedule contains only two mini-cycles, but others on the DVD have more.

After a good warm up using the same regimen employed for the tempo workout, you should be ready to begin. Race walk each interval at the pace listed in the schedule. The first few intervals usually feel fairly easy, but as you progress through the intervals, holding the same pace becomes considerably harder. After each interval, rest enough to catch your wind, thus allowing your heart rate to lower. However, do not totally recover. During the rest period, walk slowly or stretch; do not sit down to wait while time ticks away and your muscles tighten. When the rest period ends, immediately begin the next interval. Try to use a watch that stores the splits for each interval. Remember, consistency is key. Record the splits in your training log when you return home from the track.

Take caution when walking interval workouts. You might find it easy to blast the first interval, thus increasing the difficulty of the remaining repeats. Much like the distance workout, you gain more by completing the first few intervals a little slower and the next few on pace. Then, if you have some energy left, push a little faster on the last few repeats.

Sample Interval Training Schedule

Purpose:
    Become accustomed to the targeted race pace. Raise the lactate threshold.

Starting Weekly Mileage:	Maximum Weekly Mileage:	Easy Pace:
32.5 miles/week	37.5 miles/week	9:55/mile - 1st cycle 9:50/mile - 2nd cycle

Week	Sunday	Monday	Tuesday	Thursday	Friday	Saturday
1	8 easy miles	4 easy miles	1 mile warm up 3.5 miles @ 8:40/mi 1 mile warm down	4 easy miles	1 mile warm up 10 x 800 meter repeats each in 4:05 2 min. rest in between 1 mile warm down	4 easy miles
2	10 easy miles	4 easy miles	1 mile warm up 4 miles at 8:40/mile 1 mile warm down	4 easy miles	1 mile warm up 7 x 1200 meter repeats each in 5:55 2 min. rest in between 1 mile warm down	4 easy miles
3	12 easy miles	4 easy miles	1 mile warm up 4.5 miles at 8:40/mi 1 mile warm down	4 easy miles	1 mile warm up 5 x 1600 meter repeats each in 8:10 3-4 min. rest between 1 mile warm down	4 easy miles
4	5 easy miles	3 easy miles	extra day off	3 easy miles	3 easy miles	3 easy miles
5	8 easy miles	4 easy miles	1 mile warm up 3.5 miles at 8:30/mi 1 mile warm down	4 easy miles	1 mile warm up 10 x 800 meter repeats each in 4:05 2 min. rest in between 1 mile warm down	4 easy miles
6	10 easy miles	4 easy miles	1 mile warm up 4 miles at 8:30/mile 1 mile warm down	4 easy miles	1 mile warm up 10 x 800 meter repeats each in 4:05 2 min. rest in between 1 mile warm down	4 easy miles
7	12 easy miles	4 easy miles	1 mile warm up 4.5 miles at 8:30/mi 1 mile warm down	4 easy miles	1 mile warm up 10 x 800 meter repeats each in 4:05 2 min. rest in between 1 mile warm down	4 easy miles
8	5 easy miles	3 easy miles	extra day off	3 easy miles	3 easy miles	3 easy miles

When race walking intervals, be sure to walk the first few repeats no faster than the rest. However, completing the latter ones faster than the first few is fine.

The Interval Training Phase is composed of two mini-cycles. As you progress through each mini-cycle, the weekly workload increases. Then, after three weeks, you back off and recover for a week. Throughout the phase, workload intensifies in three ways. First, the distance workouts grow longer. Likewise, the tempo workouts increase by a half mile each week during each mini-cycle. The final increase occurs in the form of longer intervals. You still walk the same distance in total mileage, but each week the individual intervals lengthen.

Your workload also builds from mini-cycle to mini-cycle. The second cycle mirrors the first, just a bit faster. After adapting to the stress of the first mini-cycle and then resting, your body is ready to accept more stress in the form of an accelerated race walking pace.

 ## COACH'S WARNING

If you have problems finishing an interval workout, do not quit. Instead, consider two options. Either slow down to a comfortable pace you can sustain for the remaining repeats, or shorten the distance of each repetition. Selecting the latter option requires offsetting the dodged workout by completing additional intervals; this way, the total distance equals that of the original schedule. Finishing these difficult workouts trains your mind to focus and endure, providing great mental advantages when difficulties arise during a race.

Additional Options

If you have additional time in your training schedule and wish to add another mini-cycle to the interval training phase, feel free to do so. I recommend repeating the last four-week mini-cycle. Race walk all of the same workouts, but increase your pace for tempo and long interval days as shown in the following chart.

Week	Sunday	Monday	Tuesday	Thursday	Friday	Saturday
9	8 easy miles	4 easy miles	1 mile warm up 3.5 miles at 8:25/mi 1 mile warm down	4 easy miles	1 mile warm up 10 x 800 meter repeats each in 3:55 2 min. rest in between 1 mile warm down	4 easy miles
10	10 easy miles	4 easy miles	1 mile warm up 4 miles at 8:25/mile 1 mile warm down	4 easy miles	1 mile warm up 7 x 1200 meter repeats each in 5:40 2 min. rest in between 1 mile warm down	4 easy miles
11	12 easy miles	4 easy miles	1 mile warm up 4.5 miles at 8:25/mi 1 mile warm down	4 easy miles	1 mile warm up 5 x 1600 meter repeats each in 7:50 3-4 min. rest between 1 mile warm down	4 easy miles
12	5 easy miles	3 easy miles	extra day off	3 easy miles	3 easy miles	3 easy miles

Peak Performance Phase

The *peak performance phase* tweaks the body to excel and race your best when performance counts the most. During this phase, you walk workouts at race pace and faster. Your total mileage once again reduces before increasing slightly. Too much distance work near race day hampers your ability to walk fast. While distance workouts lengthen at first, they too reduce as you approach your race.

COACH'S TIP

Plan your peak carefully. A peak can be held for only a few weeks. Attempting to hold a peak longer risks injuries and sub-optimal performances.

Distance Workouts for Peak Training

The distance day here approximates your distance day in the base building phase; however, it gradually becomes shorter as your peak performance phase progresses. Do not increase the pace of your easy distance or recovery days during this period. Simply maintain the pace you used during the interval training phase.

Rhythm Workouts

During the peak performance phase you add another type of training: the *rhythm workout*, a somewhat complicated undertaking. Although rhythm workouts are beneficial during early phases of training, I do not usually recommend attempting them until a walker attains a good understanding of and discipline in pacing workouts. My flavor for rhythm workouts is short, quick intervals. Four sets of intervals comprise the session, all walked at faster-than-goal race pace. Each set of intervals includes sustained efforts at distances of 100 meters (110 yards), 200 meters (220 yards), and 300 meters (330 yards). The challenge of mastering this workout is completing each repetition at the same pace. Do not sprint the 100-meter segment faster than the 200-meter or 300-meter segment. Instead, determine how fast you can walk the 300-meter segment and use that as your guide for the other distances. The 100-meter interval should take exactly one-third the time of the 300-meter interval, with the 200-meter repeat taking two-thirds the time of the 300-meter interval.

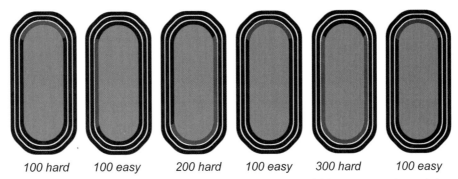

100 hard   100 easy   200 hard   100 easy   300 hard   100 easy

In between each repeat, walk 100 meters slowly until you reach the 100 meter mark, and then start the next interval immediately. When you finish a set of intervals, walk 100 meters slowly and then begin the next set of repeats immediately. Observe the chart below. It depicts one complete set of rhythm intervals, with the faster-than-goal-pace race walking illustrated in red and the recovery interval in blue.

This workout begins easy and gets tougher as you progress through the sets. If you find yourself slowing down on the longer reps or later in the sets of intervals, you started too fast. Take note and start slower next time. On the other hand, if you find your pace accelerates from set to set, go for it!

In our sample schedule for a 50-minute 10K race, we estimate that all-out walking for 400 meters—440 yards, or once around the track—can be accomplished in about 1:35. If we back off that time just a little, we arrive at a 1:40 pace as a reasonable speed for beginning repeats in the rhythm workout.

CALCULATIONS

400 meters time = 1:35
Total Seconds = 1*60 + 40 = 100 seconds
Time per 100 meters = 100/4 = 25 seconds
Time per 200 meters = 25 * 2 = 50 seconds
Time per 300 meters = 75 seconds or 1:15

If you start out a little conservatively, you might do the first set a hair slower. At the end of each set, progress immediately into the next set. No rest for the weary!

Set 1	Set 2	Set 3	Set 4
100 m - 26 seconds	100 m - 25 seconds	100 m - 25 seconds	100 m - 25 seconds
100 m - walk slowly	100 m - walk slowly	100 m - walk slowly	100 m - walk slowly
200 m - 52 seconds	200 m - 50 seconds	200 m - 50 seconds	200 m - 50 seconds
100 m - walk slowly	100 m - walk slowly	100 m - walk slowly	100 m - walk slowly
300 m - 78 seconds or 1:18	300 m - 75 seconds or 1:15	300 m - 75 seconds or 1:15	300 m - 75 seconds or 1:15
100 m - walk slowly	100 m - walk slowly	100 m - walk slowly	100 m - walk slowly

Warming up and cooling down properly remain essential, just as for the tempo workouts and longer intervals. Follow the plan outlined with tempo training.

Short Fast Intervals

Similar in form to long intervals, these shorter, faster repeats require you to walk additional intervals at a slightly faster-than-race pace. Being shorter, these intervals often prove the most fun, at least at the beginning.

Warm up well and keep in mind the same discipline as maintained during the longer repeats. Each repeat must be consistent in pace. These workouts are actually considered VO_2 Max training and thus improve the body's oxygen capacity.

Sample Peak Training Schedule

Purpose:
Tweak training over a short period of time to prepare for optimum performance.

Starting Weekly Mileage: Easy Pace:
32.5 miles/week   9:50/mile

Week	Sunday	Monday	Tuesday	Thursday	Friday	Saturday
1	10 easy miles	3 easy miles	1 mile warm up 100, 200, 300 x 4 100 m easy in between each repeat 1 mile warm down	3 easy miles	1 mile warm up 24 x 400 meter repeats each in 1:55 1 min. rest in between 1 mile warm down	4 easy miles
2	8 easy miles	3 easy miles	1 mile warm up 100, 200, 300 x 4 100 m easy in between each repeat 1 mile warm down	3 easy miles	1 mile warm up 24 x 400 meter repeats each in 1:55 1 min. rest in between 1 mile warm down	4 easy miles
3	8 easy miles	3 easy miles	1 mile warm up 100, 200, 300 x 4 100 m easy in between each repeat 1 mile warm down	3 easy miles	1 mile warm up 24 x 400 meter repeats each in 1:50-1:55 1 min. rest in between 1 mile warm down	4 easy miles
4	5 easy miles	3 easy miles	extra day off	3 easy miles	1-2 easy miles light sprints just to loosen up	Race a 50:30 10K
5	3 easy miles	3 easy miles	1 mile warm up 100, 200, 300 x 4 100 m easy in between each repeat 1 mile warm down	3 easy miles	1 mile warm up 24 x 400 meter repeats each in 1:50 1 min. rest in between 1 mile warm down	4 easy miles
6	5 easy miles	3 easy miles	1 mile warm up 100, 200, 300 x 4 100 m easy in between each repeat 1 mile warm down	3 easy miles	1-2 easy miles light sprints just to loosen up	Race a 50:00 10K

COACH'S WARNING

You are so close to achieving the goal you trained more than six months to attain; don't leave all your hard work on the track by overdoing it now! At this point in your training you become most vulnerable to injury. Listen to your body and take extra rest if you start to break down.

Picking a Race Distance and Goal Time

Deciding how far and how fast to race often seems difficult. If you decide on your first week of race walk training that you will follow the 22-minute, 5K schedule, you will not only fail, but also probably injure yourself along the way.

When selecting an initial goal, start with shorter distance races first and work your way up to longer races. The training program for each race goal includes a minimum distance to walk the first week. If you typically walk much less than that distance, you need to build up to the starting distance slowly. Add a few miles each week until you bridge the gap. Then assess your easy walking pace and try to match it to a program. This provides a fairly accurate method for determining a realistic goal.

Once you start a training program, reassess its appropriateness after about three weeks. If you feel you cannot meet most workout target times, switch to a slower schedule. Use common sense and do not train through injuries. Do not stay on a schedule if you constantly feel sore or tired, like you completed a marathon every day.

I designed each program to train walkers at the minimum sustained pace and distance needed to achieve a targeted goal. Some people need more training, others less. My programs offer a safe approximation of the work you need to accomplish to ensure reaching your goals without getting hurt or over-training.

 COACH'S TIP

How you train determines how you race. By training like you race, you maximize your chances of success. Therefore, a few weeks before your goal race, try to race walk your hard workouts at the same time of day as your race.

Cross Training

Cross training means undertaking exercise not specific to race walking. Many theories about the effectiveness of cross training exist. But remember, specificity of exercise remains the overriding rule. If you do not race walk fast when you train, you will not race walk fast enough at a race. Likewise, if you do not put enough time on your feet race walking, you will face difficulties trying to complete longer distance races.

So, why cross train? In many circumstances, cross training provides great benefits. For example, the dynamic flexibility drills or the strength training detailed in Chapters 3 & 9 are two forms of cross training. You undertake each one because it enhances your workout routine in a particular way that race walking alone cannot accomplish.

You might employ other forms of cross training for the simple reason that your body only handles so much of a specific stress, in this case race walking, without breaking down. Whether because of injury or to prevent it, we utilize cross training to increase the amount of work the body accomplishes over time without risking overuse problems. In the case of injury, cross training allows you to maintain your fitness level while your body repairs itself or heals. In the past I swam for this purpose. A mile in the pool does wonders for your body without stressing strained or abused joints.

Which activities you select for cross training depend upon your background and goals. Right now I race walk with the sole goal of maintaining fitness, so I cross train with activities I enjoy, like hiking and kayaking. I choose to avoid running. Its destructive impact on my body led me to become a race walker in the first place. However, if your running background is strong, without a history of injuries, running may be an excellent way to add a few miles and build your cardiovascular system. Many coaches start their race walkers with a running routine and then switch over to race walking. They typically use this approach with walkers who train for much longer than the three-month cycles I present above. Indeed, you could spend an entire cycle running before switching over to one of my programs.

Sleep

Paul Schwartzberg used to say, "If you train hard, you must rest hard." I couldn't agree more. Sleep represents an essential component of any training program. Everyone's needs are different; assess yourself carefully and ensure you get *enough sleep*. In college, they called me *the geek of sleep*. I slept anywhere and anytime I could. While sleeping, your body rebuilds and recovers from the hard work you put it through. No one knew this better than two-time Olympian Herm Nelson. Dubbed *The Bear,* he possessed a unique ability to hibernate all day before hard workouts.

Keeping a Training Log

Perhaps the single best tool to monitor your training is a daily log. A log also teaches you about your body's response to various training factors. I still have mine from 1986 through my competitive race walking days. I recorded *every* workout—yes, every single one. A training log can be as simple as handwriting in a notebook or as complex as maintaining a computer database. The form of the log matters little: the contents, a lot.

Your training log must describe all aspects of your workout. Start with the distance and pace of your race walk. For an interval workout, list your splits. Also, record average and maximum heart rates for each interval. Finally, documenting your body's response provides useful information down the line: did it feel very easy, painfully hard, or somewhat mixed? One good system involves rating your perceived exertion level for each workout by indicating a number from one to ten. Long, long ago, I placed a star next to those workouts I considered successful, hard conditioning. At the end of each month, I used the number of stars as a rough basis for assessing the quality of training for that period.

Serious athletes need to document even more information. When you wake up in the morning, record your heart rate before getting out of bed. Your resting heart rate serves as a barometer of your body's condition. If your heart rate rises for a few days, you could be getting sick or dehydrated. Another good habit: note the length (hours) and quality of how you slept. When you suddenly feel run down and don't seem to have any "zip" in your workouts, use your log to determine the possible cause: training too hard, or not getting enough sleep.

COACH'S WARNING

For your training log to be effective, it must be accurate. Write your results in it everyday. Do not wait until the end of the week to play catch up. By then, issues like how you felt become diluted by confusion or poor recall.

Heart Rate

Why did I wait until the end of the chapter to cover heart rate and heart rate monitors? Not because I don't believe in them. I do. I view monitoring heart rate as an incredibly effective training tool. There are two basic methods for assessing heart rate in your training program.

If you keep a good training log, then your heart rate record becomes a gauge of how hard you train or race. If you train at a 150 heart rate for your race-pace intervals, and go out at 165 for the first mile of a race, then you know you began the race too fast. Likewise, if your heart rate midway through the race remains at 140, you probably have room to pick up the pace. This simple method of using your heart rate provides an easy, effective strategizing tool.

A more complex heart rate method involves using your maximum heart rate (MHR) to help determine the appropriate heart rate for different workouts. Knowing your MHR enables you to calculate your optimal heart rate for any particular workout using a percentage of maximum heart rate (PMHR). So if you aim to walk at 70% of your MHR, with an MHR of 200, your PMHR for 70% is 140.

Determining true MHR for a person just learning to race walk is problematic. To use heart rate as a tool, you need a means of approximating your MHR. The commonly used method, found in many publications, uses 220 minus age as a formula; this method produces a lower-than-actual MHR for trained athletes and a higher-than-actual MHR for untrained athletes—not very helpful.

The following formula provides a more accurate heart rate measurement. Instead of calculating MHR, use your resting heart rate and your age as factors in calculating PHR. The formula follows:

> **Goal Heart Rate = (220 – your age – resting heart rate) * .PHR + resting heart rate where PHR is the percentage of effort/MHR at which you want to train.**

For each type of workout previously described, there exists an associated percentage of MHR, or exertion effort, at which to train. For example, if a 34 year-old walker maintains a resting heart rate of 50, then estimating proper training heart rates look like the following:

Workout	% of MHR	Heart Rate Calculation	Heart Rate
Easy Distance	70	(220 - 34 - 50) * .70 + 50	145.2
Tempo	85	(220 - 34 - 50) * .85 + 50	165.6
Interval	85	(220 - 34 - 50) * .85 + 50	165.6
Rhythm	90	(220 - 34 - 50) * .90 + 50	172.4
VO$_2$ Max	95	(220 - 34 - 50) * .95 + 50	179.2

In contrast, using the traditional HR calculation method produces lower heart rates. If you are untrained and just beginning a race walking program, these approximations are probably acceptable initially.

Workout	% of MHR	Heart Rate Calculation	Heart Rate
Easy Distance	70	(220 - 34) * .70	130.2
Tempo	85	(220 - 34) * .85	158.1
Interval	85	(220 - 34) * .85	158.1
Rhythm	90	(220 - 34) * .90	167.4
VO$_2$ Max	95	(220 - 34) * .95	176.7

Your heart rate sometimes varies from its norm, temporarily, for many reasons. In hot weather, dehydration tops the suspect list. With less fluid in the body, the heart must pump harder to get blood to your muscles. Even in moderate temperatures, you might still suffer from dehydration if you consume a little too much alcohol the night before. Assuming you do not take too many vitamins, an easy way to tell if you are dehydrated involves checking the color of your urine. Stark yellow typically indicates dehydration. As a guideline, your body absorbs one liter of fluid per hour. Electrolyte drinks are preferable to straight water to prevent a condition called hyponutremia[2]. Other reasons for an elevated heart rate include lack of sleep, mental stress, or onset of a virus or other illness.

Track lengths

Meters or miles, that is the question. When developing the training section, I faced the difficult decision of whether to use miles or meters. I chose to go with the most natural distance for each workout type. Since interval workouts usually occur on the track, I developed them with meters. Since distance workouts typically take place on roads, I used miles.

$$\text{Yards} = 1.094 * \text{Meters}$$
$$\text{or}$$
$$\text{Meters} = 0.9144 * \text{Yards}$$

So 400 meters = 1.094 * 400 = 437.6 Yards

---

[2] Hyponutremia is a condition where the body gets too much water and not enough electrolytes. It can be as dangerous or more dangerous than dehydration. See Chapter 10.

One final note on track lengths. Walking in any lane but the 400-meter lane results in a distance different from 400 meters. At almost all tracks, with the exception of Franklin Field in Philadelphia, the first lane is the 400-meter lane. Ideally, you should train in that lane. However, if you cannot, be aware that each time you shift one lane over, you walk nearly an additional eight meters per lap. The chart below lists meters and yards for one lap at each lane.

	Lane 1	Lane 2	Lane 3	Lane 4	Lane 5	Lane 6	Lane 7	Lane 8
Meters	400	408	416	424	431	439	447	455
Yards	437	446	455	463	472	480	489	498

COACH'S TIP

While there is little that you can do the week before a race to make up for a lack of previous training, there is a lot you can do to ruin the quality training already accomplished. Be careful and do not over train the week before your key race.

SPOTLIGHT ON

Howard "Jake" Jacobson was introduced to race walking by Henry Laskau in January 1957. Jacobson describes himself as a "good to very good but never great race walker," who finished in the top three to ten at many open competition races. As a master, he won a number of national titles, setting age-group records along the way. But it has been his abilities as coach, mentor, big brother, team organizer, club founder, corporate spokesperson, fitness editor, and author that have, as he says, "outshined my athletic performances."

Over a span of years beginning in 1966, he was athlete-coach for the Long Island Athletic Club. In 1977, he founded the East Side Track Club with his son, Alan. The club soon obtained the sponsorship of Adidas, Reebok and then Converse, and was able to assist the development of race walkers such as Dan O'Connor, Vincent O'Sullivan, Carl Schueler, Curt Clausen and even myself.

In 1980, his first book, *Racewalk to Fitness*, was published by Simon and Schuster. It was considered by many to have been the "bible of the sport." New York City's Central Park became a Mecca for walkers in 1979 when Jacobson founded the New York Walkers Club (NYWC) and provided free weekly clinics 50 weeks a year in up to five locations around the metropolitan area. In 1982, Jacobson coined the word *healthwalk* to describe the pursuits of those who came to his clinics seeking fitness. The NYWC grew in geometric proportions and at its peak boasted 1500 members. The club produced as many as 20 races a year.

In 1984, Jacobson rented a children's summer camp for one week to teach average citizens race walking and healthwalking. He also invited eight juniors to be coached by himself, Vincent O'Sullivan, and Gary Westerfield. Expanding his vision, Jacobson bought a 100-acre farm in the Catskills to serve as a camp for walking and weight-loss. Race walkers Nick Bdera, Dan Pierce, Dave McGovern, John Slavonic, and Curt Clausen were his hired staff, primarily undertaking construction and maintenance work, with time off for training. McGovern also assisted Coach Jake with instructing the guests during technique sessions. After six seasons, Jake closed the camp and moved back to the NY metropolitan area to become a fitness editor for the *New York Post*.

Jacobson was also the director of the Walkers Club of America and in 1985 produced The March Across America for Mothers Against Drunk Driving. The event was awarded the Silver Anvil Award as the best special event of the year by the Public Relations Society of America.

You can visit Jacobson's web site at *www.coachjake.com*.

Chapter 7 - Stretching

Ahh, the workout is over. Time to reward your body for all the hard work it has put in, loosen those muscles back up, and hasten their recovery.

Introduction

Always stretch when you have finished working out. When your muscles are tired they become tight bands that fight you, resisting forward progress. In contrast, when you loosen your muscles by stretching, you facilitate relaxed, efficient race walking; prevent injuries; and increase your range of motion. If that is not reason enough, stretch just because it feels good!

Be patient while stretching. Make certain to use good technique, as improper form leads to stretching—and possibly overstretching—the wrong muscle group.

COACH'S WARNING

Take care not to bounce your joints in an attempt to achieve a deeper stretch. You need only stretch far enough to feel your muscles elongate. If you start to feel pain, stop. You should not stretch to the point of pain.

Generally, unless otherwise noted, the stretches below should be held for 20 to 30 seconds, one limb at a time. Symmetry is key. Always start with the least flexible limb, as human nature leads you to focus longer and more attentively on the first stretch. Otherwise, by repeatedly stretching the more flexible limb—as many people do—you increase any imbalances.

Remember, stretching prior to walking is not recommended, because stretching cold muscles is less effective and leads to injuries. Instead, to warm up muscles before walking, practice the Dynamic Flexibility Drills presented in Chapter 3.

About the Model

While Jack Starr is my race walking idol, he does claim to be the least flexible person on earth. (Yes, a slight exaggeration.) So why select him as a model to demonstrate the proper way to stretch? Simple. In almost every demonstration, he shows exactly how to stretch correctly. If he can do it, so can you. Whether you stretch as far (or farther) than Jack is determined by your individual flexibility. In any case, use the same form as Jack demonstrates. Notice that in two cases, Jack uses a towel for assistance in stretching a particularly tight muscle group. Such aides enhance his ability to reach a correctly extended position. You see alternative stretches utilizing props where your lack of flexibility may cause you to require some assistance.

About the Stretches

Each stretch lists **Importance** and **Intensity** levels at **Low**, **Medium**, or **High**. Those stretches indicated as high importance should be done after every workout, while ones at low importance are used as needed for muscle tightness or injury recovery. Low importance stretches can also be alternated, cycling through the list a few each week as time permits.

Intensity specifies the forcefulness of the stretch. Lower intensity stretches are good for beginners or those with a particularly tight area that needs loosening. High intensity stretches are meant for advanced walkers who are at least semi-flexible in the area of concern.

Calf Stretches

Race walking uses calf muscles considerably more than other sports. Stretching the calves helps technique while preventing injuries. Calves are a complex muscle group, so a single stretch is not sufficient. If time permits, executing each of the four stretches presented is not overkill.

TRADITIONAL CALF STRETCH
Importance: High   Intensity: Low

Place both hands at shoulder height on a wall or pole in front of your body. Keep your arms fairly straight and your lead leg bent under your body. Now, place the heel of your rear leg 1½ to 2 feet behind your body.

Keeping your rear leg fairly straight but not locked in position, place the heel of this foot on the ground. You should feel a stretch down the outer part of your rear-leg calf muscle. If you don't, try moving your rear foot back a little farther (remember to place your heel back on the ground after you move your foot back). Throughout the stretch, your upper body should remain vertical and straight; do not bend forward.

Alternate legs when finished.

COACH'S TIP
Stretching the calves helps alleviate shin pain.

Figure 7-1

ADVANCED CALF STRETCH
Importance: Medium   Intensity: Medium

If your calves are extremely flexible, you may need a deeper stretch. Try the *Advanced Calf Stretch*. Because this stretch is relatively aggressive, you may need to build up to it by practicing the Traditional Calf Stretch first.

Place both feet as close as possible to the edge of a step or curb while maintaining good balance. If possible, use a tree, pole, or even another walker for balance

While keeping your rear legs as straight as possible, lower your heels over the curb as much as feasible. You achieve the best stretch by hanging as close to the edge as possible and lowering your heels as far as they will go. After holding the stretch for 20-30 seconds, alternate legs. If you still feel tight, repeat this stretch more than once.

This stretch is also effective if you stretch one leg at a time. The stretch is performed in the same manner, just tuck your non-active leg for balance.

Figure 7-2a   *Figure 7-2b*

INTENSIVE CALF STRETCH
Importance: Medium   Intensity: High

The third stretch is the most aggressive calf stretch included. We use it to stretch the upper areas of the calf that are not reached by less intensive stretching. Be sure to use care when first executing this stretch as you can easily overextend your calf if you bounce or move into this position too forcefully. Unlike the first two calf stretches, the advanced stretch concentrates on the muscles of your upper calf. You may want to work up to this position by practicing the other stretches for a few weeks first. Once again, you will need a wall or pole for support.

Following Jack's example, begin by standing about an arm's length away from the pole. (The closer to the wall you stand, the more you stretch the calf.) Place the heel of the first leg close to the bottom of the wall with the toes against it, as if you were trying to step on the pole. Now keep your leg and back straight and lean into the wall slowly. Being careful not to reach the point of pain, lean into your front leg until you feel moderate tension in your upper calf. Hold the stretch for 20 to 30 seconds, then alternate legs.

Figure 7-3

 ## COACH'S WARNING

This is a very intensive stretch. Do not over stretch. It is easy to overdo this one. You may skip this stretch if you are uncomfortable with it.

BENT LEG CALF STRETCH
Importance: Medium   Intensity: Low

The calf is not a single muscle; it's two, and both muscles need stretching. The previous three positions worked the outer calf muscle. The *Bent Leg Calf Stretch* may not feel effective overall initially, but it utilizes an excellent position that stretches deep in the inner calf muscle.

This stretch starts at the position in which you ended the Traditional Calf Stretch. Place both hands, shoulder high, on a pole or wall in front of your body. Keep your arms fairly straight with one leg slightly bent under your body.

Place the heel of your rear leg 1 to 1 1/2 feet behind your body. Notice this is about six inches in front of the placement for the Traditional Calf Stretch. Keeping your rear leg fairly straight and in a stable position, place the heel of your rear foot on the ground.

Now, keeping your heel planted, bend the rear leg so that your knee drops a few inches closer to the ground. You should feel a deeper stretch in your calf muscle. While not as pronounced as the other stretches, this one really works!

Figure 7-4

Shin Stretches

When race walking with any form approximating proper technique, the first muscle group to feel in need of a stretch is the shins. Your shin muscles are taxed more in walking than in almost any other sport. In fact, I found that the only athletes who begin race walking with previously developed shins are equestrians. The way their feet sit in the stirrups gives them a special immunity to the early shin discomfort found by many race walkers.

Since race walking forces you to land on your heel with toe pointed, it strains your shin. The body is clearly unaccustomed to this work and reacts by communicating its displeasure. Good stretching helps combat the discomfort. Both shin stretches below provide excellent benefits after walking and can also be executed while working out if your shins begin to burn or become otherwise bothersome.

When your shins hurt, you will find it almost impossible to walk with your toe pointed at heel strike and achieve a proper roll through to your toes. If your shins bother you enough, they may lead you to land flat footed. Most flat-footed walkers have difficulty straightening their knees and must stretch their shins or get themselves disqualified. Enough said?

SEATED SHIN STRETCH
Importance: Medium   Intensity: Medium

The *Seated Shin Stretch* is an effective stretch but has drawbacks. For one thing, you must sit on the ground. If you are in the middle of a race, this is particularly inconvenient. The other problem is, you need grass to perform the stretch, or some very tough knees. Nevertheless, this stretch is very effective in loosening over worked shins.

Start by sitting on the grass or soft carpet with your legs folded directly under your thighs. (Note Jack's foot position: shoe laces against the ground.) Use one hand to support your weight and the other to lift your knee. This lifting should send a stretch down your shin. Hold it 20 to 30 seconds, then switch legs.

Figure 7-5a

Figure 7-5b

Balance yourself near a pole or wall. Put your weight on the supporting leg. Now, touch the other foot to the ground, toe first, and pull your rear foot forward just to the point where it is about to move forward. Hold it there. You should feel the shin muscles elongate and loosen up. Do not rest on your big toe as shown in Figure 7-6c.

| Figure 7-6a | Figure 7-6b | Figure 7-6c |

Hamstring Stretches

Don't neglect the hammies. Huge muscles that can get extremely tight, the hamstrings need to be stretched every day. This is especially true if you race walk in hilly areas that stress your hamstrings more than level-ground walking. Fortunately, there are endless ways to stretch the hamstrings. Below we demonstrate a few.

The most traditional hamstring stretch starts in a seated position. Place one leg in front you. Bend your other leg with the sole of your foot facing towards your straight leg and knee pointed out. Keeping your back straight, lean forward from the hips, reaching towards your toes. Ideally, you should reach past your toes, but remember not to overstretch or bounce while trying to touch them; just stay within your comfort zone. See Figure 7-7b. Jack achieves a great position while stretching only within a few inches of his toes. Not bad for 75!

| Figure 7-7a | Figure 7-7b |

A simple variation of this stretch is to stand a few feet away from a fence or low support, placing a straightened leg on it at the foot, about waist height. This position is useful when it's wet outside or you are in the middle of a race or workout and do not wish to lose time sitting down. Both positions are equally effective.

EASY ON THE BACK HAMSTRING STRETCH
Importance: Medium   Intensity: Low

Walkers with really tight hamstrings or lower back problems may wish to start by using this low-stress stretch.

Begin by lying on the ground and positioning the non-stretching leg so that it supports your weight while making a triangle with the ground. Try to lift the other leg, holding it as straight as you can. The more flexible you are, the closer to your torso you should be able to pull your leg. Ideally, your leg should be perpendicular to the ground. If, like Jack, you can't achieve the ideal position, that's fine. Always remember, stretch within your own limits.

Figure 7-8

TOE TOUCHING HAMSTRING STRETCH
Importance: High   Intensity: Low

Remember being asked to bend over and touch your toes in gym class? Good idea, bad execution. Bending over like that might cause stress to the lower back. Instead, avoid such stress by using the Toe Touching Hamstring Stretch. Instead of standing straight up, lean against a wall or pole. Keeping your buttocks against the pole, place your feet approximately six inches to one foot away.

Continue leaning against the wall while you bend down and try to touch your toes. Focus on preventing your legs from bending. Keeping your feet away from the wall reduces the stress on your back and avoids straining the sciatic

Figure 7-9a

Figure 7-9b

nerve, one of the largest nerves in your body, located in the pelvic region.

IMPROVED TOE TOUCHING HAMSTRING STRETCH
Importance: Medium · Intensity: Medium

The Improved Toe Touching Hamstring Stretch is almost identical to the previous stretch. The improvement rests with the removal of the wall. After all, there's never a good wall around when you need one.

To ensure your buttocks stays far enough behind you to remove the stress from your lower back, cross your feet as depicted in the figures to the right.

Execute the rest of the stretch identically to the *Traditional Hamstring Stretch*.

Figure 7-10a

Figure 7-10b

BACK OF THE KNEE STRETCH
Importance: High · Intensity: Medium

Sometimes a pain creeps up on you out of nowhere, like with pain behind the knee. Race walking sometimes aggravates this area, and it sneaks up so slowly you don't actually realize it until too late. Avoid this potentially painful problem by adding the stretch below to your warm-down routine.

In a seated position, place the first leg straight in front of you. Next, bend the non-stretching leg outwards with your foot alongside the first thigh, forming a triangle. Keeping a straight back, bend from the hips and lean towards your toe. If your hamstring flexibility allows, pull your toes towards your body as I do in Figure 7-11a. If you lack flexibility in the hamstrings, you will not be able to reach your toes. Use a towel like Jack to extend your reach and get cracking on those hammies!

Figure 7-11a

Figure 7-11b

You may be tempted to disregard the exercise below, but this little gem is one of the most rewarding stretches in this book: progressing through it slowly stretches your neck, back, and hamstrings.

Begin in the same stance as with the Toe Touching Hamstring Stretch (Figure 7-12a), then lower just your head, tucking your chin towards your chest (Figure 7-12b). Slowly curl your upper body down and away from the wall. Continue to progress gradually, allowing your hands to drop to your sides (Figure 12-c).

Figure 7-12a

Figure 7-12b

Figure 7-12c

Finally, progress through figures 7-12c to 7-12f, slowly lowering your arms towards your toes. (Touch them if you can.) Try to spend 20 to 30 seconds progressing from step 1 to 6. Finally, hang for another 10 to 20 seconds before reversing the process. Be patient. Reverse the stretch very gradually, concentrating on the sensation of your vertebrae stacking as you progress upwards.

Figure 7-12d

Figure 7-12e

Figure 7-12f

QUADRICEPS STRETCH

Importance: High   **Intensity:** Medium

The most common quadriceps stretch is actually the most effective for our needs. Standing next to a pole or wall for balance, raise the first leg behind the body, grabbing your foot. The upper part of the leg remains in a vertical position as you pull the leg upward. See Figure 7-13a.

To completely stretch all quadriceps muscles, try the following variation. After completing the stretch shown in Figure 7-13a, pull your leg back as in Figure 7-13b.

Alternate legs.

In both variations, be careful not to pull your leg laterally; this puts unneeded stress on the knee.

Observe Figure 7-13c. The leg being stretched is parallel to Jack's support leg. In contrast, Figure 7-13d shows the leg being stretched pulled to the left.

Figure 7-13a

Figure 7-13b

Figure 7-13c

Figure 7-13d

Hip Stretches

It's all in the hips. (Or should I say, race walkers do it with more hip action!) Proficient race walking technique requires excellent range of motion in the hips. Stretching properly increases this range, thereby enhancing hip-motion effectiveness. Of course, stretching also helps reduce injuries—in this case, to an essential component of a powerful stride.

CURB HIP STRETCH
Importance: Low   Intensity: Low

The first hip stretch, though simple, requires a reasonably high curb. Stand at the curb with one leg on and the other hanging over it. Now, lower the hanging leg while keeping both legs straight and your foot parallel to the ground; feel the stretch in the hip opposite the curb. Repeat the exercise for the other hip.

While the second hip stretch presented is actually more effective, this hip stretch is excellent for wet days or in the middle of a workout or race.

Figure 7-14

SEATED HIP STRETCH
Importance: High   Intensity: Low

Begin the *Seated Hip Stretch* on the ground with both legs extended in front of your body. Bend one leg, crossing it over the other, and use the opposite elbow to push the bent knee towards your body. You should feel the stretch in your hip. If your shoulders are tight, you might feel a stretch here as well. Reverse legs and repeat.

A similar but alternative form of this stretch is to grab your knee and pull it towards your body. Both are effective and can be performed individually or sequentially.

Figure 7-15a

Figure 7-15b

HIP EXTENSION STRETCH

Importance: Medium   **Intensity:** Medium

This stretch provides great relief for tension in the hips. Using the front leg for support, bend the knee at a 90 degree angle and align it carefully over the ankle with your thigh in a horizontal position. Place the back leg as far behind you as possible, leaning forward on your toes. Now drop your weight so you feel a stretch across the back hip, extending down your leg. Be careful not to lean too far forward (knee in front of your ankle) or you will place added—and unneeded—stress on your knees.

Figure 7-16a

Figure 7-16b

SPOTLIGHT ON

Racewalk.com has been the single greatest resource for race walking information on the web since its inception in 1995. It was created by me and I have maintained it with the assistance of volunteers over the years. From the beginning, racewalk.com provided countless pages of free information, with articles explaining the techniques of race walking, flexibility drills, stretches, and various other important topics related to race walking.

Its critically acclaimed photo stories bring national races alive for fans across the country, with results often posted within hours of race completion. Combining high-quality digital photographs with play-by-play of the race, our unique perspective communicates both the human emotion and athletic drama of competitions short and long.

Many of the pages are updated by you, the surfer. With users maintaining pages containing race schedules, club contacts, and related web sites, racewalk.com strives to constantly improve its depth, breadth, and variety of content.

Racewalk.com is more than just free information: it's a one-stop shop for purchasing the best books, videos, DVDs and race walking apparel available anywhere.

So visit *www.racewalk.com* today!

Piriformis/Iliotibial Band Stretching

The Piriformis and Iliotibial (IT) Band are two little-known hard to spell body parts that can remain obscure until they begin causing great discomfort. The Piriformis is a small muscle in the buttocks; when tight, it stresses the sciatic nerve. The IT Band is made up of fibers that run along the outside of the thigh, attaching in the gluteal muscles and connecting below the knee. The IT Band gets irritated from either overuse or anatomical abnormalities.

The following positions provide excellent stretches for this often-inaccessible area. You may find them a bit complicated, but if you follow the instructions carefully, you'll find the effort worthwhile, I promise.

BUTT BAND STRETCH #1
Importance: Medium   Intensity: High

Using your arms to balance and sustain your body weight, reach one leg behind you for support while bending the stretching leg across and in front of your body. Slowly transfer your body weight to the front leg until you feel a stretch emanating from your buttocks. Take care not to lower your front leg onto the ground.

Figure 7-17a

Figure 7-17b

BUTT BAND STRETCH #2
Importance: Medium   Intensity: Medium

Start by lying on your back with your arms extended perpendicular to the body. Fold the leg you wish to stretch inward and bent at the knee. Place the other leg over it, using it as a weight to push the knee of the leg you are stretching lower. You should feel a good stretch down your outer thigh.

Figure 7-18

SEATED GROIN STRETCH

Importance: Medium   **Intensity:** Medium

At times race walking produces tightness in the groin. Regularly practicing this stretch reduces such discomfort while keeping this important area loose.

Start by sitting with feet turned inwards and legs bent as depicted in Figure 7-19a. Notice the knees fall as close to the ground as possible (Figure 7-19b). As a mental reminder to lower your knees, place your arms atop your lower legs. Now lean forward from your midsection, keeping your back as straight as possible. Avoid lazy stretching. Figure 7-19c shows Jack neither lowering his knees nor leaning forward. While this may produce a minimal groin stretch, the position is ineffective.

| *Figure 7-19a* | *Figure 7-19b* | *Figure 7-19c* |

Shoulder Stretches

Race walkers move their arms through a greater range of motion than runners or pedestrian walkers. By keeping your shoulders stretched and relaxed, you race walk more comfortably and efficiently.

STATIC SHOULDER STRETCH

Importance: Low   **Intensity:** Low

Many people face challenges with this stretch, which is executed from a standing position. Attempt to clasp your hands behind your back, one from above and one from below, as shown in Figure 7-20a. If you can reach, hold the position for 20 to 30 seconds; then reverse arms to stretch the other shoulder. If your hands remain a few inches apart from each other (see Figure 7-20b), use a towel to complete the stretch (see Figure 7-20c). Walk your hands up the towel, positioning them as close together as possible, then reverse arms.

| *Figure 7-20a* | *Figure 7-20b* | *Figure 7-20c* |

75

Take care to perform the Reverse Windmill slowly. Begin by placing one hand on your shoulder, arm relaxed, elbow towards the ground (Figure 7-21a). Slowly raise the elbow forward so the arm becomes perpendicular to your body (Figure 7-21b). Continue bringing the arm straight up, keeping your biceps as near to your face as possible. Slowly rotate the arm back with the elbow as close to your body as possible (see Figure 7-21c), aware it must travel outwards at some point.

Figure 7-21a

Figure 7-21b

Figure 7-21c

As the elbow passes behind your head, keep your upper arm parallel to your shoulders (Figure 7-21d). Gradually rotate the arm through a complete circle (Figures 7-21e & 7-21f) and return to the original position (Figure 7-21a). Slowly repeat the rotation ten times.

Repeat this exercise with both arms.

Figure 7-21d

Figure 7-21e

Figure 7-21f

Chapter 8 - Racing & Mental Training

After all the hard work, now you are almost ready to race. You're probably feeling a bit nervous, but that is completely normal. The only time you might not feel some nervousness is when you do not care about the race. So, treat a slight case of bad nerves as a friendly reminder that you are prepared to accomplish the goals you set so long ago.

Racing should be fun, at least early in the race. However, a good race does take thorough planning. With careful preparation, you can avoid many unexpected problems. But planning cannot start the day before the race; it must start weeks before. The first preparation is one that few people consider seriously: mental training.

Mental Training

Train the mind, you say? Read on.

I began my first season of race walking during winter track of my senior year of high school. I was completely ignorant about training philosophy, race walking technique, and race strategy. Yet I was successful. How? Aside from working extremely hard and maintaining a desire to walk fast, I chased my teammate in every race. "Stay with John," echoed in my mind. The mantra kept me focused on walking fast and using the techniques that made me fast.

By the end of the season, we reached the high-school national championships, an event for which I was totally unprepared. Only a year before, I was a complete non-athlete, opting to devote my time to computers rather than athletics. Lucky for us, the officials at nationals miscounted everyone's laps after the very first one. But I never knew. I just stared into John's back, while he was probably thinking, "Sh*t, Jeff's still with me." This interplay focused us on each other and not the officials. I can't tell you when we realized something was amiss, but at one point our coach yelled to us, "forty yards." We were leading the high school nationals by forty yards! Why? By allowing the lap count to distract them, everyone else choked. Instead, we stayed focused, finishing first and second by more than seventeen seconds.

In the case of that race, fear of my coach chastising me for not focusing ahead of me provided the catalyst for centering my attention. However, it is possible to achieve the same effect by training the mind along with our muscles. Training the mind involves multiple steps. By setting small obtainable goals and then succeeding at them, you can train the mind to be confident you will achieve your main goal.

Start by creating a list of positive mini-goals that seem attainable en route to accomplishing your primary goal. These steps start with your training, lead up to and include your race, and culminate with you reaching your goal.

A typical list may look as follows:

- ☐ Walk as far as the race distance.
- ☐ Walk further than the race distance.
- ☐ Complete an interval workout at—or faster than—race pace.
- ☐ Walk half the race distance in another race or workout at—or faster than—race pace, and feel good about it.
- ☐ Get to the race with plenty of time to prepare.
- ☐ Start the race on pace and feeling comfortable.
- ☐ Hit the splits along the way.
- ☐ Cross the finish line under goal race pace.

As you accomplish each goal, check it off the list. The pattern of succeeding with your smaller goals trains your mind to believe the final goal is achievable.

COACH'S TIP

The goals I present here are very broad in nature. When you create your list, include many more specific goals.

Concerns

Many competitors express concerns about all aspects related to race day. What are the conditions of the course? Who will be there? What's best to wear? When is the post-race party? Many of these questions can be answered, thereby relieving anxiety, others cannot. Instead of letting fear fester, learn to visualize what might happen and how to deal with it. No one can tell you exactly what will happen at any given time, so you need to prepare yourself for all possibilities. Proper preparation reduces the anxiety that builds up prior to the race and allows you to over come any distractions that occur within the race itself.

Programming the Mind

How do you prepare your mind so that you are truly relaxed on the day of the race? Simple. By exercising your mind along with your body. One technique that exercises your mind involves hypnosis. Hypnosis teaches you to be more relaxed on race day, as well as to program your mind to focus on those techniques that make you fast. Novice walkers sometimes focus only on winning. While you need a positive image of attaining your goal, focusing solely on that goal distracts you from the mechanics that enable you to achieve it. By focusing on appropriate techniques that make you fast, you become fast.

Self-hypnosis, like regular hypnosis, is just a form of relaxation. You do not accomplish it by waving a watch in front of your eyes; nor do you bark like a dog when you are through. Instead, by learning to relax deeply, your mind becomes more susceptible to suggestion. Once relaxed, by placing positive suggestions about the race in your subconscious, your mind accepts these suggestions as natural truths.

It often helps to make an audiotape of this lesson, or go through the steps in your mind. When I first began using hypnosis techniques, my coach led me through them. Later, I used a tape-recording that repeated my coach's *script*. Finally, I found the tape unnecessary, because after some practice I could simply *think through* the steps in my mind.

The best way to relax deeply is to use mental imagery. Start by finding a place to lay down undisturbed and assume a comfortable position. Next, imagine yourself in a quiet, peaceful setting, maybe on a beach or near a lake. Imagine a fire near your feet, warming them. Then begin, very slowly, to imagine the warmth from the fire traveling up your feet, through your legs, and into your upper body. Gradually, allow the warmth to travel to your arms, shoulders, neck, and head. Once you're relaxed, imagine your body getting light, and then heavy, and then light again. By this point, hopefully you feel very relaxed.

The best way to relax deeply is to use mental imagery. Start by finding a place to lay down undisturbed and assume a comfortable position. Next, imagine yourself in a quiet, peaceful setting, maybe on a beach or near a lake. Imagine a fire near your feet, warming them. Then begin, very slowly, to imagine the warmth from the fire traveling up your feet, through your legs, and into your upper body. Gradually, allow the warmth to travel to your arms, shoulders, neck, and head. Once you're relaxed, imagine your body getting light, and then heavy, and then light again. By this point, hopefully you feel very relaxed.

- Being relaxed and confident that you are accomplishing your goal.

- Seeing your training partners arriving for the race.

- Starting the race and feeling good because you trained hard and well.

- Passing the mile/kilometer markers of the race, happy at your pace and comfort level.

Once you feel comfortable with the race scene, step it up a bit. Repeat to yourself the positive suggestions you used during your training sessions. By mentally preparing advice about improving your walking stride, you automatically remember these suggestions during the race: just like having your own personal coach inside your head. Here are some potential suggestions:

- I drive my hips forward.

- I swing my arms from a couple of inches behind my hip to just above my chest line.

- I carry my foot through, low to the ground.

- I keep my head up.

78

Triggers

Triggers serve as great reminders for your subconscious to think about your affirmations. Use a common site at the race to trigger the memory of your positive suggestions. Walking around a turn, seeing a telephone pole, or passing a split are all possible triggers. What you choose to serve as your trigger is not important, as long as the object regularly repeats along the course.

Instead of just saying "Drive your hips forward," mentally program the affirmation into your head: "As I see the telephone pole, I remember to drive my hips forward, helping me race walk faster and more legally." On race day, when you pass your trigger, your affirmation rises to consciousness. So you have that going for you, which is nice.

The key to this method's success is remaining deeply relaxed throughout the exercise. If you make a tape to listen to, be sure to speak in a monotone voice throughout the session to encourage such a state. Make sure you imagine everything the way you want it to happen, all the way through to the finish line.

Back when I was in college, a professor of my *Metaphorical Thinking* class used to enjoy making me the guinea pig. He chose me, because he thought the world-class athlete was the closest thing the Western World had to the Eastern World's mental gurus. At the time, I didn't understand why. However, after traveling to the Far East multiple times, studying a bit of Buddhism, and practicing meditation, I now understand his point.

When a race walker achieves complete focus on technique, his or her mind *blanks*. Everything goes on autopilot. To achieve this, you must train your mind. Similarly, monks spend countless hours training to clear their minds of everything. With practice, monk-like mind control is within your grasp.

Acclimatization

Chronologically, the next step in your race preparation includes acclimatizing your body for various racing conditions.

Altitude

The acclimatization that takes the longest to achieve is altitude. Fortunately, few races are held at altitudes high enough to require altitude acclimatization. However, if you plan to race at an altitude of a mile or higher, you need to consider the following issues.

It takes many weeks, up to six, for the cellular adaptation to altitude to occur. When training at altitude, the lack of oxygen to your muscles causes your leg speed to suffer at exactly the time you are trying to perfect it. For example, your pace slows approximately three percent at an elevation of one mile. So while training at altitude increases the capacity of your blood to carry oxygen, your top leg speed suffers.

Here's a better solution: live at a high altitude and train at low altitude. This enables your body to profit from the physiological benefits of living at altitude, but race walk with a pace close to sea-level intensity. The problem with this solution is there are very few places to achieve this conveniently. One place is Cloud Croft, New Mexico, where living at 9,000 feet and training at 4,000 feet is accomplished with a car ride.

Is higher better? Let's all train on Everest.

More information is available at www.hypoxico.com

An interesting but expensive piece of technology solves the problem of inconvenience. The Hypoxic tent is used to simulate high-altitude living. By sleeping in a specially designed tent, an athlete sleeps at simulated altitude while training at sea level. In theory, the best of all worlds: train fast, sleep "high," and be home for mom's home-cooked meals.

One final note: while most experts agree on the benefits of high-altitude training for high-altitude racing, the benefits of high-altitude training for sea-level racing remain nebulous. Often, high altitudes create climates with low humidity and cool temperatures. If a race is set in hot, humid conditions, an athlete trained at high altitude may not be ready for these weather conditions. This leads me to the next race-day consideration.

Weather

Athletes must always factor in the impact of weather upon racing. Ideally, train in or simulate the weather conditions in which you expect to race. Unfortunately, predicting weather is quite difficult. Ironically, my 20K PR was set in temperatures hovering around freezing. A scant two days earlier, the weather was in the sixties. There was no way for me to prepare on such short notice. Fortunately, 30-degree weather swings occur rarely, so a little preparation goes a long way.

If you know your race-day weather will be hot and humid, then train in hot, humid conditions. If you plan to travel to a race where conditions differ from where you live, simulate them. When I trained for the Macabbiah Games, I needed to prepare to race across what amounted to be a desert. Living in Washington, DC, in July of 1989, I faced very warm and sticky conditions. Still, to prepare as best I could, I trained at noon in a sweatshirt every day.

When weather is cold and/or rainy, the best defense is to dress in disposable layers. This way, as you heat up after the start, you just toss your unneeded layers aside.

Time Zones

If you travel across time zones for a race or are simply racing at an unusual time of day, slowly adapt your training and sleeping schedule to the time zone and race time of the competition. By adapting slowly, you do not shock your body before the race, when you need to be relaxed and getting a good night's rest.

 COACH'S TIP

The general rule of thumb dictates that you need to arrive to your race a day earlier for every time zone you cross. However, this rule must be tempered with an athlete's individual comfort level away from home. Some athletes thrive on the change of environment, whereas other athletes benefit from the familiar surroundings of home.

On the Road to Victory

Pre-Race Checklist

Race walkers use very little in the way of equipment. Still, before you travel, make certain you prepare everything you will need. Ensure that everything you wear during your race is broken-in and comfortable beforehand. As a precaution, wear your race outfit for a hard workout before you consider wearing it during a race.

Lubricants

Chaffing during a race is quite nasty, not to mention distracting. While some people are more prone to chaffing than others, anyone can avoid this problem with a little planning and effort. First, as mentioned above, properly

80

break in all race clothing, including undergarments, before race day. Next, liberally apply Vaseline or some other lubricant to any areas that friction might cause to chafe. Be careful though, it's easy to leave some lubricant on your hand and end up with a mouthful of nasty tasting lubricant. Finally, if your race length exceeds 5K, consider storing a lubricant at a water or aid station and reapplying it during the race. By following these steps before a problem occurs, you can virtually eliminate chaffing issues.

Safety Pins
Here's one piece of equipment a novice often fails to bring along on the day of competition: safety pins. Safety pins are used to fasten race numbers to your shirt. Try to bring at least ten of them to each race. Most race walk competitions require wearing a number on the front and back of your shirt. I use eight pins, fastening one on each number's corner. Typically race directors provide safety pins; unfortunately, sometimes they grossly underestimate the number of pins they need. Don't be left with your race number flapping in the wind. Why did I say ten? Ever lose a string in your shorts? It happens more often than people care to admit.

 **COACH'S TIP**

Attach your old safety pins to your race bag. Aside from bringing good luck, this ensures you an adequate supply of pins.

Sunscreen
The need for sunscreen is debatable. Its use depends upon the distance of the race, the weather conditions, your tolerance to the sun, and how long it takes you to complete the race. When I race competitively, I rarely wear it, especially not at short races. However, if I coach a marathon and plan to be out for 10 hours or more, I almost always put some on. If you do use sunscreen, make sure it is a sport formula. Again, as with all things, try it on during a hard pre-race workout to make sure it doesn't bother your eyes or cause any other problems.

COACH'S TIP

Experiment ahead of time with sunscreen. One trick to try is putting it on no higher than the nose and below the eyes. By avoiding your forehead, you may avoid stinging from the sunscreen getting in your eyes.

Your race preparation is almost complete. It helps to use a checklist:

- ☐ Vaseline or other lubricant
- ☐ Safety pins
- ☐ Sport-formula Sunscreen
- ☐ Socks
- ☐ Shoes

- ☐ Top
- ☐ Shorts
- ☐ Undergarments
- ☐ Hat and or Shades
- ☐ Nutritional Supplements
- ☐ Heart Rate Monitor

Traveling
Traveling to a race is always a hassle. Just ask the high-school teams from Maine. They drive everywhere, often showing up in the wee hours of race day morning, a very ill advised resting strategy.

Try leaving yourself plenty of time to get to a race relaxed, but not so far in advance that you sit around a hotel room for days going out of your mind. Ideally, I like to arrive two nights before the race. This gives me one full day to serve as a buffer if there are any travel problems, or relax if there are none.

If you travel by plane, be careful of dehydration. Bring bottled water with you on the trip and drink constantly. Also, remember to stretch whenever the opportunity arises. Always request the exit row of a plane. Your legs will thank you for the extra room. Carrying baggage may be an issue as well. First and foremost, never check your essential equipment. Carry it on. If the airlines lose your luggage, you don't want to be searching for a new pair of racing shoes the day of the race. Also, try to use luggage with built-in wheels, and take care with loading and unloading. If you carry too much luggage, your shoulders are sure to cramp in the race.

COACH'S TIP

If you drive to the race, remember you still face the issues of dehydration, stretching, and carrying your luggage, just to a lesser extent.

Once at the Race Course

Once at the race site, there are a few last things to check off your to-do list. First and foremost, get to know the course. If your race is on a track, you have little to worry about. However, the majority of races today take place on a 2K or 2.5K loop course, with competitors repeating laps until they cover the total race distance. If possible, try to determine the locations of the 500M marks. These marks help you start the race on pace and maintain this targeted speed throughout. If there are no 500M marks, try to determine the loop's halfway mark. Knowing what splits are available helps your preparation. Calculate and memorize the splits for your targeted race pace. At a minimum, know the splits for each lap. Ideally, by calculating and memorizing all the splits for the race, you enable yourself to precisely gauge your progress at all points during the race.

Remember the old adage, "The shortest distance between two points is a straight line?" It may be old, but it still holds true. When racing you almost always want to walk in the straightest line possible, (known as a tangent). The only exception to this is when the terrain along the straightest path is rough or banked heavily.

Many experienced walkers struggle determining the tangents. It's a process that requires constant correction of your path. Observe the figure to the right that shows a sample racecourse and the proper tangent to walk. The course is measured along these tangents, so why walk the extra distance? Walk the course ahead of time, to determine the tangent lines and place them into your race strategy.

Tangent showed in red

 ## COACH'S TIP

Pay careful attention to the tangents of the course.

Nutrition Around Race Day

Your diet before race day, during race day, and slightly after race day must differ slightly from your norm.

Carbo-Loading

When athletes think of the pre-race dinner, they often think of carbo-loading. Unfortunately, the term carbo-loading gets thrown around so much, its true meaning is foggy. Traditionally, carbo-loading requires depleting carbohydrate reserves by eating a high-protein low-carbohydrate diet in the days leading up to a marathon.[3] Then right before the marathon, a racer consumes large amounts of complex carbohydrates to trick the body into storing more than its normal amount of glycogen. The extra glycogen helps fuel the last few miles of the marathon. This process is stressful to the body. I recommend avoiding it unless you are a very serious athlete.

Instead use common sense. Eat normally in the days leading up to the race. Ensure that you are properly hydrated and top off your tank with a nice complex carbohydrate meal of pasta the night before the race.

COACH'S WARNING

Never try something for the first time right before or during a race. Experiment with nutritional supplements, different foods, or electrolyte drinks during your training. What works for another athlete may not work for you.

---

[3] Carbo-loading is mainly used for races of marathon length or longer. There is little benefit to traditional carbo-loading until you walk at least 20 miles.

Day of the Race

Morning of the Race

How early you get up before a race depends on personal preference. Allow yourself enough time to go to the bathroom--Hell, I like to go twice before racing--eat if you need to, and get dressed and to the race with plenty of time to warm up.

Practice your pre-race routine during your training. Not all athletes' bodies respond to the physical and emotional stress of racing the same way. Some people require food in their stomach the day of the race, while others must race with the tank on empty. If you eat, usually a bland form of complex carbohydrate works best. When I raced, I ate a bagel--a New York bagel, of course--and a banana. This combination worked well for me. Both items were relatively easy to digest and seemed to settle my stomach. An added benefit was the banana's potassium, which helped prevent muscle cramps.

Finally, getting plenty of pre-race rest and sleep works to your advantage. Try to get a good night's sleep two consecutive nights before the race. More likely than not, the night before the race will not be the best night's sleep of your life. Bank a few extra hours the day before.

Pre-Race Check In

When arriving at the race, take care of business before socializing. If there is a check in, get that out of the way first. Next, while warming up, discover where the aid station(s) are located. Finally, your last to-do involves determining who is in your age group. If your goal is an age-group medal, then knowing something about your competition certainly helps.

Race Strategy

Your race tactics depend largely on your race goal. Are you racing to go the distance, finish within a specific time, or attain a top place?

Whether your racing goal is to finish or hit a specific time, your strategy is virtually the same. Ease into the race. Start the race slightly slower than goal pace, giving your body a chance to fully warm up. The adrenaline of the competition often causes you to walk faster than you expect. Temper your early enthusiasm. By starting slow, you complete the early part of the race without producing more lactic acid than your body can handle.

Gradually approach and maintain goal pace through the majority of the race, taking comfort that you practiced this pace through many workouts. If you wear a heart rate monitor, check your heart rate. It should be the same as during your interval workouts. If your heart rate is much higher, and it's still early in the race, adjust your race plan and slow down. Similarly, if your heart rate is significantly lower than that of your interval workouts, you have room to quicken the pace. Using your heart rate as a barometer provides a great gauge for your race progress.

As the final goal is in sight, push hard, at or faster than your VO$_2$ Max workout pace. If you time it right, you should cross the line exhausted but happy you reached your goal race time. Never sprint all-out during the last 100 meters. If you have enough energy to sprint hard at the end, start surging earlier. When you sprint, the risk of receiving red cards for loss of contact is high. Thus you'll fare better surging for the last 800 meters than sprinting the last 100.

 COACH'S TIP

Know your lap count. As an athlete, you hold the responsibility for knowing how many laps you have completed. If an official indicates you are done, but you feel you have a lap to go, complete it. Once you stop and end the race, you have no course of action to remediate any laps that you did not complete.

If your race goal is to place in the top three or beat a certain person, then strategy becomes a very personal plan. No strategy--ok, aside from cheating--enables you to beat a walker who typically walks ten minutes faster than you. However, knowing your competitor as well as your own limitations gives you an advantage over a realistically chosen rival. If your competitor makes a habit of starting too quickly and then slowing down, let your competitor take a lead at the beginning. Keep him/her in sight, walking within your own limits. Then, as the race progresses, catch up and pass decisively. Do not just catch up to a rival and walk together. When you make your move, it must be checkmate, with no response. Also, never be tempted to look back.

Some walkers like to suck off your pace. This creates a very frustrating situation. If your competition tries this, you have two options. Speed up and try to lose them, or slow down and make them take their fair share of the lead. Often, two walkers racing together agree to switch the lead on each lap, and then race for the victory with a few laps to go. Keep in mind, if you are racing for time and not place, keep walking at *your* pace. Use these strategies only when you race for a place.

Regardless of your race strategy, always make life easy on yourself. Walk behind or in front of your fellow competitors. Walking alongside them, unless they are on the outside of the course, is equivalent to walking in the second lane of a track; on a course as curvy as a track it costs you 8 meters every 400 meters. In a 20K race, that means a whopping 400 extra meters.

COACH'S WARNING

When following an athlete, always give yourself enough room to walk with your normal gait. Walking too close to your competitor often shortens your stride, making your technique inefficient and sometimes illegal.

Watch the Turns

How a course's turns are set up really affects a competition. Whether you face too many turns or the turns are too tight, your time really suffers. While too many turns slow you down, you can do little about the design of the course. When a turn is wide, common sense prevails: walk as close to the edge of the course as possible. However, if the turn is really tight, try not to walk around it too tightly. Walking too close causes your speed to slow and reduces your momentum once you complete the turn. Instead, take it wide enough to enable you to maintain most of your speed around it.

COACH'S WARNING

Be careful walking around the turns. It's easy to lose focus and walk without straightening the leg properly. Judges watch for this. Don't be their target.

SPOTLIGHT ON

Martin Rudow was an average runner when his college track team's manager, Dean Ingram, exposed him to race walking. For some reason race walking "just clicked," remembers Rudow.

While he understates his ability by describing himself as "a talented, but not exceptionally talented race walker," Rudow was almost an Olympian. In 1968 he was the first alternate for the 20K squad. Unfortunately, Rudow was unable to try again, as a terrible knee injury and in suing surgery ended his competitive career in 1970.

Rudow's interest in walking did not wane; instead he started organizing races and coaching. He became a judge (IAAF for nearly 20 years). From 1984-1988 he was the Men's National Race Walking Coach, during which time he wrote *Advanced Race Walking*. With no up to date training material available, previous to *Advanced Race Walking*, athletes had no printed direction for their training. Although it is now out of print, to date it sold 11,500 copies. The highlight of his post-competitive career was serving as Chief Walking Judge for the men's 20K race walk at the in 1996 Olympic Games in Atlanta.

Rudow has moved on from race walking as many of his former athletes are no longer competing. His presence is sorely missed.

The Fun and Pain of Racing Indoors

Indoor races are a great deal of fun. They also cause a great deal of pain. Most indoor races are held on tracks from 8 laps per mile to as many as a painful 11 laps per mile. The more laps, the more turns. Needless to say, all those turns really slow you down. Exacerbating the problem, many tracks are designed for runners and therefore banked. A bank is no friend to a race walker.

Not deterred yet? Still want to race indoors? Did I mention the air? As one walker at the Millrose Games recently described, "It was like my throat was bleeding." The air indoors is incredibly dry and often irritates the throat. When I raced indoors, I always developed a nice healthy cough afterwards.

Still, with all this said, it's a blast. Those fortunate enough to race in a forum like the Millrose Games at Madison Square Garden remember it as one of the most enjoyable experiences in their race walking career. Imagine 20,000 people watching you race walk. Great fun indeed.

Nutrition During the Race

Walking a few miles on a cool day does not require much thought to nutrition during the walk. However, race a 10K or more on a hot day and careful consideration is needed. Walking far or in the heat requires you to consider hydration. By the time you feel thirsty, it's too late. Plan your hydration carefully. While everyone's exact needs vary, the average person is capable of absorbing a liter of water an hour. Drinking more will likely get you sick; drink too much less and you'll dehydrate. You need a careful balance.

Take care not to drink too much water without any electrolytes. Equally as dangerous as dehydration is hyponutremia, a condition marked by low blood sodium levels. Low blood sodium leads to nausea, fatigue, vomiting, weakness, sleepiness, and in rare severe cases, even death. During the race, either consume a straight or diluted electrolyte drink, or alternate between water and an electrolyte drink.

Longer races require additional nutritional considerations. Your body stores approximately 2000 calories in the form of glycogen. Putting the rough estimate of the caloric expenditure of race walking at 100 calories per mile, after about twenty miles, you deplete your glycogen supply. Known as "hitting the wall," once reached, it is very difficult to continue racing. If you do continue, your pace slows as you burn fat instead of glycogen. Fat is less accessible and a slower fuel for your starving muscles.

The solution is to replace the glycogen with a readily usable form of carbohydrates. You already add some carbohydrates to your system in the form of your electrolyte drink. Two other forms are energy bars or gel shots. Pick your energy bar carefully. When racing, you want a bar high in carbohydrates and low in fat and protein. A gel shot is a form of simple carbohydrates that usually tastes like icing. Absorbed very quickly by the body, gel shots are best used late in a race for a final surge of added energy.

COACH'S WARNING

Be aware that many products contain caffeine. Aside from adding to the risk of dehydration, caffeine is a USATF-controlled substance. You are limited to 12 micrograms per milliliter of urine. While it takes about eight cups of coffee over several hours to reach that amount, combine a few pre-race cups of coffee with other products and you may be over the legal limit. Always monitor how much caffeine you take in.

Properly selected, energy bars provide a good source of energy during a race. However, because they take a while to chew and digest, they are best used earlier in the race so you get time to digest and utilize their energy.

COACH'S TIP

While racing, opening energy bar or gel shot wrappings is difficult. Make sure you pre-open your carbo-source to save time and frustration.

Nutrition After the Race

One last thing to think about before you warm down properly. Post-race nutrition is similar to refueling after a difficult workout. After walking hard, you must refuel your body. How quickly you refuel your body directly affects overall recovery time. As soon as you finish, replace some of the calories you just expended by consuming a small amount of carbohydrates. A carbohydrate/electrolyte drink provides a quick and easy way to get fuel back in your system. A high-carbohydrate energy bar also offers a good source of nutrients to aid your recovery.

Shortly after race walking hard, consume a source of protein to help fuel the rebuilding of muscle. Often after a hard workout, I like to eat a can of solid white tuna fish for this purpose. Of course, hold the mayo!

SPOTLIGHT ON

Racewalking International, Inc., (RWI) a nonprofit public benefit corporation, was created solely to help promote race walking for competition as well as fitness, throughout the Americas as well as the rest of the world.

Since its inception, RWI has sponsored a great many endeavors. They support existing programs financially and have also created new opportunities for race walkers of all abilities.

RWI serves to amplify the already successful program at the University of Wisconsin-Parkside. While competitively successful for decades, the Parkside program was continually hampered by a lack of funds. Today, RWI's support of the athletes' travel budget and training program furthers Mike DeWitt's hard work. But RWI's colligate support doesn't end there. Additionally, they financially support the race walking program at California University of Pennsylvania and assist some Olympic Team qualifiers.

RWI's support is not solely monetary. They oversee and operate a Youth Development Program for race walkers, ages 9 to 19, throughout the U.S. In addition, they established a nationwide Collegiate Grand Prix in 2003, offering any collegiate/university student—whether or not involved in track and field or cross country—support to compete in race walking events.

They average 20 competitions per track season, principally in the Midwest and East Coast regions. Top Five point earners in various categories receive written recognition as well as a plaque outlining their achievement. Additionally, they get updates on happenings within the sport nationwide.

RWI web casts provide an exciting event that is new to our sport, with nearly instant results from major race walking competitions around the world. The web site (*www.worldwidewalkers.net*) also offers information and feature stories on current events pertaining to the race walking community.

Chapter 9 – Strength Training

Introduction

The single best form of cross training for race walkers is strength training. Research indicates that endurance athletes improve their race times more rapidly when they add strength training to their conditioning plans. For race walkers and others concerned with speed and stamina, the key to maximizing performance is enhancing strength without dramatically increasing weight and bulk. To prevent such *bulking up* or enlarging muscle mass when training with weights, my exercises rely on light weights lifted through numerous repetitions.

I entitle the chapter *Strength Training*, not *Weight Training*, to emphasize the process of building strength to improve power and reduce the chance of injury. Some exercises utilize hand weights or machines; others rely solely on supporting body weight while working a particular muscle or muscle group. Both types of movements, in proper combination, prove very effective contributions to race walk training.

Sets, Repeats, and Circuit Training

Strength training workouts are generally performed in sets, or repetitions of one particular exercise. Each repetition involves raising and lowering a specific weight through a predetermined range of motion. My workouts typically require completing 10 to 15 repetitions of each exercise per set, for a total of three sets. Why the range of 10 to 15? Because each time we begin exercising at a new weight level, we face an increased workload that can prevent completing the full 15 repetitions for all three sets. Proper training means never setting the weight too high to complete at least 10 repetitions per set. Once we build up to 15 repetitions for all sets, we increase the weight by 2.5 to 5 pounds at the next workout.

I usually recommend taking a break for thirty seconds to one minute after each set of exercises. Alternately, circuit training provides an option to completing all the sets for one exercise at a time. Using this method, you rotate from one exercise to another, performing one set of each individual exercise with little or no rest in between each set. After you complete each circuit, take a rest of up to five minutes and then repeat the entire circuit two or three times. By circuit training quickly, you add an endurance element to the regimen.

General Rules of Thumb

When strength training, the order in which you execute the exercises matters. Always start with the legs and then proceed to the back, chest, shoulders, and arms; finish with the core, your stomach.

We perform exercises using either one or two limbs at a time. Often novices gravitate towards using both limbs simultaneously—for example, performing a leg extension with both legs at once. This approach creates problems because our strength usually varies from right limb to left limb. By exercising both limbs at the same time, the dominant one performs more work, thus adding to the strength discrepancy. Instead, wherever possible, perform each exercise one limb at a time.

 COACH'S TIP

When performing strength training exercises one limb at a time, always begin each set with the weaker limb first. Attempt only as many repetitions with the stronger limb as you complete with the weaker one. This prevents the imbalance from growing worse.

Free Weights vs. Machine Exercises

Choosing between free-weight exercises and machine-guided exercises is not just a matter of taste. Safety and performance issues must be factored into your decision, with safety always serving as the overriding concern. For reasons discussed below, free weights provide an excellent training tool; however, exercises involving weights lifted freely over the body require a *spotter* to watch over you and lift the bar if you cannot finish the exercise. Without a spotter, you may find a heavy bar of weights on your chest without a means to remove it. Since I workout alone, when I perform the bench press, I use a machine.

In most cases, however, free weights are superior to weight machines, which guide you through the proper movements of an exercise. When we use free weights, our bodies balance the weight, thereby strengthening more than just the primary target muscles. Free weights help strengthen the ligaments and tendons, as well as some secondary muscle groups. Advocates of strength training machines cite the advantages of greater control and reduced chance of injury; machine-guided workouts thus prove excellent methods for beginners or people training without anyone to spot or show them proper techniques for free weights. If you lack experience or a training partner, start with machines and graduate up as you raise your comfort level.

Stay in Control

Don't rush when strength training. When lifting weights, any slight jerk in the wrong direction creates a dangerous and potentially harmful situation. Always keep the weight in control; it's the key to gaining the most benefit from the exercise and avoiding injury.

One way to promote control is to focus on your breathing. As you exert force raising the weight, always exhale. As you lower the weight, inhale. Seemingly a simple plan, but many athletes forget about breathing, especially as they push through the last few repetitions of a set.

Working the Muscles

Unless otherwise stated, when performing each exercise, always execute each movement through a full range of motion. Make exceptions only when injured. In such cases, seek the advice of a physical therapist before engaging in strength training. The therapist can make suggestions to limit your range of motion and protect the injury.

Also, keep opposing muscle groups in mind. One sure way to injure yourself is to create muscle imbalances. When you strengthen one muscle group, you must always strengthen the opposing group. Working the hamstrings thus requires working the quadriceps. Likewise, strengthen the triceps with the biceps, the shins with the calves, and the chest with the upper back.

When to Strength Train

While you may pursue race walk training each day, do not strength train this frequently. Strength training breaks down our muscles, so we need time to rebuild them. Ideally, your conditioning plan should include strength training three times a week. Furthermore, always remember, race walking is your primary training. Choose to strength train after a hard workout (just give yourself enough time to recover), not before one. When you wipe yourself out with a strength-training workout and then try to race walk, your technique as well as your endurance suffers.

 COACH'S TIP

You can strength train six days a week if you vary your workouts. Alternating one day for the upper body and one day for the lower body facilitates rebuilding one muscles group while you work out the other. If you take this approach, lift with your lower body, after walking, on the days you do your hard workouts.

 SPOTLIGHT ON

Stella Cashman could have the most unique *How I Became a Race Walker* story. Previously, a recreational runner, Cashman was injured when a horse fell on her. She never fully recovered. Sensing that race walking was a better way to go, she has been involved with our sport for nearly two decades. She began by responding to a promotion for a race walk competition. Cashman was instantly hooked. Reaching her peak at the World Veteran Games in Australia in 1987, she earned a bronze medal for the 10K race walk with a time of 57:30.

After becoming New York City's premier race walk promoter, Cashman gave up competing and focused on helping others as a judge, coach, and race director. She has been the Metropolitan Athletic Congress Race Walking Chair for over a decade.

Cashman's club, the Park Race Walkers, consists of 50 race walkers at all levels and age groups. If you reside in the New York area and are interested in joining, contact them at (212) 628-1317 or *Francicash@aol.com*.

Shin Exercises

When I started race walking, my high school coach asked me how I was doing. I replied, "I feel fine." He then told me I was walking wrong because my shins are supposed to hurt (and they did). While my coach was not completely correct in that shin pain is inevitable, he had hit on a very common problem for novice race walkers: shin pain.

Race walking utilizes your shin muscles far more than most sports. However, proper stretching and strengthening reduces or eliminates the shin pain most beginners feel. Stretch your shins well, as illustrated in Chapter 7, and strengthen your shins with the exercises included here.

WALKING ON YOUR HEELS

Duration: **25 yards**

Purpose: **Strengthens shin muscles, helps reduce shin pain often associated with beginning race walking or increasing mileage. Balances calf strengthening.**

Probably the single easiest way to strengthen your shins is to walk on your heels.

Steps

1. Walk slowly, with a stride of no more than six inches. Remember, it's not a race.

2. Focus on how high you point your toes. The higher you point them, the better and more intensely you work your shins.

3. Maintain this technique for 25 yards.

4. If your shins can't handle this distance, stop walking on your heels briefly and stretch out your shins. Once you stretch properly, resume *heel-walking* the remainder of the 25 yards.

5. Upon completion, always stretch out the shins completely; you will feel happy you did so later.

Figure 9-1

 ## SPOTLIGHT ON

Bruce MacDonald received a scholarship to NYU as a hurdler in 1947. After graduating college, a teammate from the NY Pioneer Club asked MacDonald to compete in an all-around event that included a half-mile race walk. To prepare for the event, MacDonald and his teammate received help from the legendary Henry Laskau. After some persuasion, MacDonald gave in and eventually focused his energies on race walking. Laskau must have known what a talent his student had: MacDonald became a three time Olympian (1956 - 20K, 1960 - 50K, 1964 - 50K).

Even before MacDonald finished his elite career, he started giving back to the sport as a coach. In 1958, he was the head track and field coach at Port Washington High School. Onc of his first protégé's was Ron Daniel, who competed in exhibition events at dual meets. MacDonald was the head coach, on and off, for nearly 50 years and played a key part in getting the race walk accepted as a scoring event in the New York State High School Championships. Today he still coaches at Port Washington Middle School.

MacDonald has served as an IAAF judge and as an umpire at the 1996 Olympic Games. He has coached countless world and national class race walkers.

SHIN RAISES ON CURB/STEP

Duration: 1 set of 20 or 30 repetitions.

Purpose: Strengthens shin muscles, helps reduce shin pain often associated with beginning race walking or increasing mileage. Balances calf strengthening.

Perform this more advanced shin exercise on the edge of a curb/step. Because balance is sometimes difficult when performing this exercise, make sure you have a pole or wall to steady yourself.

Steps

1. Facing away from the curb/step, place your heels as close to the edge as possible, taking care to remain steady.

2. Pump your toes up and down as quickly as possible.

Get those toes up high! The greater the range of motion your toes pass through, the better the workout.

Figure 9-2a

Figure 9-2b

COACH'S WARNING

Keep your balance; do not fall off the curb.

Calf Exercises

Strengthening muscles involves balance. While athletes often focus on their shins, they neglect their complementary muscles, the calves.

Similar to the shin exercise, by slowly walking on your toes, you strengthen your calves.

Steps

1. Walk slowly, with a stride of no more than 6 inches. Remember, it's not a race.

2. As you walk, focus on keeping your heels as high off the ground as possible.

3. Walk this way for about 25 yards.

4. If your calves tire quickly, stop walking on your toes briefly and stretch your calves a little. Then complete the rest of the exercise. If 25 yards feels really easy, try to go a little further.

Figure 9-3

Once you finish the exercise, it's always a good idea to stretch the calves completely as shown in chapter 7.

SPOTLIGHT ON

Gary Westerfield has served our sport in almost every way imaginable. Starting as an athlete, he also has been a high school coach (Smithtown High School 1975 to 1980, and 1987 to 2000); a collegiate coach (SUNY Stony Brook 1980 to 1985); an IAAF Judge; writer of educational materials; administrator (Race Walk Chair for both Metropolitan Athletics Congress (MAC) and Long Island Track and Field (LITF), as well as current president of LITF); and race organizer.

When race walking was part of the NY high school program, Westerfield was a magnet for talent. If you were on Long Island and were serious about race walking, you sought out Westerfield. Coaching the likes of Susan Liers, Lynn Wiek, Tommy Edwards, Curtis Fisher, and even myself, Westerfield was well represented in international competition.

From 1984 to 1988, Westerfield also served as coach of the Women's National Program as well as National Team coordinator. As coordinator, he sought to bring science to the race walking world.

In 1997 he co-authored the book *Walk Like an Athlete* and has continued to write about the biomechanics of race walking since.

CALF RAISE

Duration: Each leg: 1 to 3 sets, 10 to 15 repetitions per set.

Purpose: Builds the calf muscles used in the race walking stride when your foot and toes push off against the ground for a final thrusting motion. Provides the balance that helps reduce shin problems.

Best executed with something nearby to help maintain your balance. Ideally, practice the calf raise on a curb near a pole or on a step with a handrail. This exercise is actually very similar to the *Advanced Calf Stretch* presented in Chapter 7.

Steps

1. Find a step or curb and position your toes as close to the edge as possible while still maintaining balance.

2. Next, place your heels beyond the edge, raising and lowering them through a wide range of motion.

Repeat this 10 to 15 times, taking care not to cheat by using your upper body for leverage.

Figure 9-4a

Figure 9-4b

Figure 9-4c

Options: If you feel comfortable and steady, try a modification of the simple calf exercise by completing each set one leg at a time. See Figure 9-4c.

COACH'S WARNING

Do not bounce. Be careful not to try too many calf raises the first time. You may underestimate how sore you might become in the next 24 hours.

Additional Leg Exercises

> ### STRAIGHT LEG RAISE
>
> Duration: Each leg: 3 sets, 10 to 15 repetitions per set.
>
> Purpose: Strengthens quadriceps and lower abdomen and helps the knee track better. This is an all-around great exercise. Make sure to include this in your routine.

This exercise can be done with or without a light ankle weight. Start without weight and gradually add light weights, building up to but never exceeding 10% of your body weight.

Steps

1. Start by lying on your back and supporting your body by bending one leg as shown.

2. Extend the other leg out straight.

3. Slowly raise the straight leg to about 45 degrees; hold it there for a second, and then gradually lower it.

Figure 9-5a

Figure 9-5b

COACH'S WARNING

Do not strain your lower back by lifting too much weight.

SPOTLIGHT ON

Coach Mike DeWitt was an accomplished walker in his own right, representing the U.S. at events like the World Cup. However, Dewitt's accomplishments as a coach are what landed the spotlight in his direction.

DeWitt is the women's head track coach and race walking coordinator at the University of Wisconsin - Parkside. Taking the program over from Bob Lawson, DeWitt worked and continues to work with more elite race walkers in this country than anyone else. Over half the guys at the Olympic Training Center in Chula Vista participated in DeWitt's program. Before there was a training center, Debbi Lawrence, Michelle Rohl, Jim Heiring, and Andy Kastner all graduated from DeWitt's program going on to success at the Olympics.

Those who qualify get free tuition and fees. They must have running ability as well as the desire to walk, because the DeWitt program requires running a season of cross-country and for some the running of indoor track which improves leg speed.

While not a requirement, the pattern of academic excellence is well established, with most athletes making Dean's List. If thinking of competing in college, start by contacting DeWitt at *DeWitt@uwp.edu.*

LEG EXTENSIONS

Duration: Each leg: 3 sets, 10 to 15 repetitions per set.

Purpose: Strengthens the quadriceps muscles used while extending the leg during the swing phase of race walking. Helps the knee track better.

Ideally, perform this exercise on a machine, one leg at a time. While machine makes and models differ, most are similar in structure to the one shown below. Higher-quality machines usually allow you to adjust the seat and leg roller. Set the equipment so you situate your knee on the axis of the machine, with your ankle just below the leg roller.

Steps

1. Keeping your thigh pressed against the machine, extend your leg to near locking position.

2. Lower your leg to its original position.

3. Remember to exhale as you raise the leg roller and inhale in as you lower it.

4. As you execute the exercise, make sure your ankle remains in contact with the roller and you control the weight.

Complete all repetitions of the set with the first leg before beginning repetitions for the second leg.

Figure 9-6a

Figure 9-6b

Options: If you do not have access to a machine, try this exercise on a high stool from a kitchen or bar. With an ankle weight or bag hanging from your foot, place your buttocks near the back edge of the stool. Maintaining your balance carefully, raise your foot in the same motion as demonstrated above. Pay careful attention to keeping your back straight and still.

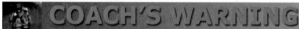
COACH'S WARNING
Do not lock the knee.

This exercise is best performed on a machine, one leg at a time. With few exceptions, most machines are similar in structure to the one shown below. Higher-quality equipment usually allows you to adjust the seat and leg roller; set them so you situate your knee on the axis of the machine, with the ankle just below the leg roller.

Steps

1. Keeping your thigh pressed against the machine, curl your leg, pulling your heels inwards so the leg roller approaches your buttocks as shown.

2. Remember to exhale as you raise the weight.

3. Complete the exercise by lowering your leg back to its original position while inhaling.

4. Always maintain contact between the roller and your leg as you execute the lift, as well as maintain control of the weight.

5. Complete all repetitions for each set with one leg before starting the repetitions for the other leg.

Figure 9-7a

Figure 9-7b

COACH'S WARNING

Keep control while raising the weight. Do not bounce the leg roller ahead of your leg.

SPOTLIGHT ON

Bev LaVeck was like many people who became infatuated with running. While she enjoyed the aerobic benefits of running, her experience with stress fractures and other running related injuries caused her to seek another activity. Fortunately, LaVeck lived in the Seattle area, where race walking was very visible. Not only did the local running magazine always have an article on it, but weekly clinics were given by Martin Rudow and Dean Ingram.

After attending one of these clinics in 1980, LaVeck was hooked. Shortly after becoming an avid Masters race walk competitor (winning many Master's national and international titles) she started giving back to the sport, teaching instructional clinics as well as officiating. Currently a Master's level judge in race walking, she is best known for her tireless efforts in promoting and recording Master's race walking. LaVeck maintains the official USA Master's race walking records, the USA Master's single age bests, and the race walk marks for the World Master's Athletics.

LAT PULL DOWN

Duration: 3 sets, 10 to 15 repetitions per set.

Purpose: Strengthens the upper back. Balances development of pectoral muscles.

Steps

1. Sit firmly in the seat provided.

2. Adjust the support bar so you do not rise out of the seat as you pull the weight down.

3. Grab the bar with palms facing outwards, and place your hands near the outer portion of the bar.

4. Pull the bar down behind your head to about shoulder height.

5. Return the bar back to start, stopping just before your arms completely straighten.

Figure 9-8a

Figure 9-8b

Figure 9-8c

Options: A variation of this exercise involves pulling the bar in front of your body to about mid-chest height. If you have time, perform both exercises. If time is limited, select one or alternate between the two.

COACH'S WARNING

Keep control while raising and lowering the weight. Don't let the bar swing back excessively as you return to a starting position.

SHOULDER PRESS

Duration: 3 sets, 10 to 15 repetitions per set.

Purpose: Strengthens the shoulder muscles used during arm swing.
Supports good posture.

Steps

1. Sit firmly planted with your back supported.

2. Place both hands on the machine so that your palms face away from you.

3. Raise the bar, while exhaling, to just before your elbows lock.

4. Lower the bar back to the starting position, inhaling as the bar lowers.

Figure 9-9a

Figure 9-9b

Options: If you do not have access to a machine, use a set of dumbbells to achieve the same workout.

COACH'S WARNING

Keep control while raising and lowering the weight. It's easy to throw your back out if you lift too much or cheat using your back muscles.

Duration: 3 sets, 10 to 15 repetitions per set.

Purpose: Strengthens the chest, thus balancing the upper back. Supports good posture.

The bench press is not usually part of a traditional race walk workout, but I include it here to balance out those exercises that develop the back. As long as you avoid the temptation to lift large amounts of weight and bulk up, it provides a fine complement to my strength-training program.

Executing a proper bench press takes a little more focus than needed for many of our other exercises. As you do with all lifts, always make sure you control the weight throughout all movements. Begin with a light weight when first undertaking the press. Then, after you feel comfortable with the exercise, increase the weight.

Steps

1. A good grip is key, so avoid laziness and use all your fingers and your thumb. The tighter the grip, the better your control over the bar.

2. Position your arms slightly wider than shoulder-width apart, with the bar positioned in the middle of your chest.

3. When lifting the weight, you can hold your arms at an angle between 45 degrees and 90 degrees to your body. I recommend holding it at 90 degrees. The closer your arms get to a 90-degree angle, the more you develop your chest muscles. While holding your arms at a 45-degree angle from your body allows you to lift more weight, you gain much less from the exercise.

4. As you execute this lift, remember to exhale as you raise the weight and inhale as you lower it.

5. Make sure you do not lock your elbows as you extend your arms upwards.

Figure 9-10a

Figure 9-10b

COACH'S WARNING

Race walkers have no reason to determine their maximum bench press. Maxing out is risky; why take the chance? Do not arch your back as you lift the weight.

ARM SWINGS

Duration: Varied. Start at two minutes, then increase the duration as you become more comfortable with the exercise.

Purpose: Strengthens the arms in the most exercise-specific manner possible.

Specificity of exercise, specificity of exercise, specificity of exercise: a maxim I keep driving into your head. The single best arm exercise for race walking is practicing the motion of the race walker's arm swings with small, light arm weights.

Steps

1. Swing the hands back and forth through the full range of motion traveled while race walking.

2. Counter your arm swing by pushing your opposite hip forward.

3. Remember to keep those shoulders relaxed!

 COACH'S TIP

Perform this exercise in front of the mirror to simultaneously work on arm technique.

Figure 9-11a

Figure 9-11b

 SPOTLIGHT ON

Tom Eastler was a grad student at Columbia in 1966 when Israeli Olympic race walker Shaul Ladany introduced him to our sport. A self proclaimed mediocre walker who doesn't even remember the times that he walked, Eastler probably would not have focused on race walking if not for the activities of his children.

His daughters Gretchen and Lauren got him involved at the Junior Olympic level at the beginning of the 1980s. As an official and coach, Eastler touched the lives of many race walkers. However, it was his tireless effort to get the race walk included in the Maine High School track and field program that will forever be his legacy. Currently, Maine is the only state to have race walking as an integral part of the state-wide track and field program. Eastler contributes his success to the presence of a very strong summer Junior Olympic track and field program in which race walking has always been a popular event.

BICEPS CURL

Duration: Each Arm: 3 sets, 10 to 15 repetitions per set.

Purpose: Strengthens the biceps muscles used to carry and swing the arm during the race walking stride. Balances the triceps muscles.

Steps

1. With your feet a shoulder's width apart, hold each dumbbell at your side using an underhanded grip. Start with the dumbbell perpendicular to the side of body.

2. Rotating the dumbbell 90 degrees, raise it as shown. While you raise the dumbbell, your elbow rotates as the dumbbell rotates; however, its position relative to your body does not change.

3. Once you completely raise the first dumbbell, simultaneously lower it as you raise the other one. One dumbbell's movement mirrors the other's. As one lowers the other raises and visa versa. Since you exert effort at all times, remember to breathe constantly.

Figure 9-12a

Figure 9-12b

Options: If you have difficulty raising and lowering dumbbells simultaneously, try lightening the weight. If you still have difficulty, it is OK to raise and lower one arm at a time.

COACH'S WARNING

Keep control while raising and lowering the weight. Don't bounce with the weights. It's easy to throw your back out if you lift too much or cheat by using your back muscles.

TRICEPS CURL

Duration: Each Arm: 3 sets, 10 – 15 repetitions per set.

Purpose: Strengthens the triceps muscles used to carry and swing the arm during the race walking stride. Balances development of biceps muscles.

Steps

1. Bend at the waist as shown and place one hand on a bench for support.

2. Keep your back straight and parallel to the ground.

3. With your legs one shoulder's width apart, hold your upper arm parallel to your back and your lower arm perpendicular to the ground.

4. Exhaling as you lift the weight, straighten your arm so that it becomes parallel to the ground.

5. Inhale while you return the weight to starting position.

Figure 9-13a

Figure 9-13b

Options: Another popular way of working the triceps is to perform this exercise from a standing position, lifting the weight up over the body. I do not recommend this for beginners, because it can easily injure your back.

COACH'S WARNING

Keep control while raising and lowering the weight. It's easy to throw your back out if you lift too much or cheat by using your back muscles.

STOMACH CRUNCHES

Duration: Varied. Start with 10, build up to as many as 100.

Purpose: Strengthens the lower abdomen to improve posture and support your lower back.

Steps

1. Start by laying down on a firm surface.

2. Bend your knees and bring both feet towards your buttocks, so your legs form a triangle with the ground.

3. Place your hands across your chest, and begin to curl upwards by *tucking* your chin to your chest.

4. Slowly roll your upper body off the ground, pressing your lower back to the ground as you curl.

5. Always exhale while curling your body upwards

6. Lower your body to its original position by reversing your movements and inhaling as your body lowers to the ground.

7. Repeat the exercise as many times as possible, but only as long as you maintain good technique. When you reach 100 repeats, stop.

Figure 9-14a

Figure 9-14b

COACH'S WARNING

If your lower back is weak, start slowly and complete only a few crunches. Increase repetitions very gradually.

Variations: There are many, many variations to this exercise. One variation involves twisting your body towards the opposite side as you raise it off the ground. Alternate sides with each crunch.

Chapter 10 – Injuries, Treatments & Nutrition

As if searching for the elusive Holy Grail, many walkers get lured into our sport by the equally elusive promise of injury-free training. The simple reality is that although race walkers experience fewer injuries than other athletes, injuries can occur just as they do in any other aerobic weight-bearing sport.

Race walking is unique in that it demands a certain symmetry of motion. Each lower limb performs similar functions; without symmetry, the alignment is thrown off. Just as potholes affect a car, walking over bumps and humps—or just walking too much without proper support or cushioning—upsets your body's alignment, causing painful strains and inflammation in muscles and joints in the process.

When injuries occur, follow these guidelines for treatment—but remember, they are not a substitute for a doctor's opinion. Always consult your primary care physician or other medical provider when front-line treatment fails to work or when the problem worsens.

Causes

There are several different causes of injury. One of the most common—overuse—occurs for several important reasons.

1. Suddenly increasing weekly mileage adds excessive stress to the leg joints. An injury is the body's response.
2. Continually increasing mileage without allowing adequate time for the body to adapt produces stress. At first, walkers feel confused, not understanding how gradual change can cause pain. However, the continual training load amasses until the body reacts with an injury.
3. Changing terrain—whether from flat to hills, soft to hard surface, or hard to soft surface–sets up an injury.
4. Shoes not properly designed to provide support might initially feel comfortable, but as they wear, they break down. Without proper support, your foot also breaks down, which can cause injury elsewhere in the body.
5. Rapidly changing your technique requires additional stretching to help your body, especially muscles, adapt to your new style. Omitting necessary stretches can lead to injury.

Some race walkers develop injuries by walking with improper technique. Fortunately, these problems can be corrected with proper planning—following the techniques in this book and my DVDs—and good coaching. Notice that my training schedules contain both easy and hard weeks. Resting the body is as important as training it.   The body requires time to recuperate.

Pay attention to the road and road surface when you walk. An accidental trip on a curb or walking into a car dents more than just your training schedule. The racing career of National Team member John Nunn encompasses a short five years. During that time he missed training due to a broken ankle, two car accidents, and bruised ribs. It's easy to get hurt if you are not careful.

When Something Hurts

In race walking, as in life, when we do not follow directions, we get punished for breaking the rules. An injury is the punishment for not following proper training guidelines. Once injured, you must treat the injury properly. Equally important, you must also reduce or eliminate stress to the abused area by decreasing or discontinuing your race walk training until the injured area heals.

Most people rationalize training through an injury to avoid getting out of shape. Not a good idea. Treat injuries with the respect they deserve. Unless you are a very experienced walker, have a knowledgeable coach, or a doctor gives you approval, do not train through an injury. Training through an injury often prolongs the injury. By the time you finally heal, you will be less fit than if you had just rested properly from the start.

Types of Injuries

Injuries fit into two categories: acute and chronic. Acute injuries occur all of a sudden, like a football player suffering a broken rib when he is head-butted by another player. Chronic injuries, more common in race walking, occur from the accumulation of stress at a specific area of the body. The same healing principles apply to both.

When you first hurt your body, tissue gets damaged, blood vessels bleed, and the injured area swells, slowing the healing process.

Once injured, you must prevent the damage from spreading. This is critical. However, preventing the body from compensating for an injury is an equally important though often overlooked treatment principle. For example, an ankle sprain causes you to limp and overuse the non-injured leg. The other foot then receives more stress and may begin to develop symptoms as well.

Common Treatments

RICE

Your front line treatment is a simple one. Follow the traditional RICE (Rest, Ice, Compression, Elevation) method. The first step in RICE is to stop the activity that caused the injury and rest.

Apply ice for several reasons. A great pain killer, ice reduces swelling by reducing blood flow to the injured area; it also slows the release of other chemicals that retard the healing process. The best way to apply ice is with an ice bath. When ice is added to water, the water turns the temperature of the ice. Water, being more malleable, makes better contact with the body and therefore delivers a better chill (as if the ice weren't cold enough). Most of us do not have a readily available ice bath or are unwilling to create one out of a household tub. The next best treatment calls for using large, soft ice packs or crushed bags of ice. They sculpt to the body easier than a bag of ice cubes. If you can't find them, use a large plastic bag filled with ice and water. For sensitive skin, place a paper towel between the ice and your body.

A complete ice treatment consists of applying ice for twenty minutes, removing it for twenty minutes, and finally, applying it again for an additional twenty minutes. Repeating this sequence a couple of times a day works best. When training resumes, ice treatments remain especially important to prevent the return of swelling and pain after exercise. Do not delay applying ice to an injury by standing around talking to your training partner.

Be aware of aliments like arthritis, where applying ice may be contraindicated. Please consult your doctor before trying this treatment on any new injury for the first time.

A second method used to reduce swelling involves taking anti-inflammatories such as ibuprofen, aspirin, or naproxen. Some athletes think they need to act macho and suffer through the pain of an injury. However, ignoring pain is self-defeating. Pain slows the healing process and forces the body to compensate for the injury. Pain killers, when combined with rest, actually may speed the healing process. Still, you must use caution and common sense. Each person's sensitivity to anti-inflammatories differs, and using a lot of this medication can irritate the stomach. Again, please consult your doctor before using this therapeutic approach.

COACH'S WARNING

Be careful when using pain killers, as they can mask the severity of an injury. Athletes often decide to go back to training too soon after an injury, misinterpreting the lack of pain as a cure. Do not walk while you are taking pain killers. The additional stress compounds the injury.

For minor injuries, sometimes the injured body part requires **compression** or immobilization. Ace wraps and taping are two of the best approaches to limit motion, add support, and allow resumption of function with limited risk of further injury. For more extreme cases, full immobilization is required in the form of a cast or non-weight bearing crutches.

Elevation always helps, but you must keep the injured body part to at least the level of your heart. This prevents fluids from running downhill and causing swelling. Sometimes this means full body rest.

When To Use Heat

Remember the trusty heating pad? Heat increases blood flow and removes waste products from around the site of an injury. However, while it has its place in treatment, if applied too early, heat can actually cause additional damage. As a general rule of thumb, wait at least 48 hours from the onset of an injury to apply heat. This allows time for the swelling to stop.

Moist heat is more effective than dry heat, with therapeutic hot tubs my preferred choice of application. If you do not have access to one, try a moist heating pad or a pad that you moisten and heat in the microwave oven.

Ultrasound
Ultrasound works by converting sound waves to heat inside the muscle tissue. Although not as convenient as home heating methods, it achieves much deeper heating of damaged muscles.

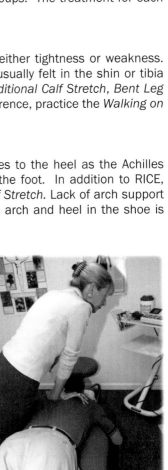

Research indicates that ultrasound is 50 to 80% more effective than superficial heat in improving range of motion to the applied area. Of course, if you do not have access to ultrasound, heating with hot packs or hydrotherapy will suffice; these tools are just less effective than ultrasound.

Many people believe that ultrasound is effective in treating pain, but few available, well-documented, scientifically sound studies support this belief.

Beware of Sports Creams
Do not be fooled by sports creams and ointments as a substitute for heat therapy. Most of these products are skin irritants that give the illusion of heat treatment; in reality, they only heat the skin's surface.

Adding Stretching As a Treatment
When the origin of pain problems stems from lack of flexibility, adding area-specific stretches to the RICE treatment often helps. A muscle strain may occur in any of the major muscle groups. The treatment for each group is the same: RICE and lots of stretching.

Shin Splints
Shin splints occur when the balance in the lower leg muscles is disrupted by either tightness or weakness. While the weakness resides in the muscles at the front of the leg, the pain is usually felt in the shin or tibia bone. In addition to RICE, include the following stretches in your recovery: *Traditional Calf Stretch*, *Bent Leg Calf Stretch*, *Standing Shin Stretch* and the *Seated Shin Stretch*. To reduce recurrence, practice the *Walking on Your Heels* exercise.

Heel Pain
Heel pain often occurs at the back of your heel where the calf muscle attaches to the heel as the Achilles tendon. This pain may extend to the botton of the heel and into the arch of the foot. In addition to RICE, stretch the calf muscles using the *Traditional Calf Stretch* and the *Bent Leg Calf Stretch*. Lack of arch support is a leading cause, so avoid walking barefoot. Finally, adding a support to the arch and heel in the shoe is helpful.

Chiropractic Therapy
Regular treatment by a chiropractor is fairly controversial. Some medical professionals do not respect the holistic practice of correcting the function of the spine and other musculoskeletal areas through non-evasively manipulating the spine.

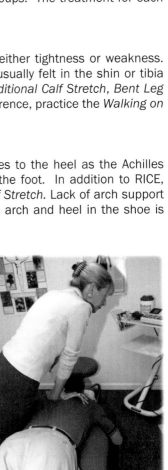

The word chiropractic's roots are in the Greek word, *Chiropraktikos*, which means *effective treatment by the hand*. Chiropractors treat by using the hand to make adjustments to the spine. Sometimes the vertebrae in your spine become fixed, thereby affecting the ability of your spine to move properly. By manipulating the spine, a chiropractor seeks to free the fixed joint and return normal function to the spine.

Personally, I have found chiropractic treatments (called adjustments) excellent for acute and chronic problems. Combing spinal manipulation with ultrasound and electro stimulation is an effective treatment for my chronic neck problems as well as some acute athletic injuries I have encountered.

Electro Stimulation

The words *electro stimulation* bring all sorts of images to one's mind, some of them quite scary. Electro stimulation actually works quite simply in concept. Electricity is used to trigger the firing of muscles in the body.

Electro stimulation occurs in many forms. For race walkers, electro stimulation is used to control pain, decrease muscular atrophy, and improve circulation.

Be wary of claims that electro stimulation gets you in shape without working out. While one form of electro stimulation, "Russian stimulation," is used to build muscle, it's used mostly for therapeutic cases where an athlete is immobilized for a period of time. Claims that electro stimulation helps you lose weight and strengthens your stomach are very misleading.

While under the care of a medical practitioner, electro stimulation proves an effective form of treatment, but the treatment is not for everyone. Do not use it without the supervision of a medical practitioner.

Massage Therapy

Everyone enjoys a good massage. Massage is growing in popularity, with many different forms of massage for many different purposes. More and more, athletic coaches recognize the benefits of massage therapy for their athletes.

Aside from the obvious relaxing effect of massage, it also:

- Increases circulation.

- Breaks up scar tissue in the muscle.

- Improves flexibility.

- Aids in the rehabilitation of injuries.

- Removes waste products.

- Improves cell nutrition.

Like all components of a training regimen, massage therapy is most effective when used regularly. One-time treatments, like the booths set up after a race, are not as effective.

COACH'S WARNING

Unknowledgeable athletes may seek massage therapy for the first time the day before a big race. This is usually not a good idea. Light massage before a race is OK, but therapeutic massage administered to an athlete unaccustomed to regular massage treatments may result in fatigue and be counter-roductive.

I use two types of massage therapy in my training regimen:

- **Sports massage** – a series of vigorous and frequent strokes, specifically designed to remove lactic acid, improve circulation, and aid in the recovery and regeneration of muscle tissue.

- **Myofacial release** - a form of ancient therapeutic massage that uses a series of soft tissue strokes to effectively treat pain syndromes in muscles, tendons, ligaments, and connective tissue.

Unfortunately, I find the latter—my preferred form of therapy—more difficult to find.

Massage is expensive and not covered by most medical insurance. Typical massages can cost between $50 and $80/hour. If you can't afford regular massage therapy, then try the North American Race Walking Foundation's *Dynamic Self-Massage for Fit and Fast Walking* video and pamphlet at *http://members.aol.com/RWNARF/* or call 626-441-5459. A great resource, it explains how to gain the benefits of massage, without the therapist.

> While the benefits of massage are vast, there are times when it is inappropriate. Massage should be avoided immediately after injuries that have bad swelling or bruises, or for athletes with open wounds or contagious skin conditions.

Other Problems

Athlete's Foot

Commonly known as "athlete's foot," this fungal infection of the foot usually begins with peeling skin and redness between the toes. Often associated with itching, athlete's foot may involve the nails as well. While athlete's foot is treated with over-the-counter powders, creams and solutions, it may reoccur. Keep your foot dry, throw your socks in the washing machine with bleach (an enemy of fungus) and use socks that wick moisture away from the feet.

Plantar Warts

Plantar warts are small thickened growths, usually occurring on the soles of the feet. Caused by a viral organism, they can be painful if located directly under the weight-bearing part of the foot. Treat them with over-the-counter solutions. Do not shave or cut them; this leads to spreading them on yourself and others. Follow the directions for treatment carefully and keep your feet dry.

Blisters

One of the most common problems faced by beginning race walkers, as well as more experienced ones, is the dreaded blister. Friction caused by improperly fitting walking shoes, particularly if one foot is larger than the other, is an obvious culprit, but it's not the only one. Irregular walking terrain also leads to blisters.

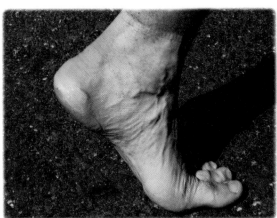

Everyone's question is to pop or not to pop the blister. Do not pop your blister! An open wound invites unwanted organisms. Depending on the size and location of a blister, usually a sterile covering protects it and prevents more friction. Soaking your foot in a salt solution may pull water out of the blister through osmosis.

If the blister is open, an antiseptic such as iodine or alcohol prevents infection. For recurring blisters, consider the source, which may involve a change in the way the foot contacts the ground in the shoe. Often, a change of shoe insoles makes a difference in the amount of friction the foot experiences.

Nail Problems

With constant pressure from improperly fitting shoes, blood vessels may break under the nail, causing blood to collect underneath. Leading to a condition called **black toenail**, this usually does not cause pain, but may lead to the loss of your toenail. If pain exists, soaking the foot in warm water may release the blood underneath the nail and alleviate the pain.

Thickening of the toenails is sometimes related to constant pressure, but occurs without the change in color. Fungus can enter into these nails, making them difficult to cut, and contributing to their loss and pain. Height as well as width of a shoe's toebox usually causes these ailments. The shape of the toes or contracture of the joints also plays a significant role.

On the Road Again

When starting back on your training regimen, do not repeat the mistakes that caused the injury. First and foremost, start back slowly. Don't give into the temptation to try to make up the time you lost by training more. You will just reinjure yourself. A good rule of thumb is to give your body a few extra days from the time you feel healed before you start back on a training program. Being pain free merely indicates that the injury is below the pain threshold; it doesn't guarantee that it is fully healed. Taking the extra time allows your body to completely recuperate. If you lose more than a few days from your training program, you may need to start your mini-cycle over or even revert to the mini-cycle before the one that caused the injury.

Dynamic Self Massage for Fit and Fast Walking is one of those products you do not even know you need, even thou you need it. It is so unique, that I have decided to spotlight it in the text.

While most of have slight aches and pains associated with training hard or non-race walking stresses, few of us can afford to go to a massage therapist on a regular basis. No worries. This guide and video come to the rescue.

Dynamic Self Massage for Fit and Fast Walking explains the primary muscles used in walking. It explains - with pictures - how and why faulty muscle use promotes disabilities and interferes with maximum performance. It also gives you a way of maintaining and, if necessary, regaining normal muscle function.

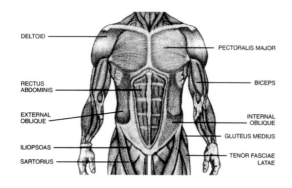 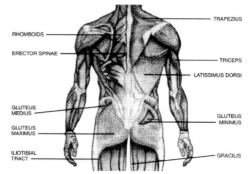

By following the instructions in the Massage Guide, you and your body can work in harmony. You won't find yourself struggling with tight, sore muscles after a walk. Within weeks, your aerobic conditioning improves, your speed improves; and your sense of vigorous well-being improves. All for less than the cost of one visit to a massage therapist!

There is more. You can see basic massage techniques in action with the guide's accompanying video. The demonstrators show you how you can easily bring regular muscle care into your daily planning. Prove it to yourself. Order the guide and video today. You can't find a better resource for preventing and healing muscle stress, fatigue and pain.

Whether you use Dynamic Self-Massage after exercise for injury prevention or use it to heal existing aches and pains, your muscles will be grateful for the care you give them. The guide and video offer you an effective, ageless way of nurturing your body so you can a walk just as fit and fast as you want.

The guide and video together, $28. The guide alone $10.00. The video alone $18.00 Shipping $4.00. Californians add 8.25% tax.

You can order them at

North American Race Walk Foundation
1203 South Orange Grove Blvd.
Pasadena, CA 91105
(626) 441-5459
narwf@sbcglobal.net

Chapter 11 - History

Once upon a time there was a magical land where the top athletes were not baseball or basketball players, but pedestrians. Pedestrians did battle using super human strength and endurance, walking in multi-day contests to determine the fittest and fastest in the land. To the victor went the cheers of tens of thousands, as well as a king's fortune. Sound too good to be true? Actually, it already happened.

The Earliest Years

Competitive race walking's roots trace back as far as 2500 B.C., when Egyptian hieroglyphics recorded the first written account of a walking competition. Similar evidence indicates that walking competitions existed in early Greek civilizations. These early contests were loosely defined. Many were simply go-as-you-please, long-distance events, with competitors alternating at will between running and walking. Clearly, the sport has evolved through several incarnations since these times.

The Gambling Invasion

One of these evolutions involved waging large sums of money on walking contests. One famous example occurred in England, 1589. An English nobleman, Sir Robert Carey, wagered he could walk non-stop for 300 miles. Winning the wager, he set the stage for even greater walking feats. In 1608 he journeyed an amazing 2000 miles across Europe in 41 days.

The 18th Century

While long-distance feats by individual walkers certainly captured the public's eye, it wasn't long before head-to-head races were scheduled. However, there was a change in players. No longer were noblemen battling it out for glory; far easier for the noblemen to enlist *gladiators* to do their bidding. The early walkers of the 17th and 18th century were often a nobleman's footmen. Footmen had a lot of occupational training; they walked alongside a nobleman's carriage and often walked ahead to ready affairs in the town before the nobleman got there. Though a far cry from the 5K weekend shuffles we are accustomed to, these early events mark the beginning of regularly held walking competitions.

The sport of pedestrianism came full circle by the mid 18th century. The second half of the 18th century saw individual walkers battling the clock in the quest for glory and riches. By 1762, the *100 miles-in-a-day* barrier was broken by Mr. John Hogue.

While single-day and speed events caught the public's fancy, it was the multi-day event that catapulted pedestrianism into its *Golden age*. As the decades passed, more and more creative walking challenges were attempted and accomplished. One quite impressive event had Robert Barclay walking one mile an hour for each of 1,000 hours. He walked a half mile out and a half mile back, cheered on by a crowd that overwhelmed nearby towns and villages for miles around the race.

The 19th Century

In the mid 1800s the sport reverted again to man-against-man competitions. With purses multiple times the size of a factory worker's yearly salary, walking attracted athletes looking for a path out of poverty. Walking continued to gain in popularity despite a brief interruption by the Civil War.

Two walking greats emerged in the mid-to-late 19th century. Edward Payton Weston and Daniel O'Leary combined to walk many feats against the clock. Amongst their other accomplishments, Payton walked 117 miles in 24 hours, while O'Leary completed 500 miles in six days. However, the public cried for a head-to-head battle. Battle they did, for six days and over 500 miles, with O'Leary finishing on top.

Today those of us fortunate enough to race indoors in front of 20,000 fans grumble at racing a mile on an 11-lap-per-mile track. These early pedestrians would mock our complaints. They often competed in multi-day events on similar tracks. While I can not conceive of circling around like a hamster on a wheel, neither can I conceive of winning the sums of money that were awarded for these competitions. At walking's peak, competitors won prizes that equaled the amount an average worker made in a lifetime.

By the late 19th century, the Golden age of walking had begun its decline. Events no longer distinguished walking from other forms of progression. While we may debate the exact reasons, the fact remains that walking never again achieved such notoriety or financial reward.

Added to the Olympic Games

Although on the decline, walking's popularity gained a little boost when it was added to the Olympic Games. Many people believe walking's induction to the Olympics occurred at the 1908 games; however, it actually occurred somewhat before that. In 1904, the race walk made its first appearance in the Olympics as an 880-yard racing event within the decathlon. It was also included in the 1906 Interim Olympic Games in Athens, but these games were never recognized as official.

Early Race Walking Rules
The rules governing race walking in the early years, while worded differently, are surprisingly similar in intent to the rules of today. While I will not list all of them here, I do list the most relevant rule pertaining to the action of the legs:

> "As the foremost foot in taking a step touches the ground, the knee must not be bent. The heel must touch the ground first and the toe be the last portion of the foot to leave it. It is imperative that the heel of the foremost foot must touch the ground before the toe of the other foot ceases to have contact with it."

Although the rule adds further restrictions to race walking, focusing on the part of the foot that makes contact during the double support phase, the rule is essentially a combination of the rules we used first in the 1970s and the latest definition of race walking instituted in 1996. This rule is in essence where the nickname *heel toe walking* derived.

While they obviously make no mention of "to the human eye," they do mention the knee straight on contact. However, they do not mention that the knee must remain straightened until past vertical. These differences are just some of the variations in race walking rules through the decades.

Another interesting point in the rules involves the carriage of the body during walking:

> "The body must be kept strictly upright. Note - Discretionary power is given to the judge or judges of walking to decide whether, in the event of the body being inclined forward, such attitude is the result of fatigue or arises from some cause beyond the control of the competitor; and if it be, and he or they are convinced that the rule has been broken for such reason only, and that the competitor is still walking fairly otherwise, disqualification need not necessarily follow from this cause alone."

While a bit subjective, this rule follows the pattern of other late 19th century and early 20th century rules for our sport: rules concerned with posture, appearances, and status, in an apparent attempt to differentiate walking from the savage sport of running. For example, *The Walking Cure*, a 1924 book on walking, dedicated an exorbitant amount of space to describing the proper attire for walking. This attire had little to do with performance; instead it concerned itself with appearances. Likewise, walkers were required to walk with dignified form. It seems the early days of our sport had noble aspirations indeed.

While these rules intended to aggrandize race walking, controversies still arose. At the peak of our sport's popularity in the 1920s and 1930s, seven hundred to eight hundred walkers typically battled it out on the streets of New York City. According to three-time Olympian Bruce MacDonald, fewer cars filled the roads, so walkers competed right down the middle of the street. However, the vast number of athletes actually led to our sport's retreat from popularity. With competitive events nearly impossible to judge, complaints of alleged cheating proliferated. When a few walkers bunch together today, distinguishing one set of legs from another becomes nearly impossible; imagine hundreds of legs racing down a crowded street.

Unfortunately, without the infrastructure to support competitive race walking, people grew discouraged and quit the sport.

RACE WALKING IN THE EARLY YEARS

From those early pedestrian days to today, the sport evolved in many ways. Its history contains a great many colorful characters whose dedication, determination, and ferocity in competition provide lessons for us all. Obviously, their knowledge of exercise physiology and technique is not on par with the accumulated research and information available to today's walkers. However, their wisdom and spirit, exhibited through many years of competition, must be made know to subsequent generations.

Our account of modern American race walking history picks up where the great Henry Laskau walked our sport out of its early twentieth-century doldrums. With no disrespect to the athletes or performances of this era, I lump the period from the late 1940s to the late 1970s together, dubbing it the Early Years of American Race Walking.

Is a Rose a Rose?

The sport characterizing this early era appeared quite dissimilar from race walking as we see it today. Thus, when evaluating early race walkers and their accomplishments, we must keep their historical context in mind. First and foremost, those associated with race walking defined the sport differently than we do today. Their definition included no reference to keeping the leg straightened after contact; nor did it permit any loss of contact (to the human eye or otherwise). Furthermore, in addition to using a distinct technique, early race walkers embraced an attitude quite unlike that of today's athletes. In our day, serious race walk competitors target a single race or two, avoiding lesser competitions, in the hopes of peaking their training to achieve a world-class performance. In the early days, as Dave Romansky says, "It was all-out war: every race, all the time."

Battle On

For example, in 1971 Romansky beat archrival Ron Laird at the 2-mile Indoor National Championships, an evening race. The next day, he walked a 40-mile workout, even though he planned to compete in a local 10 miler the following day. Competitively minded Ron Laird did not share Romansky's training plans. Instead, Laird intended to beat Romansky in the 10 miler. Romansky could have—probably should have—taken it easy in the 10-mile race. Instead, after cursing Laird out for showing up, he joined him in battle without regard for the abuse he had recently loaded on his body. The lead switched back and forth, with Romansky thinking at one point he had his opponent beat. But that day Laird got his revenge, thwarting Romansky's final efforts to hold on to the victory. Both athletes finished under 1:10: simply amazing!

While battles raged on the East Coast, West Coast walkers of this period were more laid back and less competitively active at the minor national championships. Whether from financial constraints or sport logistics, we do not know. Two-time Olympian Tom Dooley remembers the 20K and 50K Championships as rare racing opportunities to compete with the best. Until the 1970s, almost all national championship races took place back East. Without sponsors or significant club support, the West Coast walkers lacked the means to attend most national-level contests.

Working for a Living

Most American race walkers of the early years worked full-time, using their wages to fund their travels. This lifestyle contrasts sharply with that of the competition, as many German, Mexican, Russian, and Italian walkers enjoyed the advantages of government-sponsored training. Much like today's U.S. Army WCAP (World Class Athlete Program) participants, athletes from abroad earned wages solely for training and racing. Additionally, some foreign nations provided their Olympians with full-time jobs when their athletic careers ended, thus enabling their walkers to focus on their training and participate in the sport longer.

In sharp contrast, American walkers drove to races and slept six or seven to a hotel room. This sort of camaraderie created a family-like atmosphere within the clubs—of course, with all the dysfunction of biological families. However, without financial support, early organized walking followed the same pattern we see today: a small group of elite race walkers dedicating a short period of their lives to a venerated sport. Today as then, when the majority of the group moves on, the remaining community members scurry around, trying to find new athletes to allow the sport to subsist and thrive.

In countries like Mexico, the tale unfolds differently. Tom Dooley remembers Mexican Walk Week boasting 50 or so good-caliber walkers. But back in the U.S., economic viability and athletic opportunity limited the depth of the field. And while national support for competitive race walking isn't solely a numbers game, economic conditions play a part in obvious and subtle ways. Throughout the early years, countries including East

Germany, Russia, and Mexico scientifically monitored their athletes with blood and VO₂ tests. In America, no such testing took place until the late 1970s, when Martin Rudow led a U.S. attempt to modernize race walking with scientific means.

A Growing Sport?

I constantly hear people say our sport is growing. I disagree. In the early years, race walking enjoyed a far more prominent status. For example, the Millrose Games showcased the 1-Mile Race Walk during prime time, directly before the prestigious 1-Mile Run. Dave Romansky remembers fondly the attention given to race walkers because of this spotlight. Sometime during the seventies, in an elevator at Madison Square Garden, a group of fans recognized him and asked for his autograph. Another amazing story from Romansky's past: out for a pre-Olympic training walk in his hometown one morning, he covered six miles on a local highway. He received friendly beeps and hellos from 106 drivers passing by, all of whom knew who he was and why he was training. Sadly, neither incident would likely occur today.

A Note On the Selection Process

In our conceivably steroid-laced baseball league today, many fans are impressed with the per-season home run race. Far more impressive were the days of Babe Ruth, when in a single season, Ruth hit more home runs than entire teams. Mark McGwire had a peer, Babe Ruth did not. Similarly, the early performances of Henry Laskau, Ron Laird, and Larry Young must be evaluated using their contemporaries for context.

As we debate the all-time best within any sport, controversies about the selection process unavoidably occur. Some fans have short memories when it comes to the origins of the Golden age. Others remember racers with performance times less impressive than today's, but still far ahead of their peers. Fortunately, many fans of our sport have good memories, with the likes of Jack Mortland and Elliot Denman refusing to allow those who came before us to fade into obscurity.

Recently I posted a question to a few walking news groups: "Who was the best race walker ever?" Results varied, but factors respondents used to make selections included fastest times, international performance—as opposed to just participating in overseas events—and dominance within the sport over an extended period, at least in the U.S.

While I editorialize elsewhere in this book, I attempt to remain relatively objective in my selection of race walkers for this list. I avoid sorting race walkers by an overall ranking system. Instead, I present The Greats according to the first decade in which they demonstrate their prominence. When reviewing these biographies, we must keep in mind: It's all about the context.

Murray Rosenstein winning the 26ᵗʰ annual Coney Island Race Walk in 1936

HENRY LASKAU

Birthday: October 12th 1916
Hometown: Berlin, Germany

Personal Bests
10K: 47:25
20K: 1:37:04

Career Highlights
43 Senior National Titles
3-Time Olympian
Held every American record from 1 mile to 20K

No historical account of race walking in the U.S. would be complete without tribute to the *Dean* of American race walkers, Henry Laskau.

After initial success in the early Olympic Games, American race walking fell upon Dark Ages. Instead of cheers, race walkers in the 1940s and 1950s were, in Laskau's words, met with catcalls. It would take athletes like Laskau to change that.

Born October 12, 1916, in Berlin, Germany, Laskau became his country's top middle distance runner in the 1930s. Unfortunately, however, his status did not protect him from the atrocities of the Nazi Era. In 1939, he and his family were arrested and sent to a forced labor camp. There, Laskau was able to earn the sympathy of a guard who allowed him to escape. Sadly, he was forced to leave his family behind, and they later perished in concentration camps.

Laskau fled Germany, traveling to France and then Cuba before settling in the United States. In the early forties, he served in the U.S. Army, providing counter intelligence during World War II. With the war concluded, Laskau's thoughts returned again to track and field. Following the suggestion of a track coach at New York University, he decided to give race walking a try.

Laskau was a complete natural and quickly rose to dominate the sport nationally. From 1947 to 1956, he amassed 43 national championships, earning positions on the U.S. Olympic teams in 1948, 1952, and 1956. At one time or another, he held each and every American record, from 1 mile to 20 kilometers. Laskau electrified the crowds at Madison Square Garden in 1951 when he lapped walker after walker on his way to a world record for the 1 mile: 6:19.2, which stood for 12 years. His legend at Millrose lived long past his record. Even today when warming up in the bowels of Madison Square Garden, Laskau's accomplishments still loom large. Amazingly, Laskau did all this while reportedly training only three days a week!

His dominance in American race walking did not go unnoticed. In 1997, Laskau was the second race walker inducted into the U.S. Track and Field Hall of Fame.

As amazing as his performances were, Laskau's dedication to the sport during his post-competition career remains equally memorable. He continued to give back to race walking in every way imaginable. He has been responsible for converting countless runners to race walking

113

and inspiring race walkers all over the U.S. He organized and judged race walks locally and internationally and served as judge for both race walks in the 1984 Olympic Games. He was president of the Walkers Club of America, the expressed purpose of which is to encourage race walking for competition as well as fitness.

On a personal note, I consider myself very lucky to have met Laskau. In the Eighties a race was named in his honor. In 1986, one cold and miserable Sunday morning, I was fortunate enough to win the Henry Laskau 10K. I still have a piece of the race T-shirt sewn into a blanket. Years later I enjoyed the privilege of Laskau's company when he traveled with me to the Macabbiah Games, which he won all four times he competed. Laskau will forever remain within my fondest race walking memories.

Later in life Laskau suffered from Alzheimer's disease. He passed away May 7, 2000. Today, we must savor the inspirations and memories he left us.

MAJOR INTERNATIONAL EXPERIENCE

10K Olympic Games
> 1956 – 12th - 1:38:46.8 - Melbourne, Australia
> 1952 - DQ - Helsinki, Finland
> 1948 - 7th – *unknown time* - London, England

10K Pan Am Games
> 1951 – 1st - 50:26.8 - Buenos Aires, Argentina

Maccabiah Games
> 1965 - 1st - Maccabiah Games, Israel
> 1957 - 1st - Maccabiah Games, Israel
> 1953 - 1st - Maccabiah Games, Israel
> 1950 - 1st - Maccabiah Games, Israel

U.S. SENIOR NATIONAL CHAMPIONSHIPS

2 mile - Won 4 times	10K - Won 10 times	20K - Won 5 times	Indoor 1 mile – Won 10 times
3K - Won 6 times	15K - Won 5 times	25K - Won 1 time	

Laskau Winning the Longest Continuously Held Race Walk in the United States

Laskau at the 1952 Olympics

Birthday: May 31st, 1938
Hometown: Louisville, KY
Current Residence: Ashtabula, OH

Personal Bests
10K: 43:07
20K: 1:28:18

Career Highlights
64 Senior National Titles
4-Time Olympian

Perseverance is Ron Laird's middle name. Unable to qualify for his high school baseball team, he joined track and ran the half mile and mile, but his running wasn't much better than his baseball. Fortunately, Laird had other talents. While attending Parsons School of Design on a six-week art scholarship during the summer of 1955, Laird competed at AAU track meets just outside Yankee Stadium. At only 50 cents to join the AAU and 25 cents an event, he competed in all the events he could handle.

Running a few events and then throwing the discus and javelin, Laird noticed people warming up for the race walk. After mimicking their technique, he decided to give it a try. This race was handicapped, so slower walkers were granted a head start. As Laird had never race walked before, he began with a 600-yard lead. Still, Laird finished dead last. Only 17 years old at the time, he wanted to quit race walking, but two of his competitors (Elliot Denman and Bruce McDonald) talked the young athlete into pursuing the sport.

Embarrassed by the gait of race walking, Laird made progress by training at night. After a few more handicapped races, he felt ready for his first non-handicapped race, a 5K against the legendary Henry Laskau. Laskau's friendliness and accessibility impressed him. However, when race time came, Laskau was ruthless, lapping Laird three times. Still, the experience and encouragement Laird gained convinced him that he should try a 10-mile handicapped race in Philadelphia. With two weeks of training, Laird entered the race and won. He was elated, having never earned a trophy or prize before.

Returning to school his senior year, Laird decided not to compete in high school activities. Instead, he joined the New York Pioneers and trained for the race walk. A series of indoor races at the Armory and Madison Square Garden kept him busy. His biggest race of the season was the 1-mile Nationals, where he finished 5th with a time of 7:14.

Having great speed but little endurance, Laird headed to the Olympic Trials in 1956. Racing both the 20K and 50K, he struggled to finish the second race and needed to sit down several times. Determined, he marched towards his goal: a finisher's trophy. (Laird did like his trophies.) Back then, aid stations at races were nonexistent. Laird, ever resourceful, convinced a bunch of kids who were harassing him to help. They rode their bicycles to a gas station and filled empty coke bottles with water.

Laird continued to improve after the trials. He raced often and trained hard. Dropping out of college, he ended up in the Army as a draftsman.

By 1958, Laird had placed first in the 20K Nationals with a time of 1:40:09. This achievement qualified him for his first international competition, a dual meet with the USSR. Qualifying for the team meant he earned a USA team uniform, expense-paid travel, and a two-dollar-a-day stipend. He began with the team training for a week at West Point. However, flying to Moscow and then racing against the 1956 Olympic champion Leonid Spirin must have been intimidating. Laird didn't race up to his potential, walking a 1:49.

Next Laird was scheduled to race a 20K in Warsaw. However, then as now, the race walk received little respect. When officials wanted to watch other events instead of working the 20K race, they cancelled the competition. To make amends, George Hausleber invited the walkers to the national sports center, where they enjoyed themselves tremendously.

Laird soon finished his Army obligation and temporarily settled in Norristown, Pennsylvania. Unable to find steady employment, he worked where he could. He trained on the roads of the local mental institute and, sponsorless, hitchhiked to races.

Laird continued to grow stronger and by the 1960 Olympic Trials was well prepared to qualify for the Olympic team. He won the 50K, the first of the two trials, without trouble. At the 20K trial, he found himself in third place late in the race. Knowing a third-place trials finish would require him to compete in both Olympic races, he stopped to wait for the next competitor, Bruce McDonald. McDonald, who had also qualified in the 50K two weeks earlier, came across Laird lying on the ground. Concerned there was a problem, he was relieved to learn Laird's plan and joined Laird in waiting. When Bob Mimm caught them, they let him pass and finish third, relieved they would not be forced to race a double at the Olympics. In the end, Laird finished 19th at the Games with a time of 4:53:21. Today he views the race as his finest Olympic achievement.

By 1962, Laird had obtained the New York Athletic Club (NYAC) as his sponsor and moved to Chicago to once again prepare for the Olympics. NYAC provided him funds to travel to many national meets. Instead of using the payments to cover his fares, however, Laird chose to return to hitching and pocket the cash.

Laird used many unconventional methods to improve performance. A favorite was the tire pull, an exercise he employed to strengthen his hamstrings. It required race walking with a rope and tire tied to his waist. Lacking any knowledge of exercise physiology, Laird pursued all training at a brutal, full-effort pace. He knew nothing of periodization and varied workouts. And while some of the techniques Laird used to gain speed differ sharply from those we use today, others are quite the same. One technique that has gone by the wayside is how Laird pulled his heel back, even before it hit the ground, and then dug it in. This allowed him to maximize his pulling power. However, just as we do today, he did turn his hips to extend stride.

In late 1963 Laird moved to California and decided to race at the 20K distance. After all, most 20K races required travel. He won the 1964 Olympic Trials and things looked on track for his second Olympic appearance. Unfortunately, his debut at Tokyo soon became the worst day of his racing career. Up until then, he had been disqualified only once before—quite an accomplishment, considering it took only one judge's opinion to get pulled from a race. While he began the Tokyo race strong, something about his technique caught an official's eye and cost him his second lifetime DQ. Meanwhile, Ron Zinn, his fiercest competitor from 1960 to 1965, finished sixth with a great personal record of 1:32.

Laird achieved perhaps his best international performances in 1967. The first race was at Lugano, in East Germany, a meet later renamed The World Cup. Midway through the 20K he led the pack with two Russians in tow. But a white flag and the still-fresh memory of his Olympic disqualification caused him to back off. He finished third with a time of 1:29:12, setting the first sub-1:30 American record in the process. Later that year, just before Mexican race walkers became dominant, Laird earned one of a duo of gold medals at the Pan American Games, with teammate Larry Young winning the 50K.

At the 1968 Olympic Trials, Laird had the pleasure of winning the 20K twice. (That's right, twice.) The first trials were at sea level, and a spot on the Olympic Team was originally guaranteed to the winner of that race. Late in the race, Laird caught Larry Young *hurling* and nailed him, winning by five yards. Next, the top *sea-level finishers* were

NYAC Team – 1967
Laird with Bruce MacDonald & Ron Daniel

invited to a training camp and second trial race at altitude. There the athletes voted not to count the results of the sea-level race. Laird needed to race again. Justly, he won a second time.

The trip to Mexico City for the Olympic Games did not go as well, with Laird contracting strep throat early in the trip. Ironically, on race day he led the pack the first 2000 meters before breaking away and making a wrong turn. He walked a long 50 yards off course before doubling back and rejoining the race. He then faded badly, finishing near last.

Hoping to make up for his poor Olympic performance, Laird strove to make the team again in 1972. However, a hamstring injury obtained at an insignificant race put an end to his dreams. (A sad lesson to us all). He was forced to drop out of both Olympic Trial races and attend the Munich Games as a spectator. But the crafty Laird's Olympic story does not end there. His twin brother was able to acquire a press pass for the games at a cost of one bottle of whiskey. The pass and Laird's USA uniform gave him near-complete access to the entire Olympic compound, and he put it to good use.

After a year of nursing his hamstring back to health, Laird, 38, needed a new plan to combat his young and ever-improving peers. In fall 1975, he drove to Mexico City to join a small group of elite race walkers training for international competition. The group included the likes of Raul Gonzales and Daniel Bautista. Laird's training strategy worked and he finished the 1976 Trials second only to Todd Scully. For a change, Laird's performance peaked at the best time. He was the first American 20K finisher at the Games.

Laird's competitive career was all but over by the 1980 Olympic Trials. He finished second to last but was disqualified after the finish. With racing behind him, he enjoyed the honor of leading a race-walking colony of 14 walkers at the Colorado Springs Olympic Training Center from 1981 to 1984. More a manager than coach, Laird provided technical advice and helped obtain sponsorships for the walkers, who essentially trained themselves. Laird recalls that group members were not always happy. Some walkers were incompatible and refused to work together.

When all was said and done, Laird set or reset 81 U.S. records, from the 1 mile to the 25 mile. In 1986 he became the first race walker inducted to the U.S. Track and Field Hall of Fame. He currently lives in northeast Ohio and walks an hour or two per day for fitness. (Race walkers beware: Laird is considering a Master's comeback.)

MAJOR INTERNATIONAL EXPERIENCE

20K Olympic Games
1976 – 20th - 1:33:27.6 - Montreal, Canada
1968 – 25th - 1:44:38.0 - Mexico City, Mexico
1964 - DQ - Tokyo, Japan

50K Olympic Games
1960 – 19th - 4:53:21.6 - Rome, Italy

20K World Cup
1973 – 3rd - 1:30:45.0 - Lugano, Switzerland
1967 – 3rd - 1:29:12.6 - Bad Saarow, East Germany

20K Pan Am Games
1967 – 1st - 1:33:05.2 - Winnipeg, Canada
1963 – 4th - 1:52:09.3 - Sao Paulo, Brazil

U.S. SENIOR NATIONAL CHAMPIONSHIPS

2 mile - Won 4 times	15K - Won 6 times	30K - Won 6 times	50K - Won 2 times
5K - Won 2 times	20K - Won 8 times	35K - Won 6 times	Indoor 1 mile – Won 3 times
10K - Won 4 times	25K - Won 10 times	40K - Won 5 times	Indoor 2 mile – Won 1 time
			1 Hour – Won 7 times

Birthday: February 10th, 1943
Hometown: Independence, MO
Current Residence: Columbia, MO

Personal Bests
20K: 1:30:10
50K: 4:00:46

Career Highlights
3rd Place 50K - 1968 Olympic Games
3rd Place 50K - 1972 Olympic Games

Larry Young began race walking after leaving the U.S. Navy in April 1965. It is a testament to Young's achievement that, 39 years later, he remains prominent on the U.S. All Time Performers List: 10th best for the 50K.

Young learned to race walk at a summer series of open meets at local high schools in New York. Having raced the half mile and mile in high school, he remained fascinated by the race walk. Once he tried it, he became instantly hooked. Competing at local races, he quickly improved his one-mile time to just under eight minutes. At one race he met walking greats Ron Laird and Don Denoon.

Young got invited to race at the Times and L.A. Invitationals—both very prestigious indoor meets at the time—and preceded to finish dead last at each. After the race, Laird and Denoon convinced Young to walk a 10-mile handicapped race at Rose Bowl Park. (Laird must have been passing on a tradition that Bruce MacDonald had passed on to him.) Having never raced more than a few miles, Young was apprehensive. He knew nothing about training for race walking and was pleasantly surprised to finish fourth. Although he felt sore for a few weeks, he began to wonder if his talent might rest with longer distances. He proved himself very clairvoyant.

Back in the Sixties, any athlete who had not won a Senior championship could compete at the Junior level. In 1966, Young won his first championship, the Junior 30K in Pamona, CA. Later that same year in Chicago, he won his first Senior national title: the 50K championship in 4:38.24. He followed this performance with another solid 50K at the 1967 Pan Am Games: 4:26:20.8, a U.S. record at the time. The performances gave Young the confidence he needed to qualify for the Olympic team. As he put it, "Why not get a medal?"

Young considers himself fortunate that the 1968 Olympics took place at altitude in very grueling conditions. The night before the race, Young (who was not favored to finish in the top 10) ran customary pre-race drills through his mind. Meanwhile, most other athletes failed to take environmental conditions into their race strategies. On race day, when event favorite Christopher Hohne took the pack out hard, Young knew his game plan would work. Walking slowly and steadily, he let the pack go ahead, and by 35K had begun to catch them one by one. As Young passed his competitors, he noted their fatigue and lack of focus. He earned a bronze medal, finishing at 4:31:55.

Young decided to take the next year off from training and improve his financial situation. He moved back to Missouri to live with his folks. At age 26 he earned a full race walking scholarship at Columbia College, where he studied art and specialized in sculpture.

Young not only repeated his bronze medal performance at the 1972 Olympic Games in Munich, but raced in the 20K as well. He jokes that he took part in two of the most controversial Olympics. But for once, race walking did not cause either crisis. Controversy continued to follow Young, eventually causing him to retire from competition. In 1980, he decided to hang up his

Larry Young
Sculpture

http://www.youngsculpture.com/

sneakers when he learned the U.S. was going to boycott the 1980 Moscow Olympic Games due to the Soviet Union's invasion of Afghanistan.

No longer very active in the race walking world, Young today focuses his energies on sculpture. Amazingly, he holds great talents in two completely disparate fields.

MAJOR INTERNATIONAL EXPERIENCE

20K Olympic Games
1972 – 10th - 1:32:53.4 - Munich, Germany

50K Olympic Games
1972 – 3rd - 4:00:46.0 - Munich, Germany
1968 – 3rd - 4:31:55.4 - Mexico City, Mexico

50K World Cup
1977 – 13th - 4:19:56 - Milton Keynes, Great Britain
1967 – 22nd - 5:06:08.0 - Bad Saarow, East Germany

50K World Championships
1976 – 21st - 4:16:47 - Malmo, Sweeden

20K Pan Am Games
1975 – 3rd - 1:37:54.0 - Mexico City, Mexico

50K Pan Am Games
1971 – 1st - 4:38:31 - Cali, Columbia
1967 – 1st - 4:26:20.8 - Winnipeg, Canada

U.S. SENIOR NATIONAL CHAMPIONSHIPS

2 mile - Won 1 time	15K - Won 1 time	30K - Won 6 times	50K - Won 7 times
5K - Won 1 time	20K - Won 1 time	35K - Won 3 times	20K Olympic Trials – Won 1 time
10K - Won 1 time	25K - Won 1 time	40K - Won 2 times	50K Olympic Trials– Won 2 times

Young at the 1968 Olympic Trials

Young on his way to winning the 1972 50K Olympic Trials

S
U
E

B
R
O
D
O
C
K

Birthday: April 4th, 1956
Hometown: Rome, NY
Current Residence: Rialto, CA

Personal Bests
10K: 49:41.3

Career Highlights
1st Place Women's World Meeting; later became the
Women's World Cup.

Sue Brodock began her competitive career in junior high school, running track for the Fontana Cinderbells in California. Having trouble with allergies, Brodock occasionally struggled through her races, so coach Bob Bollinger suggested she try race walking. In the Sixties and Seventies, women had few opportunities to race walk. However, the AAU had an active program, and their meets were to become Brodock's main stage. In her very first year, she competed at the Nationals. And though she downplays her early success, Brodock must have been a natural.

With no grade-school or high-school walking programs, Brodock competed solely for club teams. In the early seventies, Coach Bollinger retired and she switched teams to the Realto Roadrunners, coached by David Japps. Japps' strategy was to have Brodock run two thirds of her training and walk the remaining third. He would get her in great shape first, then work on technique.

While her sisters walked well, they didn't have Sue's determination and talent. To this day, Japps claims that Brodock was the hardest-working athlete he ever coached.

Still in high school, Brodock by 1973 had moved up to the Senior level, where she found few competitions for women and instead challenged the male-chauvinist walking world of the times by racing men. Japps remembers traveling to a men's race in Arizona. Brodock walked well but was eliminated, allegedly because she was a woman. Apparently, when the judge disqualified her, he actually justified his call by claiming that no woman should be able to walk as fast as the men.

When I first heard this story, I thought maybe Coach Japps was coloring history. Sad to say, I was wrong. Gary Westerfield, coach of Brodock-rival Susan Liers, confirms that many judges in those days held a similarly disparaging view of women.

Fortunately, not everyone shared that view. Brodock was invited to the men's LA Times Invitational, a massive indoor track meet in the 70s. Racing competitively, she held her own against an all-male field. And although she did not win the race, she did earn the title, "Best Athlete of the Meet." Actually, she won this title for two consecutive years. The first year, she received a motorcycle that she sold to raise traveling funds. The following year she won a special coin that she kept.

Brodock achieved one of her greatest accomplishments early in her career. In 1974 she won what would later become the Women's World Cup. Back then, it was a 5K race named the Women's World Meeting. At first, Brodock was unsure how she would attend her first international competition, as she had no sponsors and would need to raise her own funds to cover all expenses. Typically, athletes of the time solicited support through a mail campaign, but Brodock proved much more creative. She and her coach walked door-to-door seeking to repaint addresses on residents' curbs. At just three dollars an address, that was a lot of houses to paint.

A perfectionist in her walking, Brodock's long-standing goal was to break 7:00 for the mile. After many attempts, she walked a 6:58.4 at the 1979 Los Angles Times Indoor Games, breaking the world record in the process.

Brodock gave up walking soon after becoming a born-again Christian and making her relationship with God her highest priority. She retired after the 1983 Indoor Nationals and today owns the Pretty Pet Parlor, a grooming shop in Fontana, CA. She is no longer involved in race walking, but race walking has not forgotten her. For her electrifying indoor performances she was inducted into the Indoor National Track and Field Hall of Fame. She retains the honor of holding more Senior National titles then any woman in U.S. history, although Michelle Rohl is quickly closing in on her.

MAJOR INTERNATIONAL EXPERIENCE

5K World Cup
        1974 – 1st – 24:16.2 – Stockholm, Sweden
        1979 – 22nd – 25:00 – Eschborn, West Germany

U.S. SENIOR NATIONAL CHAMPIONSHIPS

1500 M - Won 1 time	10K - Won 5 times	20K - Won 2 times
5K - Won 6 times	15K - Won 1 time	Indoor 1 mile - Won 8 times

121

Birthday: November 11th, 1958   Personal Bests
Hometown: Stony Brook, NY   5K: 23:32
Current Residence: Stony Brook, NY   10K: 48:32
College: SUNY Stony Brook

Career Highlights
17 National Titles
10 Consecutive Gold Medals, Empire State Games

Susan Liers (Reina) claims to have started race walking without knowing a thing about the sport. She began in high school, walking as fast as possible through the halls in an attempt to elude the hall monitors. However, her official race walking debut was sparked by a joke. Observing Smithtown West's High School Coach Gary Westerfield race walking during winter track practice, she mimicked him mockingly. A week later, Liers was competing at an indoor meet at the Nassau Coliseum. She finished in just over 9:23 for the mile. Amazingly, in her next race a few months later, she broke the eight-minute barrier.

In 1976, the summer after her senior year, Liers earned an opportunity to compete in the Women's World Meeting, the equivalent of the Women's World Cup. She had to fund her own travel to this European meet, but finishing fourth in the 5K, she found it well worth the expense.

The first American woman to break the 50-minute barrier for the 10K, Liers walked 49:54.2 at the 1981 National 10K championship in Maine.

Her success continued with an amazing streak of 10 consecutive gold medals at the Empire State Games for the 5K and 10K. As the race walk was the first event of the games, Liers launched herself and the sport into a bright public spotlight. In honor of her achievements, she was picked to represent New York State when Air Force One flew to Greece to obtain the Olympic Torch for the 1980 Winter Olympics at Lake Placid. The finale of the trip was participating in the torch relay and lighting the main torch with then Governor Hugh Carey.

Years later, she again was honored as she walked (race walked, of course) the torch to its ceremonial position at the 2002 opening of the 25th Empire State Games.

Liers' achievements might be overshadowed by the current lack of elite competition at Empire State race walks; however, back in the early eighties, the Empire State Games permitted guests. One year the games drew three sub-50 performances as Liers successfully battled Teresa Vaill and Sue Braddock on her home turf.

Liers was a woman ahead of her time. While the 10K stood as the competitive international distance of the day, longer races proved better for Liers. She won the women's walking division of the NYC marathon multiple times, and in 1977 defeated the entire field—all men—at the Junior National Championship 20K in Long Branch, NJ. Unfortunately, the meet organizers would not turn over the race award to a woman. After all, it was the Men's National Championship.

In the early eighties, Liers branched out into TV with a principle part in a Federal Express commercial. At the time, Federal Express ran an advertising campaign featuring a fast talking theme. So why not a fast walking campaign featuring a group of race walkers? The walkers whizzed back and forth in an office, carrying pots of coffee across the office. To the average viewer, it seemed the tape was sped up, but in reality no camera tricks were used.

When all was said and done, Liers won 17 National titles and competed in numerous international competitions.

Today Liers race walks only to race her son. She works at Computer Associates as an information technology manager. Still living on Long Island, she occasionally can be spotted at local races.

MAJOR INTERNATIONAL EXPERIENCE

10K World Cup
1983 – 41st – 51:54 – Bergen, Norway

5K World Cup
1981 – 9th – 24:15.8 – Valencia, Spain
1979 – 10th - 24:02 - Eschborn, West Germany

U.S. SENIOR NATIONAL CHAMPIONSHIPS

1 mile - Won 1 time	10K - Won 4 times	20K - Won 3 times
5K - Won 4 times	15K - Won 4 times	1 Hour - Won 1 time

DAVE ROMANSKY

Dave Romanksy was a walking machine. Training and racing hard all the time, Romansky peaked in the late 1960s and early 1970s. He competed in the 50K at the 1968 Olympics and in 1970 won seven National championships, setting twelve U.S. records and three world records in the process. His career didn't end there; in fact, it never ended. Romansky toured with the National team until he was over 40. Since then he has taken his enthusiasm and success on the Master's circuit, where he continued to win championships, set records and in 1997 earned the title National Master's Race Walker of the Year.

Romansky has never stopped giving back to the sport. Since early in his competitive days, he has donated his time and energy to promoting race walking, especially if it involved children. Today, Romansky still race walks and coaches local athletes to share the success and glory he enjoyed nearly 30 years ago.

RON ZINN

To some Ron Zinn is just a name on an award—granted, a very prestigious award. Few remember why Zinn was so revered he became the namesake of the prize for Best U.S. Race Walker of the Year for both men and women.

Ron Zinn's elite race walking career lasted a scant five years. Beginning in 1960, Zinn dominated American race walking until 1965. The top American Olympic 20K finisher for both 1960—19th overall at 1:42:47—and 1964—6th overall at 1:32:43—he put it together when it counted. In all, he won 15 National titles.

Regrettably, his career was cut short when he left to serve in the Vietnam War. He was one of the war's many unfortunate casualties.

TOM DOOLEY

Tom Dooley was an average high school and college runner when first introduced to race walking. An instant success, Dooley mastered the heel-toe form immediately and reached international competition within a year. His elite career spanned from 1966 to 1980 and amassed two 20K Olympic Teams, two Pan American Games—including a silver medal—and three World Cup Team berths.

Along the way, Dooley broke 11 National records at distances ranging from 1K to 25K.

Dooley, like many walking greats, continues to give back to the sport. He is the head walking coach for the Leukemia Society's Team in Training program—a program that has coached more people to complete marathons than any other in the world.

RACE WALKING IN THE 80s

Some view the 1980s as the hey day of American race walking. Indeed, this was probably the single wealthiest period of race walking in terms of sponsorship and organizational budgets. However, money alone did not lead to the success of athletes and programs set forth by the governing bodies of our sport. A continual stream of new talent fed the 1980s race walking scene, with more than two thirds of America's elite walkers tracing their roots to the high-school program of New York State. Unfortunately, in 1985, the race walk event was removed from the men's high school outdoor track and field competitions. The flow of athletes and the number of competitions available for youth in New York has sadly dwindled ever since.

Two organized efforts to influence U.S. performances characterize 1980s race walking. The first was highly visible. In the early eighties, America's first legitimate race walking colony was formed at the U.S. Olympic Training Center at Colorado Springs. Until the Summer Olympics of 1984, America's most talented men gravitated to the Center. Training mostly on their own, without the support of coaches, some individuals certainly thrived; however, we can only imagine the more widespread impact of an organized training program. Eventually, with a combination of athletes retiring and some allegedly poor behavior on the part of residents, the program ceased to exist.

The second trend began in 1984, when Sal Corrallo took hold of the reigns as Race Walking Chairman for TAC (The Athletics Congress), the governing body of U.S. race walking. Corrallo held a great vision and was capable of inspiring others. We used to call it "being Sal'd" when Corrallo roped you into a commitment. His vision was for a national team program, not just eight people named to a team, showing up for a meet.

The USOC and Mazola sponsored a budget of more than $70,000, far more funding than we have ever seen before or since. With the help of Gary Westerfield, Martin Rudow, Frank Alongi, and Jake Jacobson, Corrallo put together a coherent national training program. The philosophy was simple: Every athlete needs a coach, other than himself (or herself)! What's the old adage? "Anyone who coaches himself has a fool for a coach."

National coaches Westerfield and Rudow made themselves available to develop and monitor training for any seriously interested athlete. Previously, athletes would qualify for championships, then show up to races unprepared. But with Corrallo monitoring athletes closely and reporting results back to the USOC, the aim of fielding fitter teams seemed much more in reach. Unfortunately, some established walkers were not entirely receptive to the team-program approach. They felt they had earned their achievements on their own and snubbed the help of outsiders. And while no one was penalized for not participating, with funds available for national coaches to travel to international races, the upcoming athletes who embraced the program gained the advantage of familiar guidance at overseas competitions.

The program enjoyed ample funds to provide stipends for at least the top-five men and women in the U.S., as well as national coaches. Supplementing these funds, the athletes of the roaring eighties found significant sponsorship opportunities for the first time. A blessing and a curse, these sponsorships funded athletes' training and living expenses. While the financial rewards of the sponsorships certainly helped the athletes' bottom line, they started a trend that eroded the club system in America. Athletes no longer focused on team championships. They began to see their teams as paychecks rather than families. Athletes still had a family-like relationship with their training partners, but come race day, there was no team championship to bond them together.

Still, the program achieved results. In 1987, a few months after a Mazola-sponsored training camp, the American teams representing the internationally contested distances of 50K and 20K for men and 10K for women finished among the World Cup's top ten. Sadly, this was the last time America achieved such prominence. While the program offered great promise, funding abruptly dried up in 1988. A change in regime also meant a shift in the approach to developing a national team.

Corrallo had aspired to build a lasting structure that would ensure an enduring, successful program. Unfortunately, walkers weren't available to replace athletes ready to retire. Still, Corrallo's ambition and driving force planted the seeds that would come to fruition in later years. His efforts set the stage for future programs in LaGrange, Georgia, and Chula Vista, California.

Birthday: October 15th, 1961   Personal Bests
Hometown: Kenosha, WI   10K: 44:42
Current Residence: Kenosha, WI   20K: 1:33:48
College: Gateway Tech
          University of Wisconsin-Parkside

Career Highlights
3 Time Olympian

Debbi Lawrence's race walking career has spanned over 20 years. Like many others, she started as a runner and got injured. Having trouble staying injury free, her running coach Mike Dewitt and then-boyfriend Don Lawrence showed her the basics. The basics were all she needed, because in her first race she qualified for the U.S. Nationals. While not finishing in a position to guarantee her place on an international team, some women who finished ahead of her decided to race at another distance and freed a space for Lawrence to race internationally. Race internationally she did, but it was not enough to lure her to race walking permanently.

Returning to school and still on a scholarship for running, Lawrence ran cross country and indoor track. She was racing exceptionally well and qualified for Nationals in the 1500M and 3000M races. Then, once again, she injured her knees.

Lawrence started race walking again, allowing the race walk training to maintain her running fitness level. Just before nationals, she jogged and ran a little and it was enough for her to finish 3rd in the 3000M. To avoid further injury, she scratched from the 1500M. Dewitt knew that his athlete only had one good race on her knee. Even though she was the defending 1500M Champion, the 1500M had heats, whereas the 3000M had only a final race. Turned out he was right; Lawrence's knee problems continued to plague her.

With a bad knee, Lawrence focused on walking. Again she qualified for nationals and competed overseas. Over her career she has been a three-time Olympian ('92, '96, '00); eight-time U.S. Outdoor champion ('84, '86, '90, '91, '92, '93, '96, '97); four-time U.S. Indoor champion ('92, '93, '94, '97); and 1991 Pan American Games 10K silver medalist.

Not her best race, but favorite internationally was the 1992 Olympics. At the time, Mary Decker's former coach, Dick Brown, coached her. The race plan was to go out hard with the leaders. While only able to walk with the

lead pack for a short while, Lawrence felt exhilarated just to be there. Then she hit the wall and felt like dropping out. She couldn't; her parents had purchased really expensive tickets in the stadium instead of watching the race for free on the road. As much as she wanted to quit, she didn't. When she entered the stadium, the fans were cheering for her like she was in first place. Goosebumps came over Lawrence, who didn't believe she deserved the cheers.

Lawrence learned two valuable lessons that day. Had she given in to the fatigue, she never would have experienced the joy of entering the stadium. She learned to never drop out of a race. While sticking her neck way out with the lead walkers didn't pay off, she did learn the value of putting your neck out a little. Up until that point she felt she raced too conservatively. By shaking it up a little, she learned to be more aggressive.

It's a shame race walking is not prominently featured indoors as in Lawrence's day. It's possible that Lawrence was too successful for race walking's own good. In early Nineties the indoor track circuit had race walking as one of the events. Lawrence remembers how cool it was to be a competitor with Diane Dixon. That's right, competitor. Competing in the Grand Prix, you were given points for placing in Grand Prix events as well as setting records. This cross competition was great for race walking. It really got our names out in front of other track and field fans. The first year they included it, Lawrence got really sick, but the last two years she won it. Won it all. She beat out the best runners in the world for a prize of $12,000 each year. A lot of people must have complained, because they dropped the race walk from the Grand Prix and then from other races as well. Lawrence enjoyed "taking lime light away from the runners."

Late in her career, Lawrence learned another valuable lesson. One our younger walkers need to learn early. Going into the 1996 Olympic Trials, Lawrence was far from favored. The day was hot and humid, but Lawrence had a secret weapon: mental training. During 1995 and 1996, Lawrence trained her mind as well as her body. Lawrence says, "The power of the mind is amazing." She learned that when you prepare the mind to race, you can do amazing things. She claims not to remember the heat and humidity by the end of the race. She does however remember making her third Olympic Team.

In between her busy racing schedule, Lawrence's modelesque looks landed her on the cover of publications like *Walking Magazine*. She claims her best years are still coming, although Lawrence has difficultly balancing training with her busy career teaching clinics, giving teleclasses for walking over a 10-week period to people all over the world via the phone, as well as promoting healthy eating and fitness for children.

MAJOR INTERNATIONAL EXPERIENCE

10K Olympic Games
    1996 – 20th - 45:32 - Atlanta, USA
    1992 - 26th - 48:22 - Barcelona, Spain

20K Olympic Games
    2000 - 44th - 1:47:20 - Sydney, Australia

10K World Cup
    1991- 15th - 46:13 - San Jose, USA
    1989 - 41st - 48:10 - L'Hospitalet, Spain
    1987   31st - 48:16 - New York, USA

10K Goodwill Games
    1998 - 5th - 47:36.97 - Goodwill Games

10K World Championships
    1995 - 24th - 45:03 – Goteborg, Sweden
    1993 - 37th - 48:53 – Stuttgart, Germany
    1991 - 19th - 45:58 - Tokyo, Japan
    1987 - 20th - 47:31 - Rome, Italy

20K World Championships
    2001 - 19th - 1:37:57 - Edmonton, Canada

10K Pan Am Games
    1991 - 2nd - 46:51.53 - Havana, Cuba

10K Pan Am Cup
    1988 - 3rd – *unknown time* - Mar del Plata, Argentina
    1986 - 9th - 49:06 - St. Leonard, Canada
    1985 - 29th - 50:29 - St. John's Isle of Man
    1983 - 51st - 53:49 - Bergen, Norway

U.S. SENIOR NATIONAL CHAMPIONSHIPS

5K - Won 2 times   15K - Won 2 times   10K Olympic Trials - Won 2 times
10K - Won 9 times   20K - Won 1 time   Indoor 3K - Won 4 times

Lawrence at the 1988 Olympic Trials

Lawrence working it at the 10K Nationals

Whoppin it up!

Birthday: November 20th, 1962
Hometown: Pine Plains, NY
Current Residence: Gainsville, FL

Personal Bests
10K: 45:16
20K: 1:33:23

Career Highlights
2-time U.S. Women's 10K National Champion

Teresa Vaill began her 20-year elite athletic career as a high school distance runner at Pine Plains High School in Upstate New York. She entered the race walk without training, just to earn points. Then, a few weeks before the NY State meet, she began to train for the walk. This meager preparation was enough for the very talented Vaill to excel.

Vaill's walking career might have ended there, but at the 1981 Hartwick Invitational in Oneonta, NY, she met Susan Liers and her coach, Gary Westerfield. When race time came, Vaill chased Liers, then a national-class race walker. Seeing Vaill's potential, Liers promised her the opportunity to become a member of Island Track Club and travel to races. Shortly after, Vaill joined the club and raced with Liers and teammate Carol Brown to win the Women's 15K National Team title.

Mostly self coached, Vaill has never been to a training camp or tested physiologically; still, she works hard. Quiet by nature, Vaill prefers to talk with her feet. She walks hard from the gun (just look at the photo below) and keeps pushing until she runs out of gas—a formula that has served her well. Balancing the duties of her family farm with training, Vaill knows what hard work is all about. Waking at 2 A.M., her active life as a dairy farmer built her stamina and strength as a walker.

With hard work came many rewards: twelve national rankings in the 10K—1986 to 1998—and another consecutive four as a 20K walker. During this time, Vaill competed internationally, representing the United States for an amazing 13 years. In 1987, Teresa and twin sister Lisa both qualified and competed at the World Cup in New York City. What a nightmare for the judges!

A two-time U.S. Women's 10K race walk champion, Vaill at 39 was runner-up at the 2002 U.S. Outdoor Championships. Almost winning the race entirely, she lead until the final mile, when Joanne Dow passed her. She ended the season ranked second nationally by Track & Field News. Still hanging in at the top, Vaill finished third in 2003. While Vaill has been ranked #1 in the 10K women's race walk on three separate occasions—1986, 1993, and 1994—she remains most proud of her 10K victory at the 1994 U.S. Nationals. She recently rejoined Coach Westerfield at his new club, Walk USA. Still aiming to make her first Olympic Team, Vaill continues to train and race well.

Vaill launching out to a commanding lead at the 10K Nationals in Wilkes-Barre, PA

MAJOR INTERNATIONAL EXPERIENCE

10K World Championships
1995 - 22nd - 45:02 – Goteborg, Sweden
1991 – DNF - San Jose, USA

10K World Cup
1995 – DNF - Beijing, China
1989 – 23rd - 46:45 - L'Hospitale, Spain
1987 - 20th - 46:50 - New York City, USA
1985 - 24th - 49:37 - St. John's, Isle of Man

20K World Cup
2002 – DQ - Torino, Italy

10K Pan Am Games
1995 - DQ - Mar del Plata, Argentina

10K Pan Am Cup
1994 – 2nd - 46:20 – Atlanta, USA
1988 – 5th - 47:18 - Xalapa, Mexico
1988 – DQ - Mar del Plata, Argentina
1986 - 4th - 46:47 - St. Leonard, Canada
1984 - 6th - 51:29 - Bucaramanga, Columbia

20K Pan Am Cup
1998 – 2nd - 1:41:02 - Miami, USA

U.S. SENIOR NATIONAL CHAMPIONSHIPS

5K - Won 6 times
10K - Won 3 times

15K - Won 1 time
20K - Won 3 times

Indoor 1 mile - Won 3 times
Indoor 3K - Won 3 times

Vaill crushing the Women's 20K field at the 2003 Men's 50K Nationals

L
Y
N
N

W
E
I
K

Birthday: June 19th, 1967   Personal Bests
Hometown: Sayville, NY   10K: 46:13.83
Current Residence: Fishkill, NY   20K: 1:35:38
College: SUNY Stony Brook

Career Highlights
15th place at the World Championships
1 time 10K National Record holder

In the mid 1980s, a few New York high schools with coaches interested in race walking dominated the competitive scene. Weik attended such a school and at her coach's request began walking as a sophomore in 1983. At the time, she was an accomplished distance runner specializing in the 800M and one mile. The next year Weik finished 3rd at Junior Nationals, completing the 3K race walk in 15:00. Not satisfied, she returned her senior year and won the race with a time of 14:35.38. Ever the tough competitor, Weik completed this race through an injury and was carried off the track in pain after the event. Still, she broke the Junior National record and qualified for international competition, gaining a reputation for her ability to block out distractions when focusing on success. While her injury required her to use crutches for a month, she still managed to race at a dual meet with Canada.

After high school, Weik attended college at SUNY Stony Brook, a school boasting renowned race walk coach Gary Westerfield, but no athletic scholarships. After one year under Westerfield's tutelage, Weik commenced a multi-year battle with America's best. Unfortunately, she was disqualified at her first Senior-level national meet. Never disqualified before, Weik had a tough time dealing with disappointment, particularly since she believed the disqualification unwarranted. Coach Westerfield encouraged her, explaining, "Your time will come." And come it did.

In 1987 Weik broke into the Senior ranks in a big way. Early season, she qualified for her first World Cup Team, finishing 5th American with a time of 48:37. Later in the year, she readily took her place in the upper echelon of American race walking, finishing 2nd at the National 10K with a time of 47:36.5, and qualifying for several international competitions in the process. The season continued to be prosperous for Weik as she finished 4th at the Pan Am Games and 8th at the World University games.

But Weik feels her greatest accomplishment that year was the season's last race, the World Track & Field Championships in Rome, Italy. Working with Westerfield on a positive affirmation program called *Perfect Power*, the two set up a series of positive goals to accomplish before and during the race.

One of Wiek's goals for the trip was acquiring an Italian-made leather jacket. Westerfield spent many an hour shopping before the race to make sure this pre-race goal was attained so Weik could block out virtually everything but walking during the race. To this day, the only thing Weik remembers about that race is the single moment that she felt a little negative and switched on her Perfect Power. She then broke the American record. At the race finish, someone asked Weik a question about where they had walked. She could not remember. Now *that* is what I call focus.

During her training, Weik was fortunate to receive a very generous sponsorship from the Brown shoe company for a number of years. Her most memorable national championship was in 1989, when she and Teresa Vaill walked side-by-side at the halfway mark. The two competitors battled it out to the last lap, with Weik edging out Vaill by seven seconds to set yet another National record.

Weik's seven-year, back-and-forth rivalry with Debbie Lawrence, Maryanne Torrellas, Victoria Herazo and Teresa Vaill for dominance in American race walking came to an end when Weik retired from competition to focus on her family and professional life. Though she no longer race walks, she does run to stay fit. She is the proud mother of four girls and has her own pediatric physical therapy practice in Fishkill, New York.

MAJOR INTERNATIONAL EXPERIENCE

10K World Cup
1991 - 28th - 47:44 - San Jose, USA
1989 - 21st - 46:38 - L'Hospitalet, Spain
1987 - 34th - 48:33 - New York City, USA

10K World Championships
1991 - 25th - 46:48 - Tokyo, Japan
1987 - 15th - 46:51 - Rome, Italy

10K Pan Am Games
1991 - 4th - 47:54 - Havana, Cuba
1987 - 4th - 48:11 - Indianapolis, USA

5K World University Games
1989 - 9th - 22:00 - Zagreb, Croatia
1987 - 8th - 23:43 – Unknown Location

U.S. SENIOR NATIONAL CHAMPIONSHIPS

10K - Won 1 time   20K - Won 1 time   1 Hour - Won 1 time

Weik at the 1987 10K World Cup

Weik chasing Ann Peel, Teresa Vaill, and Maryanne Torrellas at the Vitalis U.S. Olympic Invitational

Birthday: **July 26th, 1958**   Personal Bests
Hometown: **Woodhaven, NY**   10K: **46:13.83**
Current Residence: **Clinton, CT**   5K: **22:10**
College: **St. John's University**

Career Highlights
Pan Am Games Bronze Medal, 1500M World Best
6 time National Champion, Mobile Grand Prix Champion

With much success as a high school runner logging a 2:11 half mile and 4:32 1500M, Maryanne Torrellas came to walking naturally, earning top rankings and a track scholarship in the process. Her cousin, Peter Timmons, a national-class race walker, introduced her to the sport of race walking and encouraged her to try it.

After seven consecutive stress fractures in her foot, Torrellas accepted Timmons' advice and began race walking to stay in shape. While she dabbled, she learned to enjoy the sport. She quickly got in shape and qualified for the 1978 Indoor Nationals. She remembers her initiation to the racing elite on a very small track where, in the middle of the pack, Susan Liers stepped on her shoe.

Lured back into running, Torrellas became distracted from athletics when she married and had a child. After the pregnancy, Torrellas described herself as a *walking house*. Recently, she showed a friend her picture from those days, and the friend didn't recognize her.

Torrellas realized she needed to get back in shape. With motivation the key to success, she set the goal of qualifying for the 1983 outdoor nationals and in the process lost 35 pounds. She qualified for the 10K by the skin of her teeth. Her goal was simple: to finish anywhere but last. Worried she was the slowest qualifier, she raced beyond her dreams and finished in the top four. This qualified Torrellas for a trip to Swedish Walk Week, where she set the American record for the 1 mile, the 3K, and the 5K. Torrellas also qualified for the World Cup that year. Hoping to break 50:00 for the 10K, she smoked the majority of the field with a 47:52, finishing 16th overall. Race walking had her hooked.

Torrellas managed to have three more children within a busy race walking career in which she won the 10K Nationals six times. After her second and third children, she kept breaking the American records and at one point held all records from 1500M to 10K.

With all her success, Torrellas never competed in the Olympics. Early in her career, there was no women's race walking event in the Olympic Games. Later in her career, a series of torn knee cartilages hampered her. Finally, after collapsing at the Olympic Trials in 1996, she was forced to retire from race walking with heart valve damage.

Today, Torrellas balances work as a massage therapist and personal trainer. She has served on the medical staff of the Olympic Games and World Championships, manages women's race walk development, and judges at the Master's level. She competes only for fun, entering Master's race walks, and even has tried the steeplechase. In 2003 she traveled to the Master's Nationals, won the walk, returned a few hours later, and finished second in her age group for the steeplechase. She was happy to need only a few backstrokes in the water pit. Torrellas says the steeples are not *that* high—unless of course you are forty-five!

As many stories come full circle, Torrellas repaid her cousin for introducing her to race walking. Timmons needed a kidney transplant and Torrellas was a match. Donating one of her kidneys to her cousin, she didn't think twice.

MAJOR INTERNATIONAL EXPERIENCE

10K World Cup
     1989 – 79th - 53:07 - L'Hospitalet, Spain
     1987 – 16th - 46:28 - New York City, USA
     1985 – 20th - 49:08 - St. John's, Isle of Man
     1983 – 16th - 47:53 - Bergen, Norway

10K World Championships
     1987 - 24th - 48:27 - Rome, Italy

10K Pan Am Cup
     1988 - 8th - 49:02 - Mar del Plata, Argentina
     1987 - 3rd - 47:35.12 - Indianapolis, USA

U.S. SENIOR NATIONAL CHAMPIONSHIPS

10K - Won 3 times   Indoor 3K - Won 2 times   Indoor 5K - Won 1 time

Maryanne Torrellas with Lynn Weik, Teresa Vaill and Debbie Lawrence at the National Invitational in Washington, DC

Maryanne Torrellas, competing with women half her age at the Penn Relays in Philadelphia

T
I
M

L
E
W
I
S

Birthday: November 10th, 1962   Personal Bests
Hometown: Shenendehowa, NY   1500M: 5:13.53
Curr. Residence: Colorado Springs, CO 1 Mile: 5:33.53
College: University of Colorado   20K: 1:21:48
                                           50K: 4:10:46
Career Highlights
American Record Holder - 20K
World Record Holder - Indoor 1500M and 1 Mile

Like many walkers of his era, Tim Lewis started race walking as part of the New York high school program. Originally a runner, Lewis saw a teammate race walking, thought it looked easy, and decided to give it a try. He spent nearly a year mastering the technique and another year competing before he was able to complete the mile in 6:48. By his senior year he was close to 6:30. Lewis also competed in the TAC (The Athletics Congress, the former name of USATF) Junior Nationals as a high school junior, setting a Junior National record that he held for many.

Lewis went to college at the University of Colorado, where he benefited from the nearby U.S. Olympic Training Center at Colorado Springs. Training with the likes of Troy Engle, Mike Morris, Jim Heiring, Randy Mimm, Marco Evoniuk, Carl Schueler, Mel McGinnis, and Don Lawrence, Lewis received an early introduction to the world of the race walking elite. At the time, Ron Laird served as the Center's race walk coach in residence.

Upon his college graduation, Lewis worked full-time in the computer field for Digital Corporation. Fitting training into a busy career, he accomplished amazing feats. Lewis dominated American race walking at all distances, from 1500 meters to 20K, for many years. In the mid 1980s athletes often competed on the indoor track circuit, where Lewis holds the world record for the Indoor 1500M (5:13.53) and 1 mile (5:33.53) race walks. After all these years, Lewis's legacy still dominates American race walking as he holds four of the top five 20K times in U.S. history.

With all of his success, Lewis always took the time to say hello. Mike Rohl grew up in the town next to him. Rohl rembers that when he was an up and coming walker, Lewis would always make sure to ask about how things were going at home. I had similar experiences when I competed as a Junior on an international team with Lewis. Lewis found our common ground of computers and started a conversation. Having the best race walker in the country speak with me as an equal was a huge confidence booster. Lewis was truly a good

Lewis training with Vinny O'Sullivan, Troy Engle, and Randy Mimm

patriarch of our sport.

He set the American record at an all-comers meet in Canada and raced his two other fastest times at the Alongi Invitational, in Dearborn, MI (1:22:17), and the World Cup in New York City (1:22:27, 13th place). Unfortunately, Lewis did not fare quite as well at his sole Olympic appearance in 1988. He raced poorly, finishing second to last.

By the early 1990s, Lewis felt he had lost much of the joy of competition. He partially retired in 1992, racing a little, and then finally called it quits in 1993. Still residing in Colorado Springs, Lewis now works for Oracle. He no longer competes in athletics, but instead runs "to keep from getting fat," plays a little soccer, snow boards, skis, and camps for fun.

MAJOR INTERNATIONAL EXPERIENCE

20K Olympic Games
    1988 - 44th - 1:31:00 - Seoul, Korea

20K World Championships
    1991 – 31st – 1:30:55 - Tokyo, Japan
    1987 – 19th – 1:26:00 - Rome, Italy
    1983 – 36th – 1:30:10 - Helsinki, Japan

20K Pan Am Games
    1991 – 7th – 1:31:07 - Havana, Cuba
    1987 – 2nd – 1:25:50 - Indianapolis, USA

20K World Cup
    1991 – 54th – 1:28:04 - San Jose, USA
    1989 – 45th – 1:27:39 - L'Hospitalet, Spain
    1987 – 13th – 1:22:27 - New York City, USA
    1985 – 28th – 1:30:02 - St John's, Isle of Man
    1983 – 34th – 1:28:57 - Bergen, Norway

20K Pan Am Cup
    1988 – 44th – 1:31:00 - Seoul, Korea
    1986 – 3rd – 1:21:48 - St. Leonard, Canada

U.S. SENIOR NATIONAL CHAMPIONSHIPS

5K - Won 2 times	15K - Won 2 times	25K - Won 2 times	Indoor 5K – Won 3 times
10K - Won 2 times	20K - Won 2 times	50K - Won 2 times	

Lewis going at it alone at the 1987 World Cup

Lewis gutting it out at the 1987 World Cup

J
I
M

H
E
I
R
I
N
G

Birthday: November 4th, 1955
Hometown: Kenosha, WI
Current Residence: Kenosha, WI
College: Univ. of Wisconsin-Parkside

Personal Bests
1 Mile: 5:41.26
20K: 1:24:51
50K: 4:03:34

Career Highlights
1-Time World Record Holder for the Indoor 1500M,
1 Mile, & 2 Mile; 3-Time Olympic Qualifier

Jim Heiring was first exposed to race walking when he watched Larry Young win the bronze medal at the 1968 50K Olympic race walk. A few years later, as a high school junior, he decided to try race walking at the Junior Olympics. At this disappointing first attempt, Heiring was disqualified for disobeying the rules that differentiate race walking from running.

Luckily for Heiring, Mike DeWitt—in his pre-*Coach DeWitt* days—was nearby to teach Heiring the correct form. The combination of Heiring's natural talent and Dewitt's technical advice paid huge dividends. Heiring won the next race, the Junior Olympics Wisconsin State Championships, and continued on to the National Junior Olympic championships, where he finished 4th.

While race walking enthusiasts today associate the University of Wisconsin-Parkside, with Mike DeWitt, back then Bob Lawson coached the team. Lawson offered Heiring a scholarship, with the deal then pretty much the same as now: run cross-country, race walk during track season.

By 1976 Heiring was a college junior. He competed at the Olympic Trials, where time standards for qualification had yet to be established. The top three finishers at the trials made the team, and Heiring finished a close 5th. This achievement lead him to the epiphany, "I might be pretty good at this." He decided to dedicate himself to race walking full time.

Heiring's commitment paid off when during his senior year, he won both the Indoor and Outdoor NAIA championships. He graduated with an Art degree and felt he had to make a choice between art and athletics. Obviously, Heiring chose athletics.

With enough harsh Wisconsin winters under his belt, Heiring moved to California where the weather was more conducive to training. He worked part-time as a commercial artist while focusing on preparations for the 1980 Olympic Games. For the most part, Heiring trained alone. A few times a month, he met with Dan O'Connor for a weekend workout. Unfortunately, Heiring was hampered by injuries and became frustrated. With no coach and no formal development program, he diligently worked alone and overcame the adversity. The 1980 20K Olympic trials found Heiring and Marco Evoniuk walking together with two miles to go. The two purposely finished in a tie.

Unfortunately, the fate of our athletes was already determined before the race began. They all were beaten by opinions—opinions that lead to the U.S. boycotting the Olympics. Heiring views the lost Olympic opportunity as one of the biggest disappointments of his life.

After the Olympic Trials, Heiring spent a year working out with the Parkside athletes before moving to the Olympic Training Center at Colorado Springs. Race walking at the national level was taking a step in the right direction by establishing a resident athletes program. During this time, Martin Rudow coached Heiring over the phone and via mail while making frequent visits to Seattle.

Heiring's training was timed perfectly for him to peak again at the Olympic Trials in 1984. Leading by a mile and a half at 10K, he was well on his way to winning his second trials when the knee problems that plagued his career flared up. He relinquished the lead, but not his long-awaited berth on the Olympic Team. He finished second.

In 1986 Heiring moved back to Wisconsin and became reacquainted with Mike DeWitt, who helped him extend his racing distance to 50K. Success followed him to this event as he walked a 4:03 in Rome at the 1987 World Championships.

When Heiring competed at his fourth 20K Olympic Trials, he decided he would just walk his own race. He walked as hard and fast as possible, holding his pace as long as he could. Finishing 4th, he ignored the murmurs he heard from the sidelines. But 3rd-place finisher Paul Schwartzberg was disqualified, making Heiring eligible for the Olympics once again.

As soon as he crossed the finish line at the 1988 Seoul Olympics, Heiring retired. He realized that continuing to race no longer made sense to him. While he walked faster than he had at the 1984 L.A. Games, he had finished 10 to 15 spots further back. Without any real hope of winning an Olympic medal, he decided to stop putting life on hold to simply participate on the team.

Heiring has since married, and he and his wife have two sons. When he reminisces about his career, the aspects he most enjoyed barely show up on the competitive radar. "Racing indoors was a blast. Madison Square Garden, with 20,000 people watching!" he recalls fondly. At one point, Heiring held Indoor World Records at the 1500M, 1-mile and 2-mile distances. It seems inconceivable now, but back then the sponsors were generous. The Indoor Grand Prix Circuit could net the top walker a good $20,000 in one year: a unique opportunity for race walkers to earn money.

MAJOR INTERNATIONAL EXPERIENCE

20K Olympic Games
1988 - 38th - 1:27:30 - Seoul, Korea
1984 - 23rd - 1:30:20 - Los Angeles, USA

20K World Championships
1983 - 19th - 1:25:55 - Helsinki, Japan

50K World Championships
1988 - 22nd - 4:03:34 - Rome, Italy
1983 - DNF - Helsinki, Japan

20K Pan Am Games
1983 - 6th - 1:34:47 – Caracas, Venezuela

20K World Cup
1983 - 16th - 1:24:51 - Bergen, Norway
1981 - 22nd - 1:30:39 - Valencia, Spain
1979 - 31st - 1:28:51 - Eschborn, West Germany
1977 - 36th - 1:33:40 - Milton Keynes, Great Brittan

50K World Cup
1987 - 29th - 4:08:15 - New York City, USA

U.S. SENIOR NATIONAL CHAMPIONSHIPS

5K - Won 2 times	15K - Won 3 times	25K - Won 2 times	2 Hour – Won 1 time
10K - Won 2 times	20K - Won 3 times	30K - Won 1 time	Indoor 2 miles – Won 3 times

Heiring leading the pack at the 1987 World Cup Trials

Heiring walking with the Who's Who of race walking at the NYC Marathon

137

M
A
R
C
O

E
V
O
N
I
U
K

Birthday: September 30, 1957   Personal Bests
Hometown: Longmont, CO   20K: 1:25:23
Curr. Residence: San Francisco, CA 50K: 3:56:55
College: University of Colorado

Career Highlights
3-time Olympian; Former National Record Holder

Distance great Marco Evoniuk actually started his athletic career as a high school sprinter, running the 220 in 22.8 and the 440 in 50.5; but his destiny was elsewhere. Growing up in the strong amateur track community of Colorado, in 1976 Evoniuk was lured into race walking by two Centurion[4] race walkers. While we very rarely hear of Centurion walkers today, like the Jedi Knights, they once were plentiful.

Dr. Amaroso and the late Chuck Hunter took Evoniuk in as their padawan learner during his senior year of high school. Evoniuk quickly became quite serious about his training. In no time at all, he was race walking distances—long distances. With strong family support behind him, he excluded everything except his studies. He recognized that as a sprinter without a distance base, he needed to train hard. Feeling he needed a diverse training program, he combined running and walking workouts to master the distance and form of race walking.

On Saturdays, Evoniuk chased master's running-great Bob Green for about 12 miles, running 5:30 per mile while Green *smoked* him. On Sundays, Evoniuk joined the Centurions. Battered from his runs, he typically ambled 20-mile walks at a 10-minute pace. "I couldn't go any faster," remembers Evoniuk.

In all, Evoniuk ran and walked for a combination of approximately 70 to 90 miles per week. With the exception of his weekly distance day with the Centurions, Evoniuk didn't believe in Long Slow Distance (LSD) workouts. "I just go fast, everyday," Evoniuk recalls. He felt this training approach worked best for him, perhaps because of his sprinting background. Racing whenever he could—practically every weekend—Evoniuk bounced between racing at high school all-comer meets to race walking a series of 10K running competitions in the Denver area.

These races must not have been enough of a challenge, because soon Evoniuk ran the Denver marathon (finishing in 2:40), "Just to build confidence." He soon taught his mentors who the new master was.

In 1977 Evoniuk finished second at the 100K National Championships with a time of 11:19. While finishing second in such races represents a significant achievement, to be a true master of the sport, Evoniuk needed to succeed at the Olympic distances of 20K and 50K. His big breakthrough came in 1978, when he finished fifth at the U.S. 20K Nationals at UCLA to qualify for his first international race, the Swedish Walk in June.

The international experience really helped Evoniuk mature as a competitor. Placing at national competition provided little challenge for the upstart: the very first time he raced the 50K Nationals, he won. Still a relative unknown in 1978, he took most of the 50K field by surprise. After Nationals, in typical Evoniuk style, he drove all night to join a training camp with the top Mexican race walkers. Gaining international exposure with the likes of Mexican walking greats Daniel Bautista and Raul Gonzales added to his confidence.

By the end of the seventies, Evoniuk knew he had made it and could compete with the best in the U.S. Late in the race at the 1980 Olympic Trials, he dueled it out with Jimmy Heiring along a hilly Eugene, Oregon course. The judges really held the two competitors down, and they entered the stadium together. With

---

[4] A race walker who completes 100 miles in a single day is given the title *Centurion*.

nothing truly on the line because of the Olympic boycott, in the end, they decided to finish in a tie. Evoniuk, ever the optimist, figured he could do it all again in 1984.

En route to the next Olympics, the World Championships in Helsinki furthered Evoniuk's fortitude. Finishing 9th against the world's top walkers—and under very hot conditions—his confidence rose to an all-time high. By the time he became a resident at the Olympic Training Center in 1983, Evoniuk was at the top of his game. His goal was no less than medaling at the 1984 Olympic Games. Considering himself better at the 50K than 20K, he believed the boycott by the Soviet Union and other Eastern Block countries only improved his chances. Accomplishing a lot at the Center, Evoniuk remembers "working hard and having some fun." Although Evoniuk claims to have missed a lot of the fun, he loved to play the prankster. One day he showed up to training with bleached orange hair, driving a different car, "just to do things to make it interesting."

Evoniuk won both Olympic Trial races in an impressive way. With oppressive heat each day, Evoniuk set the stage with a 10-minute victory at the 50K. At first it looked like a double triumph was out of the question. However, after Jimmy Heiring built up a huge lead, his knee problems forced him to fade. Evoniuk not only won the 20K, but also set an Olympic Trials 20K record that stood until 2000.

Evoniuk's Olympic experience was eventful—and not just because he was competing in two events. While out on the town, he and Mike Morris participated in another form of walking: jay walking. Apparently the L.A. police didn't find Evoniuk and Morris' antics amusing and escorted them downtown "to get it taken care of." With such distractions behind him, Evoniuk got down to business.

Conditions were hot, but Evoniuk liked it hot. He finished 7th in the 20K. However, being a 50K specialist, he wondered if he should have competed in the shorter race. He had only one week to recover before the 50K event, and while he felt physically recovered, he felt mentally unprepared to put it together for his favorite event.

To this day, Evoniuk doesn't know what happened during the 50K. He believes it was not the pressure: he had raced too much for that to be a factor. Basically, he felt unable to regain his focus and dropped out of the race early. He "just couldn't get going again" after the 20K, he recalls.

Typical of a post-Olympic Year, 1985 was a down time for Evoniuk. But at the start of 1986, he began a multi-year training cycle with the aim of taking another shot at an Olympic Medal. Building a solid fitness level, Evoniuk felt the key was to increase speed. He never did LSD. He used the 20K as a tool for good leg speed, but put little importance on the National Championships at this distance. He believed they were too early in the season. Instead, he focused on international competition. Amazed by the likes of Ron Laird and Tim Seaman competing in so many national championships, he regarded the key, instead, as focusing on a single goal.

Evoniuk's plan succeeded. At the 1988 Olympic Games in Seoul, he set a new American record. Unfortunately, the plans of his international competitors also succeeded. With race walkers across the world growing faster, Evoniuk finished further back in the pack. By his third Olympic Games in 1992, one might expect him to have the routine down. However, although he trained well leading up to the race, Evoniuk just could not get moving. He dropped out of the race, his last Olympic appearance.

For all his success, his inconsistency in international competition plagued Evoniuk throughout his career. He believes there were just too many races over too many years to stay focused. Looking back, he remains amazed he was able to maintain focus across such a long period of time.

Evoniuk continued to work hard, but the next generation of walkers gained prominence. In time he found it "so much more difficult to do the distance." He felt his workout recovery time increasing and his body wearing out. Still, without the pressure of being on top, he experienced the fun of his sport once again.

No longer competing, today Evoniuk runs, walks, and lifts weights to stay in shape. He is glad the days of extreme mileage are over! He now works as a financial planner in San Francisco, California.

MAJOR INTERNATIONAL EXPERIENCE

20K Olympic Games
    1984 - 7th - 1:25:42 - Los Angeles, USA

50K Olympic Games
    1992 - DNF - Seoul, Korea
    1988 - 22nd - 3:56:55 - Seoul, Korea
    1984 - DNF – Los Angles, USA

50K World Cup
    1997 - 68th - 4:17:24 - Podebrady, Czechoslovakia
    1995 -47th - 4:11:31 - Beijing, China
    1991 - DNF - San Jose, USA
    1987 - DNF - New York City, USA
    1985 - 16th - 4:11:03 - St. John's, Isle of Man
    1983 - DQ - Bergen, Norway
    1981 - 13th - 4:07:44 - Valencia, Spain
    1979 - 35th - 4:12:37 - Eschborn, West Germany

20K World Championships
    1983 – DNF - Helsinki, Japan

50K World Championships
    1987 - 17th - 3:57:43 - Rome, Italy
    1983 - 9th - 3:56:57 - Helsinki, Japan

50K Pan Am Cup
    1998 5th - 4:36:53 - Miami, USA
    1996 8th - 4:40:18 - Manaus, Brazil
    1988 DNF - Mar del Plata, Argentina
    1986 2nd - 4:05:56 - St. Leonard, Canada

20K Pan Am Games
    1983 – DNF – Caracas, Venezuela

50K Pan Am Games
    1991 - DNF - Havana, Cuba
    1979 3rd - 4:24:23 - San Juan, Puerto Rico

U.S. SENIOR NATIONAL CHAMPIONSHIPS

20K Olympic Trials - Won 2 times   30K - Won 1 time   50K – Won 4 times
50K Olympic Trials - Won 1 time

C
A
R
L

S
C
H
U
E
L
E
R

Birthday: February 26th, 1956
Hometown: Ann Arbor, MI
Curr. Residence: Colorado Springs, CO
College: Frostburg College

Personal Bests
20K: 1:25:04
50K: 3:57:09

Career Highlights
6th Place - 50K, 1984 Olympic Games

Talking with Carl Schueler, you would never guess what a fierce competitor he once was. Synonymous with success as a distance walker throughout the 1980s and into the 1990s, Schueler displays a laid back attitude that can mislead you. The four-time Olympic Games qualifier had a long and successful career race walking, while balancing a *real* career and life outside of race walking.

Carl Schueler may have started race walking with the biggest and shortest splash in race walking history. While a 9th grader at a four-year Catholic high school in Ann Arbor, Michigan, Schueler was running a workout. He was told to jog the curves and run the straight-aways, but he was having trouble. His coach mocked, "You're race walking," challenging him to a quarter-mile race. Schueler walked a 1:58. Assuming his technique was legal, the performance must be some kind of unofficial record. Even if it was not legal, it's impressive that anyone could even come near race walking so fast on their first attempt.

Schueler's initial race walking career fizzled out as quickly as it started. He graduated high school and attended Frostburg State College, a small school in Maryland, where he ran cross country and track before becoming injured his sophomore year. When he noticed that the NAIA Frostburg included race walking on its board of events, he became intrigued. Schueler had not race walked a step since his first experience in high school. As his good fortune would have it, a teammate had a minor interest in the sport. He wasn't very good, but he introduced Schueler to Bob Kitchen, Sal Corrallo, and the rest of the race walking community. Training mostly on his own, Schueler achieved a 7:09 mile by Christmas of 1975.

Realizing that his quarter-mile experience was not a fluke and that his talents lay more with race walking than running, Schueler trained for the NAIA Indoor Nationals. In February of 1976, Schueler finished second behind Jim Heiring, just a few short months after he had started to race walk.

Schueler continued to progress, winning the 25K at what in those days was called a *B Championship*. B Championships were similar to what Larry Young called *Junior Championships*. You could compete only if you had not won a Senior national title. As Schueler humbly recalls his success, "I won those kinds of things." *Those kinds of things* also included a trip to compete at Mexican Walk Week in 1977 and Swedish Walk Week the following year.

Graduating college in 1978, he began working for the U.S. Department of Defense. By 1979, he had walked five 50K races—none all that fast, according to Schueler. At the World Cup he seemed as if he was going to have a breakthrough. On four-hour pace for most of the race, he unfortunately faded badly at the end, finishing in a time of 4:27:24.

Schueler taking a dip with Mark Fenton and Tim Lewis after the World Cup Trials

Deciding to focus his energies on the Olympic Trials, in January 1980 Schueler arranged to work four-hour days and train the remainder of the time. He quickly became a lot faster. In less than six months he improved his 50K time from 4:24 to 4:06. Putting it all together at the 50K Olympic Trials of May 1980, Schueler walked an impressive 3:59:33. While he had sacrificed in his career, essentially training full time, he was not rewarded. The U.S. boycotted the Olympics. Schueler also raced at the 20K Olympic Trials, but had not yet perfected the 20K distance and thus finished sixth.

After the Trials, he temporarily retired from race walking and entered a graduate program for regional and urban planning at the University of Michigan. Not training, he did join the occasional Alongi Invitational. After finishing all but his practicum in 1983, Schueler had nothing else to do, so in the spring he began working out again. He trained in Ann Arbor that summer, and then in September moved to Colorado Springs for an opening in a residence program at the USOTC. At that time, specific time standards weren't required to be a resident; he was accepted on his past credentials.

The training center environment proved beneficial for Schueler. Although he claims to have mostly self-coached, he acknowledges receiving a lot of physiological help as well as other assistance from numerous people, then and over the years.

Going into the 1984 Olympic trials, Schueler was the man to beat. He had won the National 35K with a very fast 2:41, but then had a terrible race at the Trials. He became dehydrated and lost to fellow residents Marco Evoniuk and Vinny O'Sullivan. Fortunately, Tommy Edwards just didn't have enough speed to catch him.

At the Olympic Games in L.A., Schueler showed why he had been the favorite at the trials. Under very hot conditions, competitors kept dropping out around him. It was a war of attrition. As the race went on, hopes rose for an American medal. Schueler finished sixth, just two minutes away from fourth place. America had been one DQ and two minutes away from its first Olympic race walking medal in years.

Schueler pretty much took 1985 off and, as a testament to his amazing ability, still won the National 50K, "Drinking beer, hanging around, and working full time," as he puts it. (I am sure somewhere in there he managed to get in a walk or two.) His success was contagious. In 1986, Schueler met his future wife, Debbie Van Orden, and infected her with the race walking disease. He likes to think of it as his curse.

Shortly after, Reebok and Rockport started sponsoring walking. With more money pouring into the sport than ever, Schuler started to train again. Wanting to give up the 50K for a while, he focused instead on the 20K. In 1986, he established his 20K PR of 1:25:04. However, he was soon back to the distance that proved so successful for him, racing the 50K at the World Track and Field Championships in Rome. He set his PR of 3:57:09 at that event.

As the 1988 Olympic Trials approached, Schueler again turned up the effort. He returned to working part time, this time six-hour days. This break from work proved enough to get him in "very strong shape." He won the Trials, but at the Olympics didn't place anywhere near as high as before. The combination of international race walkers getting faster, the additional walkers returning after the 1984 Games boycott, and a respiratory problem lead Schueler to finish twenty-third. He thought he was in 3:52 shape, but felt flat and walked 3:57:44.

Schueler battling Tommy Edwards at the 1984 50K Olympic Trials

After 1988 Schueler returned permanently to working full-time. In late 1989, he was hit by a car and seriously injured. He took some time to get back in form and in 1991 qualified for the World Championships. After completing all of the approximately forty 50Ks of his career, Schueler DNF'd for the first time. Remarkably, to that point he had never been DQ'd in a 50K.

In 1992, he gave the Olympics one last attempt. Although he was working full time, he was able to break four hours for the 50K. The four-hour time standard and a placing at the Trials were now requirements for making the Olympic Team. Schueler won the Trial race, but conditions at the Olympics were so terrible that he wanted only to see what he could do. Finishing twenty-third once again—this time at 4:13:38—Schueler knew his career had peaked.

Still, Schueler couldn't let race walking leave his life. He returned for a few more World Cup teams. Training with the help of his friend Andrzej Chylinski, he got into competitive shape again in 1996, but his hopes at a fifth Olympic team were thwarted by a hamstring injury. Schueler blames the injury on a combination of getting old and stress from work. His last international event was the World Cup held in Prague in 1997.

After 1997 Schueler gave up competing as a race walker for good. However, he coaches Kevin Eastler, America's current top-ranked 20K race walker. Of course, says Schueler, he coaches "in a low key sort of way."

MAJOR INTERNATIONAL EXPERIENCE

50K Olympic Games
    1992 - 23rd - 4:13:38 - Barcelona, Spain
    1988 - 23rd - 3:57:44 - Seoul, Korea
    1984 - 6th - 3:59:46 - Los Angeles, USA

50K World Championships
    1991 - DNF - Tokyo, Japan
    1987 - 16th - 3:57:09 - Rome, Italy

50K World Cup
    1997 - 72nd - 4:19:46 - Podebrady, Czechoslovakia
    1995 - 42nd - 4:06:45 - Bejing, China
    1991 - 31st - 4:08:51 - San Jose, USA
    1987 - 24th - 4:03:02 - New York City, USA

    1985 - 19th - 4:13:14 - St. John's, Isle of Man
    1979 - 44th - 4:27:24 - Escborn, West Germany

20K Pan Am Games
    1987 - 5th - 1:29:53 - Indianapolis, USA

20K Pan Am Cup
    1990 - 7th - 1:28:21 - Xalapa, Mexico
    1988 - 6th - 1:31:39 - Mar del Plata, Argentina
    1986 - 9th - 1:25:04 - St. Leonard, Canada

50K Pan Am Cup
    1992 - 10th - 4:24:46 - Guatemala City
    1984 - 4th - 4:20:56 - Bucaramanga, Columbia

U.S. SENIOR NATIONAL CHAMPIONSHIPS

25K - Won 1 time   35K - Won 1 time   50K - Won 7 times
30K - Won 2 times   40K - Won 3 times   50K Olympic Trials - Won 3 times

Schueler at the 50K Nationals

Schueler battling Herm Nelson at the 1992 50K Olympic Trials

Schueler finishing the 1987 50K World Cup

143

D
A
N

O'

C
O
N
N
O
R

Birthday: March 29th, 1952
Hometown: Wantagh, NY
Current Residence: Bellmore, NY
College: University of Tennessee, Knoxville

Personal Bests
20K: 1:25:56
50K: 4:09:29

Career Highlights
14 Senior National Titles
1-Time National 20K Record Holder

Dan O'Connor was at the University of Tennessee on a running scholarship when, just before the Division I NCAA cross-country championships, he stepped in a pothole and twisted his ankle. The trainer taped him up so tight that he lost all flexibility in his ankle. Barely able to finish his race, he aggravated a cyst and damaged his knee. O'Connor managed to limp through two more seasons before accepting that he could no longer run competitively.

Luckily for O'Connor, he had race walked briefly in high school with instant success. Having trained for only three days as a senior, he walked a 7:15 mile and earned a N.Y. State high school record. This experience made O'Connor's decision to return to walking easier. He felt no pain and amazingly was able to immediately translate his running workload to walking. When O'Connor uses the term *workload*, he says it flippantly, but his workload was one hundred miles a week!

Once he became a race walker, he never looked back. While he worked full-time, he trained the only way he could to fit in long miles. He carpooled to work and then walked the 15 miles from Far Rockaway back to his home. The approach paid off, as he qualified in both Olympic race walking events in 1980, only to miss the Games because of the boycott. However, he did realize his Olympic dreams in 1984 when he qualified and competed in the 20K at Los Angeles, finishing 6th.

Over the course of his career, O'Connor amassed 14 national titles, including one 50K, one 20K—with a record-breaking time of 1:26:26 in 1980—and four consecutive 40Ks. *Track and Field* magazine ranked him nationally for 20 consecutive years, dubbing him *Mr. Longevity*. Today he remains the only track and field athlete in any event to have achieved this milestone.

Eventually, family obligations became more pressing and O'Connor gave up competitive race walking. He is now the head girls' track coach for Far Rockaway High School, and two of his relay teams won at the Penn Relays in 2003. He is the proud father of four children who each ran the mile competitively by age six. O'Connor no longer walks, but jogs to stay fit.

O'Connor at the 1987 World Cup in NY

O'Connor with Paul Wick, Mike DeWitt and Herm Nelson

MAJOR INTERNATIONAL EXPERIENCE

50K Olympic Games
 1992 - 23rd - 4:13:38 - Barcelona, Spain
 1988 - 23rd - 3:57:44 - Seoul, Korea
 1984 - 6th - 3:59:46 - Los Angeles, USA

50K World Championships
 1991 - DNF - Tokyo, Japan
 1987 - 16th - 3:57:09 - Rome, Italy

50K World Cup
 1997 - 72nd - 4:19:46 - Podebrady, Czechoslovakia
 1995 - 42nd - 4:06:45 - Bejing, China
 1991 - 31st - 4:08:51 - San Jose, USA
 1987 - 24th - 4:03:02 - New York City, USA
 1985 - 19th - 4:13:14 - St. John's, Isle of Man
 1979 - 44th - 4:27:24 - Escborn, West Germany

50K Pan Am Games
 1987 - 5th - 1:29:53 - Indianapolis, USA

20K Pan Am Cup
 1990 - 7th - 1:28:21 - Xalapa, Mexico
 1988 - 6th - 1:31:39 - Mar del Plata, Argentina
 1986 - 9th - 1:25:04 - St. Leonard, Canada

50K Pan Am Cup
 1992 - 10th - 4:24:46 - Guatemala City, Guatemala
 1984 - 4th - 4:20:56 - Bucaramanga, Columbia

U.S. SENIOR NATIONAL CHAMPIONSHIPS

5K - Won 1 time	25K - Won 2 times	35K - Won 1 time
20K - Won 1 time	30K - Won 3 times	40K - Won 5 times
		50K - Won 1 time

O'Connor at the 1986 Pan Am Cup

*O'Connor at the
1980 U.S. 50K Nationals in NY*

O'Connor at the 1984 Olympic Trials

GARY MORGAN

Morgan got his start race walking at a 1975 AAU track meet where he competed at the age of 15 in the 1 mile walk. Morgan's first race was clocked at 10:45 and he never looked back. His career spanned 17 national titles and peaked when he won the 1988 Olympic Trials. The race was described by most as a death march: 95 degree heat - nearly 100% humidity. The heat was so bad, he doesn't remember his time. Of course he does remember the Olympics!

Morgan went on to finish 2nd in the 1992 Olympic Trials, however he did not have the qualifying time standard now required by the IOC. Again in 1996, Morgan finished top three at the Trials, but did not get to go to the Olympics, because once again he did not have the qualifying standard. Morgan went on to qualify for the Olympic Trials two more times for a total of five. He continues to train and race. He has given numerous talks as a motivational speaker and has had the honor of carrying the Olympic Torch in 1996 and 2002.

RAY SHARP

One of the fastest young American race walkers of the 1980s and winner of 14 Senior national titles ranging in distance from 2 miles to 100 kilometers, Ray Sharp was long on potential but short on consistency in major domestic races.

The solidly built Kentuckian compiled a record of strong performances on foreign soil while competing in two IAAF championship races (Indoor and Outdoor, 1987), two World Cups (1981, 1987); two Pan Am Cups (1986, 1990), the inaugural Goodwill Games (1986); and many other international meets.

Sharp's career could be remembered for his three failed Olympic Trial bids. His career might also be remembered for the way he could take charge of an indoor race with a trademark final-lap burst of speed, and for the intensity and zeal he brought to every race and workout. However, I will always remember Sharp as the star of one of the best documentaries of race walking ever made, *The Long Walk to the Olympics*.

PAUL SCHWARTZBERG

Paul Schwartzberg was one of the many elite race walkers produced from the New York State high school program. In Schwartzberg's senior year of high school, he won the mile walk at the New York State Track and Field Championships. After high school, Paul attended Amherst College, where as a freshman he placed second in the 10K walk at the Junior National Championships. As a sophomore, he jumped up to 20K races and made his first National Track & Field Team.

Paul's greatest accomplishments came in 1988, during his senior year at college. That year, he won the National 20K Invitational Race Walk at Washington, D.C. with a personal best of 1:26:49. Schwartzberg also won the Metropolitan 15K Race walk Championship, setting an American record of 1:02:39 in the process. While he made the National Track & Field Team for his third time that year, controversy was in the air. Paul finished the 20K Olympic Trails thinking that he had made the team as he crossed the finish line. Having picked up two DQ calls early, Paul had slowed down to ensure a place on the team. Ever the sportsman, Carl Schueler, having already made the 50K team waited for Paul at the finish line and allowed Schwartzberg to cross the line in third. Schwartzberg thought his Olympic dreams were fulfilled. Unfortunately, he received a late DQ card, his third, and was disqualified. After college and the Olympic Trials, Paul's racing walking career came to an early end. However, recently he has been seen race walking in Central Park. Is a comeback in the making?

RACE WALKING IN THE 90s

In 1992, the International Olympic Committee (IOC) radically changed the method through which race walkers qualified for the Olympics. No longer were the top three finishers at the Olympic Trials guaranteed a spot on the Olympic Team. Instead, the IOC, using the IAAF, established qualifying standards that ensured a minimum performance level for Olympic athletes. For some events, like the 100-meter run, the standards did not affect the composition of the American team. Many American athletes can meet or surpass the standards for running. However, within race walking events, the new standards proved a serious impediment in conjunction with the lack of depth in our race walking field. The U.S. team faces many challenges in developing three walkers, for each distance, who can achieve the qualifying standards at the appropriate time in the Olympic cycle.

The IOC intended for the new standards to raise the level of competition. In actuality, however, many in the U.S. race walk community believe they brought about an opposite effect. Certainly a few athletes feel pushed to excel and reach the standards needed to make the team. However, the daunting times required discourage many more race walkers who retreat from the scene without ever trying to qualify. Indeed, the new time standards dramatically changed the complexion of the Olympic Trials race. Today, the quest to hit the standard often takes precedence over competitive results, with the end result a race of less importance.

Needless to say, in the early nineties, USATF faced quite a challenge. Not helping matters were the great reductions in the budget and external financial support. Considering these obstacles, the leadership duo of Bruce Douglass (Chairman from 1988 to 1996) and Rich Torrellas (National Team Coordinator from 1988 to 1996 and Chairman from 1996 to 2000), accomplished much.

As do all new regimes, Douglass and Torrellas filled the top spots of the organization with those they trusted—in this case, Gwen and Lawrie Robertson. The new team at first concentrated on establishing yearly training camps for Senior athletes. These camps focused on teaching the biomechanics of race walking, filming and reviewing workouts, and using scientific testing to enhance athletes' performances.

Time passed, and elite athletes gravitated to international coaches and permanent training centers. As the Atlanta Olympics approached, the Center of Excellence concept originally proposed by Sal Corrallo gained momentum. As a result, LaGrange and its colony of athletes under Polish coach Bohdan Bulakowski achieved national prominence. Their success represents the dramatic progression of a group of senior elite athletes benefiting from a strategic program with leadership and focused direction.

Unfortunately, as the 1996 Olympics came to an end, local financial support for the LaGrange program evaporated. However, the memory of LaGrange's impact and the dedication of the athletes remained strong. Having seen the writing on the wall, Bruce Douglass met with Philip Dunn, Andrew Hermann, and Tim Seaman at the Atlanta Olympic Trials. The group hammered out a proposal to present to USA Track and Field, requesting support for a residency program to be located at the new U.S. Olympic Training Center at Chula Vista.

Torrellas carried the vision of Douglass and our elite athletes to fruition. His number one priority as the newly elected chairman in 1996 was to secure the Chula Vista Training Center as the race walkers' training camp site. Few people understand how much effort this took. Torrellas spent more hours working on this project than on his day job of teaching. (People tend to forget the Chairman position is a volunteer position: Chairs earn nothing for their grief). Torrellas relied on his personal relationships, stubbornness, and salesmanship skills to obtain the program's approval.

But Torrellas was not the only person making sacrifices to ensure the program's success. In the first year, Bulakowski earned little more than basic room and board, while Elaine Ward established NARI (North American Race Walking Institute) to raise funds for the program. Since that time, NARI has continued to fund the residency program, as well as other race walking ventures.

The program was taken to the next level in 1998, when Enrique Pena replaced Bulakowski as the new coach in residence at the Center, where he remains in residence to this day.

With the Senior athletes in permanent camps, the administration changed its focus to the Juniors. Around the same time, the Maine Principles' Association, the state's high school track and field organization, added the race walk to their program, spurring a welcome influx of young, new, talented race walkers. Started in 1995 as an exhibition, the 1600 M race walk became a scoring event for both girls and boys in 1999, through the hard work of Tom Eastler.

Week long training camps evolved to encompass Juniors and a few up-and-coming Senior athletes. Building on the roots of my predecessors, I was fortunate enough to hold the position of USATF Junior National Race Walk Coordinator. While I did coach some of the Juniors at this time, my overall role was not that of coach. Rather, I sought to coordinate training camps and international races, and above all, to communicate. Young people stay interested if you make them aware of the many opportunities they possess, such as training camps as well as domestic and international races.

One of the biggest Junior events developed during this era was the *U.S./Canada Junior Dual Meet*. When Torrellas was National Team coordinator, he badgered Douglass for funding to establish this competition. Going strong since 1989, this event offers Juniors great international experience early in their careers.

In many regards, the Junior program of the Nineties was a success. The comprehensive weeklong camps at the U.S. Olympic Training Center provided the young athletes a week of constant contact and twice-daily workouts. The participants absorbed and applied a great amount of technical information on the biomechanics of walking, proper stretching, nutrition, and strength training. Unfortunately, when the Juniors returned to training at home, they often lacked the reinforcement required to maintain their training center improvements.

Further complicating sustained progress towards developing race walking in the U.S. was the lack of a comprehensive collegiate program. While some colleges have formal race walking programs, the majority do not. Without a means to keep competing, many of the Juniors stop race walking upon high school graduation. This problem remains the single biggest impediment to the growth of our sport.

Birthday: November 12th, 1965
Hometown: Beaver Dam, WI
Curr. Residence: Mansfield, PA
College: University of Wisconsin-Parkside

Personal Bests
10K: 44:17
20K: 1:31:51

Career Highlights
3-Time Olympian; 4-Time US 20K champion
1995 - Pan American Games silver medalist

Most novice race walkers begin participating in the sport without a long, thought-out plan. Michelle Rohl is no different. Already an accomplished runner and 15-time NAIA All-American, she had never entertained the idea of race walking before an injury her senior year forced her to begin cross training. While she began race walking regularly to train, remarkably, she graduated from the University of Wisconsin-Parkside, in 1989 without ever having competed in the event.

Coach Mike DeWitt thought she had a talent for race walking. The following year, when Rohl had trouble qualifying for Nationals as a runner, he suggested she try qualifying as a race walker. She did, still intending to return to serious running the following season. While Rohl ran a bit over the years—even qualifying to run the Olympic Trials marathon—she never seriously trained to run competitively again.

Rohl stayed at Parkside through the 1992 Olympics. However, during training she went down to train in New Orleans to get ready for the heat and humidity. In one of the best stories of gorilla marketing I have ever heard, her husband turned a bad situation into a sponsorship and great exposure for race walking. After running up a large phone bill with MCI, Mike called them and asked them to help out. AT&T was a major Olympic sponsor. He proposed that helping the Rohls would be great advertising. They not only took care of the bill, but signed Michelle to a multi-commercial contract. It featured the story of Michelle being separated from her family and calling home, of course using an MCI calling card.

After the Olympics they relocated again to LaGrange, Georgia, where she joined a group of elite American race walkers training for the 1996 Olympics. She qualified for these games as well, finishing the highest of any of her Olympic appearances. Having the Olympics in Atlanta couldn't have worked out any better. Michelle's dad came to the race; it's the only international race he has ever seen his daughter walk.

After the 1996 games, the group moved to the new Olympic Training Center in California. Rohl could not join them, however, because she was married and had children—two circumstances unwelcome at the center.

The Rohl clan trained in Northern Wisconsin for a period before heading to Cloud Croft, New Mexico, where Michele lived at 9,000 feet while training at 4,000 feet. Very few places in the world provide the benefits of high altitude living and lower altitude training. Rohl qualified for her third Olympic Games (2000) there and planned to stay indefinitely. However, her husband Mike received an offer to head the track program at Mansfield University; with Michele offered an assistant track coach position with Mike, the Rohls moved to Mansfield, PA, where Michele now trains to qualify for her fourth Olympic games. She is the proud mother of four children. That's right, four!

MAJOR INTERNATIONAL EXPERIENCE

20K Olympic Games
2000 – 17th – 1:34:26 – Sydney, Australia

10K Olympic Games
1996 – 14th – 44:29 – Atlanta, USA

20K World Championships
2001 – DQ – Edmonton, Canada

10K World Championships
1995 – 15th - 44:17 – Goteborg, Sweden

20K World Cup
1999 – 46th – 1:36:50 – Mezidon, France

10K World Cup
1995 – 34th –45:57– Beijing, China

20K Pan Am Games
1999 – 3rd – 1:35:22 – Winnipeg, Canada

10K Pan Am Games
1995 – 2nd – 46:36.52 – Mar del Plata, Argentina

20K Pan Am Cup
1999 – 8th – 1:37:49 - Poza Rica, Mexico

10K Pan Am Cup
1996 – 2nd – 49:10, Manaus, Brazil

10KGoodwill Games
1998 – 4th – 46:04:15 – NYC, USA
1994 – Unknown Place – 44:41.87, St. Petersburg, Russia

U.S. SENIOR NATIONAL CHAMPIONSHIPS

5K - Won 1 time
10K - Won 2 times

15K - Won 2 times
20K - Won 2 times

20K Olympic Trials - Won 1 time
Indoor 3K - Won 5 times

Birthday: March 19th, 1964
Hometown: Manchester, NH
Current Residence: Manchester, NH
College: University of New Hampshire

Personal Bests
10K: 45:36.92
20K: 1:32:55

Career Highlights
Gold Medal, 1998 20K Pan Am Cup

In 1994, while teaching a fitness-walking class, Joanne Dow met some members of the New England Walkers Club and became interested in race walking. Not long after, she attended a clinic presented by Martin Rudow, former Men's National Race Walking Team Coach. Rudow announced to the participants that those who walked fast but had horrible technique would get the most out of the class. Dow identified with this description completely.

During the clinic, Rudow told Dow she had the potential to race with the best women in the sport if she decided to train. That weekend she walked a relatively mediocre 10K (54+ minutes); in a very short time Dow would enter the World Cup trials and finish seventh.

Vastly improved and just two places from making the team to compete at Beijing, Dow wasn't disappointed. She had created a stir, and word spread about this newcomer to the race walking scene. She took the comments in the best possible light and felt more motivated than ever.

Dow next walked a sub-48 minute 10K at the National Invitational in Washington, DC. Finally comprehending her potential in the sport, she realized she needed a coach and fortunately found Mark Fenton. Sadly, her timing couldn't have been worse. Like many newbie race walkers, Dow had become great very quickly, but at a cost: she tore her hamstring, an injury requiring a lengthy recovery. After nearly a year—and without a good training base—Dow entered the 1996 Olympic Trials. Her tenth-place finish and berth to the U.S. Women's National Team could be considered a great success.

The following two years proved very fruitful as the combination of Fenton's guidance and Dow's hard work paid off. She achieved personal records, walking the 10K in 45:36 and the 20K in 1:33:27. Though proud of the times she walked, Dow feels even prouder of her ability to pull things together under pressure. Representing the U.S. at the Pan Am Cup in Miami, she was concerned about finishing the 20K distance in the heat. She believed the international contestants would be more adapted to the hot and humid conditions. When the field went out conservatively, Dow took the lead. As the race progressed she continued widening her gap, never looking back as she achieved her first international gold medal. She continued her winning ways at the Goodwill Games, winning the bronze medal at her first-ever track 10K and beating all the Americans and two Russians in the process.

By the end of 1999, Dow had raced many a good race. Too many, in fact. She had competed in five 20Ks in a span of six months. By the end, she was tired and her technique reflected it. At the World Championships the unimaginable happened: she DQ'd 6K into the race. Upset, she nonetheless learned a valuable lesson: racing a lot does not work! She came to understand the importance of recovering physically, psychologically, and emotionally.

While Dow regrouped for 2000 with the goal of making the Olympic team, an early season knee surgery unfortunately derailed her plans. Recovering from the surgery, she gave it her all but fell just short, finishing 4th. The finish qualified her for further international competition, but she opted out to rest and fully recover from her surgery.

After going through the motions in 2001, Dow came on strong in 2002, winning the U.S. 20K Nationals and competing on the World Cup Team. Unfortunately, difficulties in meeting with her coach forced her to look for a new one. She turned to her alma mater, the University of New Hampshire. She found a new coach and new outlook, just what she needed. At the time this book is going to press, she is the only American woman with the A standard required to qualify for the 2004 Olympic Games.

Dow says, "Race walking is just a piece of my life." Her priority is "being a wife and mom." Married to Tim Dow, she has two children: Hannah, born 1989, and Timmy, born 1992.

MAJOR INTERNATIONAL EXPERIENCE

20K World Championships
   2003 - 24th - 1:36.?? - Paris, France
   1999 - DQ – Seville, Spain

20K World Cup
   2002 - 50th - 1:41.00 - Torino, Italy
   1999 - 53rd - 1:38:08 - Mezidon, France

10K World Cup
   1997 – 61st - 47:23 - Podebrady, Czechoslovakia

20K Pan Am Games
   2003 - 3rd - 1:35.47 - Santo Domingo, Dominican Republic
   1999 - 5th - 1:36:35 – Winnipeg, Canada

20K Pan Am Cup
   1998 - 1st - 1:38:57 - Miami, USA

Goodwill Games
   1998 - 3rd – 45:36.92 - Moscow, Soviet Union

U.S. SENIOR NATIONAL CHAMPIONSHIPS

10K - Won 1 time   20K - Won 2 times   1 Hour – Won 1 time
                                                        Indoor 3K - Won 3 times

*Dow battling Michelle Rohl
at the 2003 U.S. 20K Nationals*

Dow in the heat of it at the 2003 Pan Am Games

Dow going at it alone at the 2003 Pan Am Games

*Dow racing alone at the
National Invitational in Washington, D.C.*

V I C T O R I A   H E R A Z O

Birthday: June 2nd, 1959
Hometown: West Palm Beach, FL
Curr. Residence: Las Vegas, NV
College: Animal Health Technology;
Pierce College

Career Highlights
Holds second-most women's National titles

Personal Bests
10K: 45:04
20K: 1:35:39

Victoria "Tori" Herazo and her 21 National titles are as much a product of her hard work and determination as of her coach, Jim Bentley. Bentley was there from the beginning. While out running in late 1987, Herazo noticed him coaching age-group athletes and thought she would like to help. Bentley quickly converted Herazo to race walking and the two formed a very successful bond.

Herazo mastered the technique of race walking quickly. She qualified for the 1988 L.A. Times 1-mile walk, finishing 5th. She was hooked. Bentley laid out his philosophy: Work on technique, break records, and win national titles. Herazo was a quick study. She continued to improve and qualified for the USATF Indoor Nationals. Not finishing top-three didn't bother the upstart; there were many many more races to come.

By 1989, Herazo began racing internationally, her first experience Swedish Walk Week. Finishing in the top three, her confidence continued to build. That same year on the domestic front, Herazo started racking up National titles, winning both the 5K and the 15K.

In 1991, Herazo went on the world tour. She returned to Swedish Walk Week, but it was no longer her final destination. Instead she traveled to Seville, Spain, for the World Indoor Championship. The many walkers on the small track required heats. Finishing 6th in her heat, Herazo was confused by the finals qualifying requirements. It wasn't until later that evening that she was informed she had another race to walk. After a rough first race, Herazo wasn't sure what was left for the final event. But with a gutsy effort and a few disqualifications in front of her, she finished 9th in the world.

Herazo continued to showcase her talent on the world stage, finishing 28th in the Outdoor World Championships later in the year. She remembers that she and teammate Debbie Lawrence were seeded far back in the pack. Not understanding why, Coach Bentley jokingly suggested it must have been their height. Lawrence and Herazo were amongst the tallest in the field.

Herazo, however, did not remain in the back of the pack for long. The following year, she started off strong and finished 3rd in a tough battle with the Mexicans at the Pan Am Cup. The race remains one of the greatest highlights of her career. Walking at altitude in a Mexican-friendly environment, Herazo snuck between the favored trio of Mexicans to capture the bronze medal.

Coach Bentley convinced Herazo that she had Olympic potential. The two moved to Las Vegas to train in the heat and acclimate to conditions Herazo would face and the Olympic Trials and Games. The move paid off as Herazo became one of three women to walk in the inaugural women's race walk at the 1992 Olympic

Games in Barcelona. The games were "such a thrill", because unlike her teammates Herazo was not an elite runner throughout college. She had never dreamed of being an Olympian. With a tough uphill climb for the last two kilometers, Herazo battled the heat, hills, and competitors to finish 28th.

The following Olympics were not as successful; unfortunately Herazo was disqualified late in the race. Not feeling "right" at the starting line, she never got in her grove.

After battling injuries in 2000 and failing to qualify for her 3rd Olympic Games, Herazo refocused on school. The many hours of training required to be competitive at an international level just didn't hold a high enough priority in Herazo's life. She is currently finishing her undergraduate requirements for admission into veterinary school. While school still takes up a great deal of time, she hopes to one day soon regain her form and race in some shorter National competitions. After all, she only needs one more title to match the Broddock's record holding the most women's National titles. She better watch her back though, because Michelle Rohl also competes for the same crown.

MAJOR INTERNATIONAL EXPERIENCE

10K Olympic Games
    1996 – DQ – Atlanta, USA
    1992 - 28th - 48:26 – Barcelona, Spain

10K World Championships
    1997 - DQ - Athens, Greece
    1991 - 27th - 47:10 – Tokyo, Japan

10K World Cup
    1997 - 50th - 46:31 – Podebrady, Czechoslovakia
    1995 - 41st - 46:25 – Beijing, China

10K Pan Am Games
    1992 -3rd - 47:42 - Guatemala City, Guatemala
10K Pan Am Cup
    1998 - 11th - 1:48:02 – Miami, USA
    1996 - DQ, - Manaus, Brazil
    1992 - 8th - 47:48 – Atlanta, USA

US SENIOR NATIONAL CHAMPIONSHIPS

5K - Won 7 times   1 Hour - Won 6 times   15K – Won 5 times
                                                          20K - Won 3 times

Herazo winning the 5K Nationals an amazing 7 times

S
U
S
A
N

A
R
M
E
N
T
A

Birthday: September 19, 1973
Hometown: Riverside, CA
Curr. Residence: Rialto, CA
College: Cal State, San Bernardino

Personal Bests
20K: 1:34:44
50K: 4:39:39

Career Highlights
50K National Champion and American Record-Holder

Susan Armenta became a race walker to escape injuries caused by running high school cross country. She was fortunate to go to one of the few colleges that provided both a race walking scholarship and excellent coaching: the University of Wisconsin, Parkside. She took to race walking quickly and in 1992 qualified for the World Junior Championships, where she placed 20th. As a freshman she also competed in the Olympic Trials race walk, finishing an impressive tenth place.

After starting her second year at Parkside, Armenta missed the warmth and sun of California and decided to head home and train on her own. While she found the California climate more enjoyable, it was not as conducive to successful race walking. Instead, Armenta excelled running cross country at her new school, California State Polytechnic, Pomona, where she was the top runner on her team.

In 1995, Armenta used her fitness level from running as a springboard to train more seriously for the race walk. Still coached by mail by Mike DeWitt, Armenta qualified for the World University Games and finished 17th. Her next goal was the 1996 Olympic Trials. Without training very seriously, Armenta managed to finish in 9th place. However, when the international race distance switched from 10K to 20K, Armenta decided to take training more seriously. She moved to the U.S. Olympic Training Center in Chula Vista, CA. Armenta enjoyed the distance more than the shorter events and at the 1998 Pan Am Cup Trials finished 3rd, her highest national finish to date.

Armenta repeated her third-place finish at Nationals in 1999 to qualify for the World Championships. There she thought she had a great race, despite very hot conditions. She finished as the top American, 31st overall.

After a disappointing finish at the 2000 Olympic Trials, Armenta planned to retire from race walking. But in 2001, USATF recognized the 50km race walk championship for women, motivating Armenta to attempt the new distance. Her efforts were successful, as she established the American record of 4:49:57, bettering her performance the following year with a time of 4:39:39.

Armenta decided to continue training for the 20K race at the 2004 Olympics, while attending school full-time. She recently graduated from Cal State, San Bernardino's Kinesiology program (December 2003) and will attend graduate school in Exercise Physiology there.

MAJOR INTERNATIONAL EXPERIENCE

20K World Championships
    1999 - 31st - 1:40:20 – Seville, Spain

20K World Cup
    2002 - 54th - 1:42:14 - Torino, Italy

20K Pan Am Cup
2003 - 11th - 1:49:03 - Chula Vista, USA
2000 - 10th - 1:39:55 - Poza Rica, Mexico
1998 - 6th - 1:44:58 - Miami, USA

U.S. SENIOR NATIONAL CHAMPIONSHIPS

40 - Won 1 time

50K - Won 2 times

Susan Armenta, our cover girl, in the 2002 1 Hour / 2 Hour Championships

Armenta practicing at the US Olympic Training Center in Chula Vista, California

CURT CLAUSEN

Birthday: October 9, 1967
Hometown: Stevens Point, WI
Current Residence: Chula Vista, CA
College: Duke University

Personal Bests
20K: 1:23:34
50K: 3:48:04

Career Highlights
1999 World Championships 50K bronze medallist
3-Time Olympian, Trials winner in 2000 & 2004 50K

Curt Clausen has been race walking since he was 12 years old. Participating in the Stevens Point, WI, summer track and field program, Clausen was first introduced to the race walk in the summer of 1980.

Growing up, Clausen found the proximity of the University of Wisconsin at Stevens Point provided many fine race walking role models. He originally competed in distance running, but a demonstration by NAIA Nationals champ Jeff Ellis of Steven Point sparked his interest in walking. The following summer session, Clausen began race walk training with Coach Dave Bachman. Balancing running and race walking each summer, he experienced little success.

This pattern continued until Clausen, 17, headed for the 1985 Junior Nationals. His race plan was to stick with Tony Englehart, the 1984 champ. Unfortunately, Englehart wasn't ready to duplicate his previous feat and Clausen found himself too far behind to challenge for the lead.

A few months later, Clausen put it all together. Instead of running cross-country and track as he had in previous years, he decided to concentrate solely on race walking for his senior year. His focus paid off as he led the Junior squad at the North America's Cup to an overall U.S. Team Championship.

His goal was to win the Junior Nationals and qualify for the World Junior Championships in Greece, which is exactly what he did! After high school, he enrolled at Duke University, where he continued walking, training hard only three to four months a year. Although few people remember it, Clausen won the Intermediate Age Group Championships as a freshman. The ill-fated race was sparsely attended. I should know, I was the only other race walker.

In 1988 Clausen entered his first Olympic Trials and finished the 50K in 15th place. Shortly afterwards he won his first National title at the 40K National Championships. But this successful experience was not enough to motivate Clausen to stop dabbling and focus on race walking. For the next few years he raced the indoor circuit, became fit by June, raced at Nationals and participated in the U.S. Olympic Festival.

Unlike many New Year's resolutions that go by the wayside, Clausen's 1995 commitment to dedicate himself to race walking proved true. At first he found it tough, but by June he finished 5th at Nationals. For more than a year preceding the 1996 Olympic Trials, Clausen trained continuously for the first time in his life, replacing running workouts with a lot more race walking.

By March 1996, Clausen had attained the initial step—on his first attempt—by meeting the time standard required to participate in the Olympic Games at the National Invitational in Washington, D.C. With the standard out of the way, all he

On his way to becoming a 3- time Olympian

157

needed to do was win the Olympic Trials. He remained in North Carolina to acclimate to the heat and practiced on the Atlanta racecourse where the Trials would be held. He developed his race plan and a related mental image. Realizing that at one time or another he had beaten all top U.S. race walkers, including the #1 ranked Allen James, Clausen set his sights on training harder to achieve this goal. And beat James he did, winning the 1996 20K Olympic Trials and making the Olympic team.

Clausen's first Olympic experience was disappointing. Frankly, he got his ass kicked. The reason? While Clausen trained for the Olympic Games, he worked 40 to 60 hours weekly and coached himself. Meanwhile, other Olympic athletes trained full time with the guidance of a coach.

Clausen wanted to return to the Olympics, and not as an *also walked*. He wanted to know that he had tried everything he could to achieve all he could, so he packed up and moved to Chula Vista, California, home of a new Olympic Training Center. In 1999, Clausen had three quality breakthroughs. Under Coach Bhodan Bulakowski, he developed a strong base. Coach Enrique Pena tweaked it to perfection. At the 35K mark of the 50K Nationals, he was on pace to walk 4:00. In the final 15K, he made up six minutes to finish in 3:54.

Brimming with confidence, Clausen excelled. Walking a 19-and change 5K the day before a 2:14 30K workout, Clausen felt he was ready for the World Cup, but then the ceiling caved in. Clausen felt his entire body was broken down. With only two weeks to the World Cup, he decided to take five days off to recover. With low expectations, Clausen started the race with the second pack, walking a surprising time of 3:48 and finishing 11th.

Next Clausen set his sites for the World Championships. His plan from the start was to beat Robert Korzeniowski, who apparently had made a derogatory comment to Clausen's coach Bulakowski at a previous race. Clausen matched Korzeniowski stride for stride until the unexpected happened: Korzeniowski DQ'd at 37.5K. Without a game plan, Clausen ground it down, making sure no one caught him. Walking a 3:50:50 in 106-degree heat, Clausen crossed the line fourth, feeling "the most dead" he had ever been. Justly, he was eventually awarded the bronze medal when another top finisher failed a drug test.

Clausen also qualified for the 2000 Olympics. Unfortunately, after mid-July knee surgery, he couldn't walk a step until eight weeks before his race. Needless to say, he was not happy with his results. He finished 22nd: an improvement over 1996, but not where he wanted to be.

Clausen leading the pack at the 2002 2-Hour Championships

In 2001 Clausen returned to the World Championships, finishing 7th. After his return to top-ten status internationally, his next two years proved disappointing, with a series of setbacks hampering his progress. Bronchitis just before the World Cup, a disqualification at the World Championships, and a controversial disqualification 48K into the Pan Am Cup have kept Clausen hungry.

Now, in 2004, Clausen has his sight set on one last attempt at an Olympic medal. The Olympics will be back in Greece, where he has competed more than once. He looks to the heat and a tough course as an advantage: the *equalizer,* as he puts it.

Clausen has already hit the first milestone on his 2004 quest for Olympic glory. In the 50K Trials race, he battled early stomach problems and stiff competition. The elder statesman of our sport overcame it all, walked negative splits, and qualified for the Olympic Games with a time of 3:58:24.

MAJOR INTERNATIONAL EXPERIENCE

20K Olympic Games
  1996 – 50th - 1:31:38 – Atlanta, USA

50K Olympic Games
  2004 – TBD – Athens, Greece
  2000 – 22nd - 3:58:39 – Sydney, Australia

50K World Championships
  2003 – DQ – Paris, France
  2001 – 7th - 3:50:46 – Edmonton, Canada
  1999 – 3rd - 3:50:55 – Seville, Spain

20K World Championships
  1997 – 34th - 1:32:05 – Athens, Greece

50K World Cup
  2002 – DQ - Torino, Italy
  1999 – 11th – 3:48:04 – Mezidon, France

20K World Cup
  1997 – 60th – 1:24:41 - Podebrady, Czechoslovakia

20K Pan Am Games
  1999 – 6th – 1:23:39 - Winnipeg, Canada

20K Pan Am Cup
  2003 – 15th - 1:30:45 - Chula Vista, USA
  2000 – 12th – 1:29:59 – Poza Rica, Mexico
  1998 – 10th - 1:37:11 - Miami, USA
  1996 – DQ – Manaus, Brazil

50K Pan Am Cup
  2003 – DNF – Tijuana, Mexico
  2001 – DQ - Cuenca, Ecuador -
  (while leading the race @ 47 km)

U.S. SENIOR NATIONAL CHAMPIONSHIPS

5K - Won 3 times
10K - Won 5 times
15K - Won 1 time

20K - Won 4 times
30K - Won 2 times
40K - Won 3 times

50K - Won 6 times
2 Hours - Won 1 time
20K Olympic Trials - Won 1 time
50K Olympic Trials - Won 2 times

Clausen cruising at the 10K Nationals

*Refueling at the
2004 50K Olympic Trials*

*Clausen pulling away at the
2002 2-Hour Championships*

TIM SEAMAN

Birthday: May 14, 1972
Hometown: North Babylon, NY
Current Residence: Chula Vista, CA
College: University of Wisconsin-Parkside

Personal Bests
20K: 1:23:40
50K: 4:05:35

Career Highlights
3-time U.S. 20K Champion
6-time U.S. Indoor Champion

Seaman began his track career as a miler on his high school team. His coach, however, soon realized he could score more points for the team by excelling at the race walk event. As a junior in high school, Seaman initially disliked the idea of race walking, but grew more fond of it as he became more successful.

The summer after his senior year, Seaman won the Junior National title. Unfortunately, however, his time did not qualify him for the World Junior Championships, and instead the 2nd-place National finisher Philip Dunn made the cut. Refusing to let this setback slow him down, Seaman answered Dunn's performance with one of his own, breaking the long-standing Junior 10K record set by Tim Lewis while walking 44:25 on the road a few months later.

Success followed Seaman to the University of Wisconsin-Parkside, where he set three more Junior National records. Returning to the Junior Nationals after his freshman year, he won, walking faster than the qualifying time standard for the World Junior Championships. Unfortunately for Seaman, they were not held that year. Instead, Seaman raced at the Junior Pan American Games, where he finished 5th—no small task with the likes of future Olympic Gold Medallist Jefferson Perez atop the podium.

While on a college scholarship, Seaman became the first four-time NAIA race walk champion. Earning a degree in political science, he put his financial pursuits on hold to focus on his Olympic quest. He moved to Georgia, where his hard work under coach Bhodan Bulakowski cut more than five minutes off his 20K time within one year. With financial support limited, Seaman ate peanut butter and jelly for both lunch and dinner while he trained. Unfortunately, the sacrifice was not enough to make the 1996 Olympic Team. But Seaman had caught Olympic fever.

Recognizing the benefits provided by a training group, Seaman and training partner Andrew Hermann spearheaded the formation of the ARCO Olympic Training Center Residency Program. Seaman moved to Southern California to train at the Center while pursuing his Master's degree in International Relations.

In October 1998, Seaman had surgery to solve lower abdominal pain that had plagued him for sixteen months. While the surgery at first seemed successful, after eleven months the symptoms returned. In November 1999 Seaman again had surgery in Milwaukee, where Dr. Richard Cattey discovered five hernias in his lower abdomen. With his health problems finally behind him and new coach Enrique Pena in residence at ARCO, Seaman reached his Olympic dreams in 2000 when he won the U.S. Olympic Trials, turning in a meet-record performance.

After competing in the Olympics, Seaman returned to the U.S. to marry Leticia Felix Reyna, whom he had met at Mexican Walk Week in 1997.

Currently, Seaman is working towards his second Olympic berth. To keep up on the latest Seaman happenings, check out his web site at http://www.TimSeaman.com.

Seaman at the 2004 50K Olympic Trials

MAJOR INTERNATIONAL EXPERIENCE

20K Olympic Games
2000 – 40th – 1:30:32

20K World Championships
2001 – DQ – Edmonton, Canada
1999 – 24th – 1:35:58 – Seville, Spain

20K World Cup
1999 – 35th – 1:27:20 – Mezidon, France
1997 – 103rd – 1:31:12 – Podebrady, Czechoslovakia

50K World Cup
2002 – DNF – Torino, Italy

20K Pan Am Games
1999 – 9th – 1:28:28 – Winnipeg, Canada

20K Pan Am Cup
2003 – 4th – 1:25:24 – Chula Vista, USA
2000 – DNF – Poza Rica, Mexico
1996 – 13th – 1:41:41 – Manaus, Brazil

US SENIOR NATIONAL CHAMPIONSHIPS

5K - Won 1 time
15K - Won 2 times
20K - Won 3 times

30K - Won 1 time
40K - Won 1 time

20K Olympic Trials - Won 1 time
Indoor 5K - Won 7 times

Seaman at the 2002
2-Hour National Championships

Seaman on his way to finishing 2nd
in the 2004 50K Olympic Trials

Seaman out for a stroll during the
2003 50K Nationals

Birthday: April 14, 1964
Hometown: Seattle, WA
Curr. Residence: Sanborn, NY
College: Western Washingtion University

Personal Bests
20K: 1:24:26.9
50K: 3:55:39

Career Highlights
2-Time Olympian; Former 50K National Record Holder

Allen James was exposed to race walking early, first learning the technique at the age of ten but not actually racing for another two years. When his coach asked him to race the 800-meter race walk at a meet, he won his division, but lost to two girls from an older age group. While not exactly a politically correct motivation, losing to girls was not something James wanted to happen again.

In high school James skipped track to concentrate on cross country, soccer, and swimming. Attending Western Washington University, he quickly became a thorn in the University of Wisconsin – Parkside's plans for dominance. By the time James graduated from Western Washington University in 1987, he was a four time All-American. Armed with a degree in Business Administration, James went to work for Athletes in Action and became a player on the U.S. walk scene. In 1990 he broke into the top-10 rankings for the U.S. at 20K, holding the number one spot from 1992 until his retirement from full-time training. When James decided to finally give the 50K walk a try back in 1994, he went after the 31 miles-plus race in a big way. Speeding up over the second half of the Palo Alto, California race, he clocked 3:55:39, taking more than a minute off the American record set by Marco Evoniuk six years earlier.

For the first time since Tim Lewis, excitement about U.S. race walking grew. James followed with National titles at both Olympic distances: 20K and 50K. In 1995, he broke the four-hour barrier again with his 3:59:27 for 6th at the Pan American Games. Hopes soared for the U.S. to contend at the 1996 Olympics in Atlanta. Who would have a better advantage than James, who was nearby, training in the oppressive heat and humidity?

After years spent training to race the 50K at peak fitness in the searing heat of Atlanta, James won the Trials with the fastest U.S. time of the year. However, the best laid plans of mice and men often go astray. On August 2nd, the heat in Atlanta lifted.

Hoping for a hot day, James instead received what most athletes consider a gift: an unusually cool day. The race was a very fast one, but James had prepared for a battle in the heat. Finishing 24th with a time of 4:01:18—a solid performance—he still wished he could do better. Shortly afterwards, James went into "semi-retirement." He now considers walking a hobby that helps keep him in shape. His so-called retirement includes a few more Millrose Games titles, several fine finishes at national championship races, and the Penn Relays. Training as time allows, he averages less than 20 miles per week.

James works for the New York State Office of Parks, Recreation, and Historic Preservation, where he recently accepted a transfer to become the Director of Marketing and Special Events at Niagara Falls State Park and the Niagara Region. He and his wife Laura have three children: Teisha, age 12; Denae, 8; and Axel, 6.

MAJOR INTERNATIONAL EXPERIENCE

20K Olympic Games
> 1992 – 30th – 1:35:12 – Barcelona, Spain

50K Olympic Games
> 1996 – 24th – 4:01:18 – Atlanta, USA

20K World Championships
> 1993 – 17th – 1:26:53 – Stuttgart, Germany

50K World Championships
> 1995 – DNF – Goteborg, Germany

20K World Cup
> 1995 – 40th – 1:25:54 – Beijing, China
> 1993 – 47th – 1:32:24 – Monterrey, Mexico
> 1991 – 67th – 1:30:25 – San Jose, USA

50K Pan Am Games
> 1995 – 6th – 3:59:27 – Mar del Plata, Argentina

20K Pan Am Games
> 1995 – DNF – Mar del Plata, Argentina

20K Pan Am Cup
> 1996 – 6th – 1:34:46 – Manaus, Brazil
> 1994 – 14th – 1:30:01 – Atlanta, USA
> 1992 – DNF – Guatemala City, Guatemala

U.S. SENIOR NATIONAL CHAMPIONSHIPS

15K - Won 1 time	30K - Won 1 time	20K Olympic Trials - Won 1 time
20K - Won 4 times	50K - Won 3 times	50K Olympic Trials - Won 1 time
		Indoor 5K - Won 4 times

James strutting it at the Penn Relays

James at the 10K Nationals

James on his way to winning the 20K Nationals in 1995

Birthday: June 12, 1971   Personal Bests
Hometown: Eugene, OR   20K: 1:26:36
Current Residence: San Diego, CA   50K: 3:56:13
College: Carleton University

Career Highlights
2001 U.S. 50K Champion
Bronze Medal, 1999 Pan American Games 50K

Like many race walkers, Philip Dunn happened upon the sport by accident. When Dunn was 10 years old he entered the Junior Olympics 1500 meter run. Later he saw on the schedule the 1500 meter race walk. Young Dunn was confused. It was the same distance he had just run; why would they be having another run? So, his dad explained and showed him what little he knew about race walking. Dunn jumped into the race and won it. As a 10 year old, he thought that was cool. Dunn was encouraged to participate in the state meet, and came in 3rd. His immediate success was not enough to pull Dunn from running, but he added race walking to his routine.

Dunn stepped up to the regional, and then eventually went to Nationals in Provo, Utah, where he finished 2nd to another walker from Oregon. In Dunn's third and fourth years at the Junior Olympics, he achieved the gold.

In 1989 Dunn graduated to the next level and competed in the Junior Nationals. His second year at the Junior Nationals he placed second behind Tim Seaman. This didn't sit well with Dunn, motivating him to push for a qualifying time for the World Junior Championships, something neither Seaman nor Dunn had accomplished previously. After a few attempts Dunn qualified for the World Juniors, walking a 44:38, well under the 45:00 time that was required. Still on a high from qualifying, He raced a few days later and set an American Junior 5K record with a time of 21:14. Dunn raced in the World Juniors in Bulgaria, finishing 16th in a field that included three future Senior world champions.

Dunn entered college in 1989 and while he never really stopped thinking about race walking, he didn't do much walking until he entered a study abroad program in Dublin, Ireland. He competed in a few races there, but his focus was on running track and cross country while in college. Dunn ran a 4:00 1500M, and was a member of a Div III cross country team that qualified for the Nationals.

By the summer of 1993, Dunn's interest in race walking reemerged when he moved to Lake Placid to train with Bob Ryan. Dunn was part of a small group of up and coming race walkers that included the likes of Andrew Herman, Will Van Axen, Melissa Baker, Yariv Pomeranz, and Elliot Taub. Claiming he would never walk a 50K, Dunn was coerced when on the way to Lake Placid he and Hermann were invited to compete in the 50K at the U.S. Olympic Festival. They headed for San Antonio and Dunn finished in a time of 4:52 with Hermann just a few minutes back.

Dunn had enough of the 50K and switched back to training for the 20K. He figured he would give race walking his all for one year, achieving a 4th place finish at the Nationals in Knoxville. With the Olympics coming up in 1996, Dunn extended his commitment and followed his coach to Virginia. While not qualifying for the Olympics, he finished a respectable 6th place at the Trials.

In 1997 he regrouped, moving out to the ARCO Olympic Training Center to train for the 2000 Trials. On a steady trajectory upward on the American and world race walking scene, Dunn broke through in 2000 by making his first Olympic team in the 50 km. When Dunn is asked how he qualified for the Olympic Team, he replies, "Count to 7." This is because in the 4-hour race to quality for the team, he snuck under the standard by only 7 seconds.

Since then he has steadily improved, winning the 2001 U.S. 50km title and finishing as the top U.S. walker at the 2002 World Cup with a personal best of 3:56:13. He ended the season with his first-ever #1 U.S. ranking.

Dunn's family is a source of inspiration and support. His twin brother, Malcom, also walked and ran competitively, and is now a cross country and track coach. His mother competes in marathons and his father races sailboats. Dunn married his college sweetheart, Liz Flynn, on September 22, 2001 in Alexandria, Va. Together they enjoy traveling, kayaking, hiking, snorkeling, reading and visits to the San Diego Zoo. Dunn graduated cum laude and received his B.A. degree in English from Carleton in 1993.

MAJOR INTERNATIONAL EXPERIENCE

50K Olympic Games
2000 – 28th – 4:03:05 – Sydney, Australia

20K World Cup
1997 - 76th - 1:26:36 – Podebrady, Czechoslovakia
1995 – 80th - 1:35:40 – Beijing, China

50K World Cup
2002 – 13th – 3:56:13 – Torino, Italy
1999 – 45th – 3:59:53 – Mezidon, France

50K Pan Am Games
1999 – 3rd – 4:13:45 – Winnipeg, Canada

20K Pan Am Cup
2001 – 11th – 1:38:20 – Cuenca, Ecuado
2000 – 19th – 1:35:10 – Poza Rica, Mexico

50K Pan Am Cup
2003 - 4th – 4:15:01 – Tijuana, Mexico
1998 – 4th - 4:25:30 – Miami, USA

U.S. SENIOR NATIONAL CHAMPIONSHIPS

25K - Won 2 times   2 hour - Won 1 time   40K - Won 1 time
                                                  50K - Won 1 time

Dunn cruising at the
2003 2 Hour Nationals

Dunn gutting it out late in the 2004
50K Olympic Trials

Dunn training on the track at the
ARCO Olympic Training Center

H E R M   N E L S O N

Birthday: September 20th, 1961
Hometown: Seattle, WA
Current Residence: Escondido, CA
College: Western Washington University

Personal Bests
20K: 1:26:41
50K: 3:59:41

Career Highlights
2-Time Olympian

Two-time Olympian Herm Nelson claims he was forced into race walking in 1986 by his Western Washington University coach. Nelson was a man without an event, bested by teammates at both his specialties, the steeplechase and marathon. His coach, eager to replace the points that he would lose when team member Allen James graduated, picked an event for Nelson. The coach made a wise choice.

Graduating college in August 1987 and searching for a job, Nelson devoted his efforts to training for the upcoming 50K Olympic Trials. He placed 5th, missing the team by one spot with a time of 4:15:51 as Jim Heiring, 4th place, elected to compete in the 20K. This small taste of Olympic glory was enough for Nelson to commit to seriously training for the 1992 Games.

Nelson made 1989 his breakout year. Competing and racing well at both the World Cup and the USSR National Championships in Leningrad, he recorded personal bests for both races. He then completed the hat trick by breaking not only his personal best again, but also the American Record for the track 50K with a time of 4:04:24.

After competing so strongly in 1989, Nelson felt his body take the toll. He spent most of 1990 recuperating from a back injury sustained at the end of the previous year. Recovering by 1991, Nelson began the long preparation for the upcoming 50K Olympic Trials. By 1992 the International Olympic Committee had added the qualifying standard requirements. Nelson squeaked by. He finished 2nd at the trials with a time of 4:04:39, meeting the A standard by 21 seconds in the process. Unfortunately, he did not fare well at the Olympic Games, finishing 32nd out of 45 starters and 32 finishers.

During the Games, Nelson was bothered by gall bladder problems that had been coming on for some time. He had planned to retire after his race, but finishing last left a bad taste in his mouth. Resolute, he committed to training for another four years. Wanting to tear it up on the home turf, he qualified again in 1996 with an improved time of 3:59:41, but had another disappointing experience. He was disqualified.

Nelson felt ready to hang up his shoes for good when he was given advice by four-time Olympian Abdi Bile from Somalia. Bile said, "If you feel you still can do it and want to do it, don't give up." Taking the advice to heart, Nelson planned to go for it in 2000.

Struggling with a groin injury after the Olympics Games in 1996, Nelson never fully regained his top form. Realizing his competitive career was almost done, he wanted to complete his race walking career on a high note, so he headed north for the Canadian 50K National Championship. End on high note he did, winning the race in 4:33, although they could not give him the title.

Nelson knew that with a final 50K win under his belt, it was time to move on. Affectionately called "The Bear" for his hibernation-like napping, he dusted off his physics degree and is now a process engineer in Laser Optics for Mellisgriot Corporation in Carlsbad, California. He still hears the call of race walking and apparently has not completely escaped its grasp. Rumor has it he may emerge from his cave for the 10K Penn Relays race walk this year.

MAJOR INTERNATIONAL EXPERIENCE

50K Olympic Games
    1996 – DQ - Atlanta, USA
    1992 - 32nd - 4:25:48 - Barcelona, Spain

50K World Championships
    1993 - 31st - 4:21:08 – Stuttgart, Germany

50K World Cup
    1993 - 51st - 4:27:44 - Monterrey, Mexico
    1989 - 41st - 4:12:24 - L'Hospitalet, Spain

50K Pan Am Games
    1997 – DNF - Manaus, Brazil

50K Pan Am Cup
    1992 - 11th - 4:32:42 - Guatemala City, Guatemala
    1988 – 5th – 4:15:01 – Mar del Plata, Argentina

U.S. SENIOR NATIONAL CHAMPIONSHIPS

2 Hour - Won 2 times

30K - Won 1 time

Herm Nelson battling Carl Schueler at the 1992 50K Olympic Trials

Nelson getting some fluids and a bath from teammate Sara Standley at the 50K World Cup in 1993

Nelson in the heat of it at the 50K World Cup in 1993

Herm Nelson and Jonathon Matthews at the 1994 50K Nationals

DEBBIE VAN ORDEN

Debbie Van Orden led an active life before finding race walking. She combined running, swimming, and riding her bike to stay in shape. Even though race walking great and future husband Carl Schueler worked on the floor where she worked, it took a walking/running event sponsored by Rockport for Van Orden to first gain entry to race walking.

After dabbling in the sport for a few years, she became serious in 1990 when Schueler started coaching her. She had a real breakthrough at Nationals, walking 48:29 to qualify for the Pan Am Cup team.

With a bit of international experience under her belt, she set her sites on the Olympics. Finishing 4th at the 1992 Trials, she felt excited just to have placed so well. In 1996, however, she focused on making the team. Finishing 4th again was a huge disappointment, but Van Orden keeps things in perspective. From the day she started race walking, she loved everything about it. "You have to love the process," she says, "love working out and love racing." The end product was not what it was about. Van Orden can teach us all this valuable lesson.

JONATHAN MATHEWS

Jonathan Matthews arrived on the national race walking scene in 1992 at the age of 36, an experienced athlete with competitive running and National Team bicycle racing careers. Self coached, from 1992 to 2000 he made himself a strong presence at the national level. Aside from an injury-hampered 1996 season, each year Matthews placed in the top 3 at the U.S. National Championships for at least one--and often both—Olympic-distance walks for men, 20 Kilometers and 50 Kilometers.

During this eight-year period he won 3 National Championships and set 4 American Records—the fastest American ever at 3,000 meters, 5,000 meters, 1 hour on the track, and 5K on the road—and 22 Master's American Records. Representing the U.S. in international competition, Matthews has been the top American finisher in his event at the Pan American Race Walking Cup (twice), the World Cup of race walking, and the World Athletics Championships. He is also a two-time Olympic Festival champion. In 1993 Jonathan won USA Track and Field's Ron Zinn Award, recognizing him as the top American race walker for the year at 50 kilometers. In 1996 and 1999, Jonathan received USA Track & Field's Master Race Walker of the Year award.

DAVE MCGOVERN

What can we say about Dave McGovern? From his trademark Mickey Mouse sunglasses to his hurling at the side of the road, Dave McGovern is a landmark in our sport.

Well known for his longevity at the top of American race walking, McGovern is equally recognized for his coaching abilities, writing, and traveling race walking clinics.

As an elite athlete, McGovern peaked in 1996 when he walked a 1:24:27 20K, to rank as the 6th-fastest 20K race walker in U.S. history. In all, he amassed 11 national records and has been on the elite circuit for over 20 years.

McGovern is still going strong. He recently finished 7th at the 2004 50K Olympic Trials with a time of 4:37:30.

RACE WALKING BEYOND 2000

Race walking in the new millennium contrasts sharply with race walking just a few decades ago. With sponsorships and opportunities at an all-time high in the 1980s, we might expect by the new millennium that American race walking would have flourished and our athletes would be on par with the best represented countries in the world. Unfortunately, with the exception of a few hopefuls, this is far from the case.

While the upper echelon of American race walking remains comparable to athletes of the 1980s and 1990s, the U.S. currently has only about one third as many elite race walkers at the top ranks as it did twenty years ago. For many years, standards to qualify for the National and Olympic Trials got faster. Then they reversed. Today, they are slower than they were in the 1980s.

The one bright spot is the training group at the Arco Olympic Training Center in Chula Vista, California. Led by internationally renowned race walking coach Enrique Pena, a group of dedicated athletes strives to reach excellence in international competitions. Curt Clausen leads the group with a bronze medal at the 1999 World Championships. Training partner Philip Dunn had similar success at the 1999 Pan Am Games. While neither athlete has repeated his peak performance, they both look to the 2004 season to regain international acclaim. Following in their footsteps are Tim Seaman, John Nunn, and Sean Albert. All have dedicated their lives to full-time training and hope for big breakthroughs this year.

The problem is that beyond these few dedicated athletes and a scattered representation of women across the country, there is no depth. The sport is dying because it's not available to the young. The removal of the race walk as a scoring event in the New York High School program has finally taken its toll. The last products of that program are all but gone. Thanks to the efforts of Tom Eastler, Maine now has the race walk as a high school event. Indeed, Ben Shorey, one of our top prospects, is a product of that program. Time will tell if a state as thinly populated as Maine can produce enough race walkers to refill the ranks of our elite.

So is all doom and gloom? Certainly not. As we move forth, we must focus our energies at providing opportunities for young race walkers. The key remains as it always has: we need a movement to get the race walk included in the NCAA. With the walk included, many more top athletes will gravitate to the sport.

In lieu of achieving a spot in the NCAA's, we need our Master's movement to produce younger walkers. For many reasons, our sport enjoys a great number of Master's- level race walkers in the U.S. To produce more young walkers, we must leverage that infrastructure.

Leadership at the top has been sparse. The last U.S. Race Walking Chair of USATF, Dan Pierce, resigned in the middle of his term. Picking up the pieces, Vince Peters has taken over the top spot. We hope his leadership will help. In the meantime, organizations like NARI and RWI have filled the void. Both have provided the funds lacking from USATF to sponsor events and athletes.

Hopefully, with the hard work and dedication of athletes, coaches, and organizational leaders, American race walking will improve to rank among the best in the world.

Best of the Best. Our future, the 2002 World Cup Team.

Birthday: November 4th, 1979
Hometown: Greendale, WI
Current Residence: Cudahy, WI
College: University of Wisconsin-Parkside

Personal Bests
20K: 1:35:59

Career Highlights
4th place - Pan Am Games, 2003
Ranked #2 in the U.S. in the 20K, 2001

When Amber Antonia headed to college she had no interest in race walking. She was quite an accomplished runner and intended to run cross country and track during her tenure at the University of Wisconsin - Parkside. Unfortunately, she developed a stress fracture in her foot, so she took up race walking to stay in shape. She hopped in a 1500M race and finished 2nd in a little over 7 minutes.

Upon the suggestion of her coach, Antonia decided to try to qualify for the 2000 Olympic Trials in the 20K race walk. At the last minute she entered a 20K with other would-be qualifiers. Antonia walked a minute and change under the 1:48 standard required to enter the Trials, where she competed without any intention of making the Olympic team. She remembers it was "the coolest thing just being there."

The experience inspired her to continue pursuing race walking. Antonia combined race walking and running in the following year, with great success at both. She returned to the NAIA Indoor Nationals and won the 3K race walk. Her season continued with a unique double at the Penn Relays. She placed 3rd in the 5K race walk and ran the 10K with a PR of 36:28.

Antonia refocused on race walking. As a warm up for the 20K nationals, she competed at the National 15K and finished 4th. Realizing that training alone was not the best way to go, she moved out to the Olympic Training Center in Chula Vista, CA. The move paid off as Antonia finished 2nd at the 20K Nationals with a time of 1:36:37. She was in a position to qualify for World Champions, but had not met the required A standard.

The following season did not fare too well for Antonia's running career. Fortunately for Antonia, when running wasn't going so well, it seemed her walking was. Later that year, she set a meet record on her way to winning the NAIA Indoors Nationals with a time of 13:56.06. Shortly afterwards, she improved her time to 13:15 with a 2nd-place finish at the USATF Indoor Nationals. Antonia's success continued outdoors, where she won the NAIA Championships, the Penn Relays, and the 15K USATF Nationals. Her success continued with an excellent showing at the 20K Nationals with a time of 1:35:59. The 3rd-place finish qualified Antonia for the World Cup.

Unfortunately, her season would take a turn for the worst when a month before the World Cup she injured her shin. After having to drop out of the World Cup at 8K, Antonia didn't start training again until April of 2003. "It super sucked," remembers Antonia. She moved back to the Olympic Training Center and was amazed to take 4th at Nationals with a time of 1:39:55. She finished her season racing at the Pan Am Games, where she finished 8th with a time of 1:42:40. Antonia recalls that "it was nice and hot there too." She is now focused on achieving the A standard required to qualify for the 2004 Olympic Games.

K E
E A
V S
I T
N L
  E
  R

Birthday: October 14, 1977   Personal Bests
Hometown: Farmington, ME   20K: 1:22:25
Current Residence: Fort Collins, CO
College: U.S. Air Force Academy

Career Highlights
2nd Fastest 20K time in U.S. History
Achieved the A standard for the 2004 Olympic Team

Kevin Eastler started race walking at the age of nine, following in the footsteps of his older sister, Gretchen. He earned many age group records and All-American titles before entering the U.S. Air Force Academy in the summer of 1995.

Eastler won the 10K U.S. Junior Nationals in 1996 with a time of 47:57. He also qualified for the U.S. vs. Canada dual meet and led the Juniors to victory. While walking an excellent race, he lost to me for the second time in a row. Eastler is looking for a rematch, so I have challenged him to a winner-take-all 1-mile race 10 minutes after the 2004 20K Olympic Trials. Think he'll take up the challenge?

During his first three years at the academy, Eastler's race walking took a back seat to his academics and cross-country skiing. However, upon reaching his senior year, he started training to race walk seriously, qualifying for the World Cup by finishing 5th at Nationals. Finishing 71st at the World Cup marked his first international experience at the Senior level. The team leader was veteran race walker Carl Schueler, who began coaching Eastler in the fall of 1998.

Eastler graduated with a Bachelor's of Science degree in Mechanical Engineering and a commission as 2nd Lieutenant in the Air Force. He spent his first assignment with the World Class Athlete Program at Chula Vista. Training full-time for the 2000 Olympics, he finished in second place at the Trials but was denied a spot on the Olympic Team as he failed to meet the required time standard.

Recovering from injuries sustained in 2000, Eastler stopped race walking for over a year until he was reassigned to F. E. Warren Air Force Base in Cheyenne, Wyoming. Training was difficult. He worked in a very confined space for 24 hours or longer, training before he went on duty or after. While his father Tom would like us to believe he trained in the missile silo, Eastler trained on the track or road.

In 2003, now a Captain, Eastler recorded the second-fastest time in American 20K history and is the only walker so far to achieve the qualifying standard required to make the 2004 20K Men's Olympic Team. Back in the World Class Athlete Program, he currently trains full time for a hopeful berth on the Olympic Team.

The U.S. Air Force recognized Eastler's excellence in 2003 when they named him Male Athlete of the Year.

ANNE FAVOLISE

Anne Favolise is one of America's top collegiate race walkers. Starting in the Maine high school program, Favolise began seriously training for race walking when her high school added it to their track and field program during her sophomore year. Excelling early, Favolise traveled quite a bit to race against America's best at the National Scholastic Championships, Junior Olympics, Penn Relays, and U.S. Junior Nationals.

By her freshman year at the University of Wisconsin – Parkside, she had begun to break into the Senior ranks. She placed 5th at the U.S. 3K Indoor Nationals and has since progressed to the U.S. 20K Outdoor Nationals. Favolise's future looks bright; she may well be America's hope for the 2008 Olympics.

JOHN NUNN

In grade school, your teacher tells you that the shortest path between two points is a straight line. John Nunn took his time learning that lesson. Nunn first learned to race walk as a child, but as with many of his fleeting interests, he stopped pursuing the sport early. Instead, he became a very accomplished runner in high school and was offered a race walking scholarship to the University of Wisconsin - Parkside. Having no real competitive experience in race walking, he was expected to contend with the best collegiate athletes in America.

After a year of walking for Parkside, Nunn enjoyed great success and won the U.S. 10K Junior Nationals. However, he would not continue on his collegiate career. Instead, in the fall of 1997 he fulfilled one of his religious beliefs by participating in a two-year mission for the Church of Jesus Christ of Latter-day Saints. As soon as his mission ended, Nunn moved to the Philadelphia area where he trained for the 2000 Olympic Trials. In his first official 20K, Nunn walked a sub 1:30 performance to qualify for the Trials. However, at the trials themselves, the lack of a distance base took its toll and Nunn finished a respectable 6th. A week later he married and shortly after joined the Army and the WCAP program. Nunn now trains at the ARCO Olympic Training Center. His progress has been incredible at times, walking a 1:24:48 in Europe last season. He is now focused on achieving the time standard required to compete at the 2004 Olympic Games.

BEN SHOREY

Ben Shorey is one of America's top young male race walkers. A product of good timing and hard work, he started race walking as a high school freshman when the Maine high school track and field program added the event.

After a slow start with a coach just learning the sport, Shorey accomplished a lot. He won the State High School Championships and the U.S. Junior Nationals twice. However, Shorey was not content with age-group victories alone. When he raced at the Penn Relays, he won not only the Junior division, but the Open division as well.

Shorey has continued to develop and now races amongst the best in the country. In 2003 he moved up in race distance to the 50K Nationals and finished 3rd. Although he didn't finish as high at the 2004 50K Olympic Trials, his 6th place finish in 4:27:38 was a huge breakthrough. Shorey competes at the 2004 20K Olympic Trials later this year. With two solid 50Ks under his belt, he has the stamina to walk with America's best.

Bibliography

Anderson, Owen. "Heat Therapy and Ultrasound." *Sports Injury Bulletin*. 2004. <http://www.sportsinjurybulletin.com/archive/heat-therapy-ultrasound.html>.

Brooks, George. *Fundamentals of Human Performance*, New Jersey: Prentice Hall, 1987.

Daniels, Jack. *Daniel's Running Formula*, Champaign, IL: Human Kinetics, 1998.

Foot Glossary: Shoe Selection and Other Things You Need to Know. Gear West Bike and Triathlon. 2004. <http://www.gearwest.com/footglossary.htm>.

"Laskau, Henry." *American Jewish Historical Society*. Ed. Meir Ribalow. November 2003. <http://www.jewsinsports.org/olympics>.

Luttgens, Kathryn. *Kinesiology – Scientific Basis of Human Motion*, Dubuque, IA: Brown & Benchmark Publications, 1997.

Mcardle, William. *Exercise Physiology: Energy, Nutrition, and Human Performance.* 4TH ed. Baltimore, MD: Williams & Wilkins, 1996.

McGovern, Dave. *The Complete Guide to Race Walking Technique and Training*, Mobile AL: World Class Publications, 1998.

McGovern, Dave. 2004. <http://www.racewalking.org>.

Peterson, Connie. *Determining Your Foot Type*. 2003. <http://www.arches.uga.edu/~lnavits/foottype.html>.

"Race Walk Officiating." *USA Track & Field Handbook*. Indianapolis, IN: USATF, 2000.

Rudow, Martin. *Advanced Race Walking*, Seattle, WA: Technique Publications, 1987.

Salvage, Jeff. 1995-2004. <http://www.racewalk.com>.

Salvage, Jeff. "Predicting Race Walking Performance," *The Race Walk Coach*, 3 (1989): 38.

Salvage, Jeff, et al. "Racewalking." *USA Track and Field Coaching Manual*, Champaign, IL: Human Kinetics, 2000. 281-286.

Salvage, Jeff, and Gary Westerfield. *Walk Like an Athlete*. Medford, NJ: Walking Promotions, 1996.

Schroeder, Karen. July 1999. *Massage Therapy for Athletes*. March 2004. <http://www.somersetmedicalcenter.com/13945.cfm>.

Steckel, Mark. 2004. *What is Chiropractic?* 2004. <http://www.spinalhealth.net/chiro.html>.

Sweazy, Glenn, "Two Hundred Years of Competitive Walking." Unpublished. 1987-1989.

Wallace, William G. "Racewalking in America Past and Present." Diss. U of Texas, 1989.

Ward, Elaine. North American Race Walking Foundation. 2004. <http://members.aol.com/RWNARF/>.

Westerfield, Gary. 2002. *The Straightened Leg: The Intent of the Rules and Use of Biomechanics to Make "Bent Knee" Calls in Race Walking*. March 2004. <http://www.walk-usa.com>.

NOTE: The historical information presented throughout the book was compiled from my personal interviews, with the assistance of Josh Ginsburg, and correspondence with profiled athletes, their coaches, peers and family members. Information was gathered between July 2003 and March 2004.

About the Author

Jeff Salvage pursues his interests—photography, computer technology, and the outdoors—with a focus and intensity that can only be described as passionate. With race walking, this passion becomes an obsession. Whether he's flying across the country to support and document a National Team race, pacing a protégé through a half-marathon, or serving up electrolytes through a rainy 50K, Salvage smiles through it all—typically with camera, cell phone, and computer notebook within reach.

Salvage claims that "no one who knew him as a kid" could conceive of his 20-year immersion in the world of athletics. But at age 16, he arose from behind his computer to join his high-school cross-country team. Salvage enjoyed running, but his knees gave out early. So when he started race walking his senior year of high school, no one expected much. Salvage surprised them all, breaking the 7:00 min/mile barrier and finishing second at High School Nationals his very first season race walking.

With his newly discovered "raw talent for race walking" as motivation, Salvage focused much time and energy on developing his skills. He improved rapidly. Unfortunately, he struggled with injuries each time success seemed within reach. Having competed internationally and achieved one of his main goals—winning the Maccabiah Games—Salvage decided not to fight the fates and returned to his computer career. Still in college, he formed the club PHAST (Philadelphia-Area Striders Team) and led the resurgence of race walking in Philadelphia.

Graduating college in 1992, he balanced his information systems career—consulting, teaching and writing several college textbooks—while serving as Mid Atlantic Race Walking Chairman and Director of Race Walks at the Penn Relays, a position he still holds. In 1996 he became U.S. Junior National Race Walk Coordinator, coaching many top Juniors while running training camps for promising young athletes at the U.S. Olympic Training Center in Chula Vista, CA. Meanwhile, Salvage spearheaded his sport's presence on the Internet with *www.racewalk.com* serving as the USATF race walking committee's official site for nearly a decade. Today this site remains a primary source of free information on race walking technique, training, club programs, and national competition.

In 1996 Salvage coauthored *Walk Like an Athlete*, the basis of the race walking chapter of the USATF coach's manual. Soon after he produced a two-part video by the same name. While this package served as a springboard for his current book/video/DVD series, Salvage's recent products represent a wider synthesis of cumulative knowledge delivered with his expert flair for photography, computer graphics, and expository writing.

Today Salvage teaches computer science at Drexel University while pursuing numerous consulting, writing, and creative projects. His additional interests include kayaking and trekking, and his international travel photos recently appeared in *What Digital Camera* magazine.

COMPLETE YOUR RACE WALK LIKE A CHAMPION COLLECTION
ORDER THE DVDS TODAY!

If you didn't order the DVDs along with this book, then you've missed out. The two volume *Race Walk Like a Champion* DVD set bring the descriptions of this book to life. The DVDs set is packed with information explaining of all aspects of race walking in DVD quality video. However, the benefits of the DVD format do not end there.

The DVD's interactivity makes it a coach in a box. Its friendly menus allow you to watch exactly the section you wish over and over with no rewinding! Have a technique problem, just drill down through the interactive menus and your ever-present coach is there to assist.

No where before have so many detailed training schedules been available at the click of your remote. Simply select your race distance and then your race time and a day by day training schedule is presented. The DVDs guide you from the first steps of a base phase all the way through your race day.

Add in the audio/video photo stories of the all-time best walkers in America along with a documentary of the top athletes training at the Arco Training Center and you will have a new appreciation for our sport. Learn everything this set has to offer, and maybe you'll be in the next DVD!

Don't wait, order them today. 24 Hours a Day / 7 Days a Week

$24.95 per volume or $39.95 for the two volume set + $4.50 shipping & handling. Either order them online at www.racewalk.com, toll-free at 800-247-6553 or fax at 419-281-6883. Of course, if you prefer the old fashioned way, you can order by mail:

Walking Promotions
79 North Lakeside Drive
Medford, NJ 08055

While the quest to climb Mt. Olympus calls many to its base, a heartbreaking few reach its summit.

May all those who journey up the treacherous path learn to appreciate the beauty of the ascent, regardless of the outcome.

In memory of our dear friend *Al Heppner.*

He left us much too soon.